Hugh Cleghorn, 1752–1837

An Enlightened Scot

Hugh Cleghorn, 1752–1837

Aylwin Clark

BLACK ACE BOOKS

First published in 1992 by
Black Ace Books
Duns, TD11 3SG, Scotland

© Aylwin Clark 1992

Foreword © Nicholas Phillipson 1992

Jacket illustration © Simon Weller 1992

Typeset in Scotland by Black Ace Editorial

Printed in Great Britain by Martin's The Printers
Berwick Upon Tweed, TD15 1RS

A CIP catalogue record for this book
is available from the British Library

ISBN   1–872988–01–6

Dedicated to

Hugh and Elizabeth Sprot

In gratitude for

Their kindness and generosity

CONTENTS

ILLUSTRATIONS

*The author and publishers gratefully acknowledge
the sources and permissions detailed below.*

Photographs

FRONTISPIECE

Hugh Cleghorn, 1752–1837. Artist Unknown. Portrait in the possession of Major Hugh Sprot. Photographed by St Andrews University Photographic Unit (SAUPU).

CENTRE PLATE PHOTOGRAPHS

1 William Hamilton, 1669–1732. Great-grandfather of Hugh Cleghorn. Professor at, then Principal of Edinburgh University. Artist unknown. From an engraving in *The Moderators of the Church of Scotland from 1690–1740* by John Warrick, Edinburgh 1913, p 240. SAUPU.

2 Miss Sarah Cleghorn, 1727–1825. Aunt of Hugh Cleghorn. Portrait by Sir David Wilkie, in the possession of Major Hugh Sprot. SAUPU.

3 Rt. Hon. William Adam of Blair Adam, 1751–1839. Engraving by S W Reynolds, after a portrait by John Opie. Scottish National Portrait Gallery.

4 Adam Ferguson, philosopher, 1723–1816. Friend of William Cleghorn, and taught Hugh Cleghorn at Edinburgh University, 1768–72. Portrait by Sir Henry Raeburn, in the possession of the University of Edinburgh. Photographed by permission.

5 Plan from Hugo Arnot's *History of Edinburgh*, 1788. The Number '15' shows where Society stood. SAUPU.

6 Adam Smith, 1723–90. Rachel Cleghorn related to him on the Douglas side. Janet Douglas and the Cleghorns were beneficiaries of his will. From John Kay's *Original Portraits*, Adam & Charles Black [Edinburgh], 1877, Vol.I, Part 1, p 75.

7 John Millar, 1735–1801. Professor of Law at Glasgow University, 1761–1801. His thought strongly influenced Cleghorn's St Andrews lectures. Paste Medallion by James Tassie. Hunterian Museum, University of Glasgow.

8 Edward Gibbon, 1737–94. Visited by Cleghorn in Lausanne, 1788. Artist unknown. National Portrait Gallery, London.

Maps

Family Trees

ACKNOWLEDGEMENTS

I have thoroughly enjoyed the opportunity, through the kindness of Major and Mrs Sprot, to delve into the papers of Hugh Cleghorn, Hugh Sprot's ancestor. But the full-scale biography which the papers warranted would never have emerged in book form without the invaluable co-operation and skill of Hunter Steele of Black Ace Books.

It is also a real pleasure to acknowledge here all the help I have had in writing this book.

The Headmistress and Council of St Leonards School allowed me to consult the title deeds of St Leonards and among the private owners, the name that stood out from among the lawyers, landowners and academics who had bought St Leonards, was that of Hugh Cleghorn, 'late Secretary of State to the Government of Ceylon.' My neighbour Mrs Nancy Waterston, a close friend of the Sprots, asked them if they had any papers which would show whether Cleghorn had actually lived in St Leonards and they produced a stout wooden box *full* of papers concerning Hugh Cleghorn, his son Peter and grandson, Hugh Francis Clarke Cleghorn. Hugh Sprot then most kindly agreed that the papers should be deposited on loan in the University Library archives. Mrs Nancy Bampton, the aunt of Hugh Sprot, who has answered so many of my queries and with whom it has been a delight to discuss Cleghorn's life, put me on to documents in the Manuscript Department of the William R. Perkins Library (Duke University, Durham, North Carolina) and through them to the Ames Library of South Asia (in the University of Minnesota, Minniapolis), who were also most helpful. I am also most grateful to Mrs Claudine Reynard, Hugh Sprot's sister, for the way she retrieved more of Cleghorn's papers from an attic in England.

I am very glad to have here the opportunity to thank Mr Robert Smart, Keeper of Manuscripts and University Muniments, who not only agreed to house the papers safely but once I was past the research stage, read each chapter as I finished it and thrust it upon him. He pointed out some of my odder errors of interpretation (while in no sense being responsible for those that remain) and also took endless trouble to answer my numerous queries. Mrs Christine Gascoigne (Assistant Librarian in the University Library) has never failed either in humour or in helpfulness and has been most constructive over illustrations. Over these, I am most grateful to Mr Peter Adamson and his allies in the Photographic Unit of St Andrews University for their skill and care. Mrs Priscilla Jackson, Mr Kenneth Fraser and other Library staff have always helped encouragingly.

In following up the trails of the clues in the papers, I owe a special debt to Sonia Anderson, Assistant Keeper, Royal Commission on Historical Manuscripts, London, who guided me in the right direction to valuable sources – the papers of Frederic North, for instance, which the Archivist of Kent County Council had copied for me. Dr Elizabeth Hallam Smith of the Public Record Office, Kew, was also most co-operative.

I should like to thank all those in the record offices and libraries I have consulted: the staff of the Scottish Record Office, both in Register House and in Charlotte Square; those in the National Library of Scotland; the Archivist of Buckinghamshire County Council; down in London, the staff of the India Office Library and Records and those in the British Library. Both the National Portrait Gallery of Scotland and that in London responded efficiently to my pleas and again, as I searched for portraits, the Hunterian Gallery of Glasgow University and the Pictures and Galleries Committee of Edinburgh were most helpful, as was the University of London's Courtauld Institute of Art.

I am very conscious of the debt I owe to the curators, librarians, archivists and photographers of Neuchâtel: to Mlle Helen Kett, Conservateur du musée militaire, Château de Colombier, who obtained the kind permission of M. Guy de Meuron to include in this book photographs of portraits of his ancestors, Charles-Daniel, Comte de Meuron, and his brother, Pierre-Frédéric; to Hubert Frydig, whom Mlle Kett asked to carry out the photography; to M. Jaques Hainard, Curator of the musée d'ethnographie, and Alain Germond for his skill in photographing the Hôtel du Peyrou and La Petite Rochette; to M. J. Courvoisier, Archivist of the Services des Archives de l'Etat; to M. Jean-Pierre Jelmini, Conservateur des Archives et Estampes Historiques de la Ville; to Mme Maryse Schmid-Surdez, Bibliothèque publique et universitaire; to the publishers of Les Editions Ides et Calendes for permission to use a photograph of a portrait of Mme du Peyrou.

For practical aid and comfort in typing the book, I owe a great debt of gratitude to my neighbour, Miss Mary Taylor. I appreciated enormously the interest and ingenuity that Maureen and Bruce Milne showed when on their holiday in Malta they tracked down and photographed the lazaretto where Cleghorn spent his quarantine – and their many other kindnesses. To Elizabeth Grace I can only say a totally inadequate thank-you for the readiness she showed in turning my tentative maps of Cleghorn's journeys into professionally skilled productions, and for all the interesting conversations that seemed to spring from our meetings. I feel great gratitude to Simon Weller for responding to my plea to design a book cover. It was not easy for him in the circumstances – with Helen being so ill – but he just got on with reading the book (which he did most perceptively), and producing a cover which gives me real enjoyment whenever I look at it.

Finally it was good of Dr Nicholas Phillipson to be ready, in a very busy life, to write a foreword to this biography – it is the best possible way of recommending it to Scottish readers, and I am most grateful.

It can be seen how much help I have had in my treasure-hunt. I found it invigorating and have thoroughly enjoyed making the acquaintance of such a spirited and enterprising character as Hugh Cleghorn, who played his part, briefly but brilliantly, in strengthening British interests in the east – before circumstances brought him back to Fife, and kept him there.

Aylwin Clark
St Andrews, 1992

FOREWORD

I doubt whether many will have heard of Hugh Cleghorn, the hero of Aylwin Clark's biography. But anyone who knows anything about the age in which he lived will know it as one of the formative periods of Scottish history. When Cleghorn was born, in 1752, the western world was beginning to realise that in spite of losing its political independence, Scotland was becoming one of the most important centres of enlightenment. At the same time, an increasing number of well-educated and ambitious Scots were taking the high road to London, North America, the Caribbean and India, in search of the sort of fame and fortune that could be sought in professional life. For enlightened culture was providing Scotland with a new national identity and its young men with practical and marketable skills which were much in demand in a world being transformed by war, commerce and the growth of empire.

Cleghorn was a child of the Scottish enlightenment. Like so many of the Scottish intelligentsia, he belonged to the 'middling ranks' of Scottish society and came from a family with roots in trade and academic life. He was educated at Edinburgh in the 1760s, when the University was attracting international attention on account of an innovative new curriculum which seemed particularly well designed to prepare boys for useful careers in public life. He was to spend fifteen years as a professor of civil history at St Andrew's – retailing, without much apparent originality, the extraordinary philosophical history which Adam Smith, John Millar, William Robertson and Adam Ferguson had intended to serve as a vehicle for teaching the principles of politics and government.

After fifteen years of university teaching, the drudgery of Cleghorn's academic life became too much for him and, like so many of his fellow professors, he left – in his case to become tutor to the young Earl of Home, supervising his tour of Europe in 1788–90. As he was obviously competent and well-connected, it was probably only a matter of time before Cleghorn caught the eye of Henry Dundas, James Boswell's 'Harry IX', who was responsible for the government of India as well as Scotland. It was Dundas who sent him to India and, later to Ceylon – as Secretary of State to the new British government of Ceylon. He had realised that Cleghorn was a trustworthy man with a trained, practical mind: a man who could provide him with regular and reliable information about Indian problems at a time when Dundas was largely responsible for establishing British rule over that vast, turbulent, strange sub-continent.

Overall, Cleghorn's career was useful rather than glorious. He was clearly a decent if unoriginal university teacher and his career in India and Ceylon comes over as that of a competent civil servant who eventually found himself out of his depth. But even so, it is an interesting and unusually well-documented career, which sheds fascinating light on enlightened values in Scotland. For Cleghorn went to India with the sort of mind that the great Scottish philosophers had sought to train. They had taught him to take the world as he found it, discover how it worked and consider how those lessons could be applied to the problem of managing, and, if possible, improving it. It is the great value of Miss Clark's book that we are able to see an enlightened mind in the making.

Cleghorn came of good radical stock. His uncle, William Cleghorn, professor of Moral Philosophy at Edinburgh, had been a noted radical Whig; and his own professor at Edinburgh, Adam Ferguson, had been his uncle's most distinguished pupil and admirer. And so it is hardly surprising that, on his European tour with Lord Home, he should have fallen in love with Switzerland. For Cleghorn had clearly been brought up in the classic view, beloved of Scots through the ages, that true liberty could only be found in small republics. By the time he had begun to teach civil history at St Andrew's, he had learned to temper this somewhat old-fashioned and sentimental view. Those great architects of Scottish political and historical thought, David Hume, Adam Smith, Adam Ferguson, and John Millar had shown that true liberty was the product of good laws and regular government, and they had asked how it could be cultivated in the 'enormous monarchies' of a world which was being transformed by war, commerce and the growth of empire. It must have been a tremendous shock for Cleghorn to be catapulted by Dundas into a continent which represented everything he had been taught to distrust and abhor. For, in contemporary eyes, India and Ceylon were part of a vast, decaying oriental despotism, which was riddled with superstition and corruption, and was now only held together by an imperial army and bureaucracy.

Until the disastrous last year of his Indian career, Cleghorn seems to have adapted himself to this alien world with some skill. He had all the enlightened Scottish virtues. He was intelligent, observant, pragmatic and methodical; and more than a touch pedantic too – a fault that was to be his undoing. But while those very virtues would be the life-blood of the Victorian civil service, India was not Britain; and political survival, there, depended on mastering other, more political skills. Cleghorn's tendency to pedantry got on the nerves of the young, intelligent Governor General of Ceylon, Frederick North, who became determined to get rid of him. And the charges of corruption which ultimately felled him – he was accused of stealing pearls from the fisheries he was supposed to have been managing – sound like the result of a fatal failure to appreciate the delicate distinction between perquisites and pilfering – a nuance which had to be grasped, if one was to prosper as well as survive. Cleghorn's story is thus that of an innocent radical Whig, schooled in the most sophisticated science of politics available in the western world, and broken on the wheel of oriental despotism. It was a sad fate for an enlightened Scot.

In 1800 Cleghorn returned to Scotland and St Andrew's, and it was there, on the large and expensive estate he bought at Stravithie, that he spent his last thirty-seven years. Stravithie, his family and friends were to be the focal points of his life; Stravithie a constant worry; family and friends a corresponding joy and consolation. Cleghorn took to the business of improving his estate with a reckless enthusiasm which overstretched him financially, and would have broken him entirely – if he hadn't been bailed out by his son Peter (who had accumulated considerable wealth from his legal practice in Madras, where he was Registrar General of the Supreme Court). However, Cleghorn's ghost can take wry satisfaction from the fact these worries, and the correspondence they generated, throw fascinating light on the hazards as well as the pleasures of landowning in early nineteenth-century Scotland. And anyway, without Stravithie his family and social life would have been much the poorer. Although his children were constantly worried by their father's endless financial crises, the family was clearly a close one, and Cleghorn found in his grandchildren a source of constant delight. For Stravithie was above all a family house: always open to the large circle of friends which remained at the centre of the life of a much-liked, hospitable and decent man.

Cleghorn died in February 1837, a few months before Queen Victoria's accession, leaving behind him a remarkable archive, and descendants who have had the good sense to keep it together. In Aylwin Clark he has found the biographer to give him, and us, a vivid and perceptive portrait of an enlightened Scot, who lived during what Lord Cockburn liked to call 'the last purely Scotch age'.

Nicholas Phillipson
Edinburgh, 1992

1

Edinburgh Family Background
1718–52

A marriage of town and gown

In June 1827 Sir Walter Scott wrote in his journal: 'Mr. Hugh Cleghorn dined at Charlton and I saw him for the first time, *having heard of him all of my life.*'[1] This comment by one of the most eminent Scotsmen of his day is a little unexpected, on a man who had spent the first thirty six years of his life in university circles and the last thirty-six years as a Fife landowner improving his estate. Hugh Cleghorn's own reflections on universities on the one hand, 'with their seclusion and endowments producing only the jargon of technical language and the impertinence of academical forms'[2] and on the other, on 'that most deplorable of all characters, a country laird'[3] are crisp enough to suggest that he chafed at the limitations of both ways of life – especially in comparison with the whirl of activity into which he plunged for twelve years of his life as traveller, government intelligence agent, empire-builder and administrator. The rest of Scott's comment fills out the picture a little: 'He is an able man, has seen much and speaks well . . . ' He wrote well too, with an eye for what was significant and the historian's instinct to record – as is shown in the papers kept by his family.

Hugh Cleghorn's upbringing was in Edinburgh and his family connections and education meant that he accepted as natural the enjoyment of vigorous debate and the lively social life of what was, in the middle of the eighteenth century, among the most intellectually adventurous capitals of Europe. 'I believe there is hardly a man who has more academical blood in his veins than I have,'[4] Cleghorn wrote with some justification. His great grandfather, William Hamilton, had been Principal of Edinburgh University; his grandfather, William Scott, Professor of Moral Philosophy there, as was his uncle, William Cleghorn. His uncle on his mother's side, also William Scott, had been Professor of Greek and in Aberdeen his cousin, Robert Hamilton, Professor of Mathematics and author of an important work on the National Debt.

The founder of the family fortunes, however, was William Cleghorn, a brewer. His first brew-house was in the Cowgate, for in 1689 he asked the Edinburgh Council for permission – in return for 20 merks yearly – to convey the overflow of the fountain at the head of West Bow and the trough at Crosswell to his Cowgate brewery by lead pipes. As he pointed out in his petition, the overflow was a nuisance to everybody: 'It freezes in winter time and puts people in hazard of breaking legs and arms and in summer time it spoils the whole street at that place.'[5]

Cleghorn's business prospered, and eight years later – in 1697 – he and his wife, Bethia Brand, acquired for 20,600 merks a much bigger site which was to become the family home, as well as their place of business, well on into the nineteenth century. This was: 'the parcel of land called the Society, with the houses, brew-houses and coppers and other brewing looms belonging thereto: malt barns, lofts and kilns built thereon.'[6] The name 'The Society' came from the first commercial company to be incorporated in Scotland: 'the Fellowship and Society of Ale and Beer brewers of the Burgh of Edinburgh,'[7] established in 1598, dissolved in 1619, but not before it had drained the Meadows and fixed its name firmly on that part of Edinburgh where Hugh Cleghorn passed his boyhood and to which he returned when he needed to stay in Edinburgh. Indeed, in the last letter of his addressed from Society – in 1829 – he speaks warmly of it: 'I could nowhere be more comfortable than here – a large airy apartment and the command of books from the Library of Writers to the Signet.'[8] It was in the span of his lifetime that George Square, which included the Society on one side, became fashionable enough for the professional and elegant families of Edinburgh to develop their own social life and amusements and to bother little about what was happening north of the High Street, with the building of the New Town.

Neither William Cleghorn nor his son Hugh, nor his grandson John, seems to have had much civic ambition, although William did a stint of duty as Treasurer of the University in 1684–5.[9] Before he died, however, in 1718, he had extended his premises and was paying tack on eleven common mills at the water of Leith, with a windmill and stables thrown in.

The marriage which brought the Cleghorns and Hamiltons together took place in 1718 – seven months after William Cleghorn's death – between Hugh Cleghorn, William's son, and Jean Hamilton, daughter of William Hamilton, who was an interesting figure in the Church of Scotland for his role in paving the way for the emergence of the Moderate Party.

Born in 1669, to Gavin Hamilton and Jane Montgomery of Hazlehead, he was baptised at a Covenanting conventicle and was educated at the College, Edinburgh, being ordained in 1694 to Cramond. In 1709 he was appointed Professor of Divinity in Edinburgh, an office he retained for twenty-three years – until he became Principal in March 1732. The tributes of his students suggest that he was a good teacher; he certainly had ample opportunity to influence the attitudes of many ministers, for his classes sometimes numbered up to two hundred.[10] In a preface to a book of sermons by Dr Leechman, his biographer James Wodrow writes: 'I have heard Dr. Leechman say that he was under great obligation to Professor Hamilton; that he learned much from him in many points about which the Professor spoke his mind openly and that, young as he was, he learned something also in other points about which the Professor said nothing. The silence of such a man struck him, it would seem, and led him to investigate the causes of it.'[11] Hamilton would never, for instance, speak slightingly of Covenanting enthusiasm;[12] he 'cautioned against too much positiveness';[13] he told the Assembly in 1728 that: 'I am persuaded the support of our doctrine needs no personal injuries to promote it.'[14] His approach civilised and liberalised the temper of generations of ministers.

In 1727 Hamilton and James Alston, minister of Dirleton, were given royal chaplaincies, a gift which was the occasion of Hamilton's writing to his son-in-law, the first Hugh Cleghorn, one of the early letters in the Cleghorn Papers, dated 31 October 1727. He and his wife made the journey to London about his warrant of chaplaincy and there they heard the news of 'Jeanie's safe delivery of a daughter' (probably Sarah, because in 1825 the second Hugh Cleghorn, writing to his son Peter, says of Aunt Sarah that 'two or three years will complete her hundred'[15]). In his letter Hamilton wrote: 'I regret my not being home to partake in person with you in your joy. I am sure it would have been much more comfortable to me than to be here for all the fine things I see in this place. Yesterday we had one of the most magnificent shows in Europe upon the occasion of the King and Queen with the whole court going to the Lord Mayor's Feast but I reserve particular description of it till meeting . . . ' He went on to say that he hoped the precedent provided by Mr Alston might settle the question of the warrant and he asked Hugh to prompt Baron Clerk to see 'if it can be passed this term so as I can be put on the establishment for what will be due at this Christmas quarter'.

With the death of Principal Wishart in 1730, Hamilton saw an opportunity to free himself from 'the multitude of students' with which he had been burdened for the last twenty-one years.[16] But he did not want to accept a drop in salary, and negotiations dragged out – the Principal's place remaining vacant until 1732, when Hamilton gave up his Chair, became minister of the North New Church and was made Principal, an office which he formally held only for three months before his death in November 1732.

He and his wife Mary had a large family of sixteen children: they naturally absorbed her interest. One of her letters, written in a very clear hand, survives in the Cleghorn Papers.[17] She was writing from London to Jean (directing it to Mrs Cleghorn at the Society) on the death of Jean's sister and her own younger daughter, Anne Horsely, in February 1736. In this she describes how Anne: 'sent for her child the day she died to give her last blessing and prayed earnestly he might be preserved from the vices of the age and that he might live to be as his grandfather had been. She had her father much in her thoughts . . . ' (The child in fact grew up to be a bishop in the Church of England: Samuel Horsely (1733–1806), Bishop of St Asaph and editor of Sir Isaac Newton's work and writer on mathematics and theology.) Two other letters of Mary Hamilton that survive were to her son Alexander, who had gone out to Annapolis in Maryland, where his brother John had preceded him. These two letters to 'Sandie' are a little plaintive in tone because she has not heard from him, but she is busy collecting together 'a little box of bed and table linen' and sending off linen to be whitened to make shirts for him.[18] Gilbert, Alexander's brother, reporting on the family to him, says of Mrs Hamilton in 1749: 'Your mother is well and has the pleasure of seeing all the families descended from her in a prosperous situation.'

Alexander, out in Maryland, though he may not have been a good correspondent, yet kept in touch sufficiently to send a contribution to the building of the Royal Infirmary in Edinburgh (1742), and took the 'Physical News' from there.

Gavin Hamilton, eight years his senior, was a staunch Whig and a man of enterprise and public spirit.[19] In 1729 he went to Europe to learn about the book trade at first hand. He made useful contacts and, on his return, set up as a bookseller. His shop in the High Street became a place of great resort for students, men of letters and city worthies – and the Duke of Argyle is said to have 'sat for hours there, writing letters, talking to Hamilton and commenting on the characters who flowed past the window'. He served on the Town Council and during the Porteous Riots was the Bailie on duty and in the thick of the tumult was nearly brained by an axe. He was one of the booksellers who helped to break the Londoners' monopoly of the book trade in Scotland by appealing to the patriotism of the Scots. In all his manifold activities he was a vivid example of many aspects of the Scottish Enlightenment of the mid-eighteenth century.

Jean, the grandmother of the subject of this biography, was the eldest daughter of the Hamiltons. No personal letters of hers survive, but there are in the Cleghorn Papers some pages sewn together and labelled 'a copy of a paper in Aunty Jeanie's writing', which contain a religious testament of formidable piety, beginning: 'Eternal and Almighty God, behold a poor creature that is lost and undone by Adam's fall', and continuing for seven pages in the same vein – to the solemn conclusion: 'Let this covenant be a fountain of comfort to me all my life, at the hour of death and through all eternity.' Not for nothing was her father baptised in a Covenanting conventicle! By her marriage in 1718 to Hugh Cleghorn she had four sons: William, John, James and Patty (who died almost at the same time as his father), and two daughters, Jean and Sarah (described as 'fine girls' by their Uncle Gilbert) of whom, 'the eldest is of a comical turn and obliging in her temper; the youngest good-natured and pretty.' When Hugh died suddenly in 1734 it was Jean Cleghorn and John, their second son, who took over the running of the brewery and evidently maintained its prosperity. Gilbert reported of her to his brother Sandy: 'Jean Cleghorn . . . manages the business of a Distillery with her second son John and lives very genteelly by it.'[20]

Jean seems to have been the business-woman of her generation, being named in three Cleghorn wills and taking over the management of her mother's financial affairs in 1758, 'to relieve Mrs. Hamilton in her straits.' Gilbert was ready to help but obviously thought Jean quite capable of managing: 'If you will make up', he writes to her, 'two or three sheets of paper into a little Octavo Book or buy a Three penny Octavo paper book in my brother's shop, I will put you upon an easy method of keeping it when I come to town.'[21]

That she liked to have everything legally as well as financially clear, is shown in the Charter of 30 December 1760 in favour of Jean Cleghorn in life rent and John Cleghorn in fee, granted by the Lord Provost, George Drummond, Bailies, Councillors, etc, of Edinburgh.[22] It is this charter which gives a legal description of the exact location of the Society and which clears Jean Cleghorn's right to sell tacks or grant subfeus of the lands in question and to contract debts to the value of these lands, 'without the advice and consent of the said John Cleghorn.' It also tidies up any ambiguity left by the death of 'William Cleghorn, Preacher of the Gospel in Edinburgh, then eldest son to the said deceased Hugh Cleghorn as lawfully charged to enter heir in special' to his father.

It was this William Cleghorn in whom, amid all his other relatives, Hugh Cleghorn seems to have taken most pride. He was too young to remember his uncle personally, because he had died in 1754 at the age of thirty-five, when Hugh was only two. However, among the Cleghorn Papers is a coverless notebook which on the first inside page has 'Will Cleghorn' written large, with 'Willy' tried out above. Below this is inscribed '1738' twelve times and then, below again: 'Anno 1739 Domini, January 1st, 12 o'clock at Night.' It evokes a vivid picture of the nineteen-year-old student elated, both at what he has achieved so far and at the prospect of entering at the first stroke of the New Year into his proper realm of learning, under his masters, the great philosophers. This was to be the first volume of his Commonplace Book, his 'Adversariorum Methodus Promptuarium', and the excerpts include a most catholic variety. Here are some chosen at random: Scepticism (*Shaftesbury*); Amsterdam (Ray's *Travels*); pleasure (Montaigne's *Essays*); knowledge (Locke); atoms (Democritus and Aristotle); Saracens (Ockeley); Spinoza ('the first man who ever reduced atheism to a system').[23] In its own way this notebook is an impressive testimony to the intellectual vigour and adventurousness of this first professor on the Cleghorn side of the family. He left almost no published work – in this like his grandfather, William Hamilton. There was an Inaugural Dissertation written before taking his degree as Master of Arts which, though in the catalogue of St Andrew University in the 1770s, was missing from the shelves when Hugh looked for it.

Professor Lee sent to Hugh in 1836 William Cleghorn's 'Address to some Gentlemen immediately after the Rebellion'. Acknowledging this gift, Hugh said about his uncle: 'I got many anecdotes concerning him from our friend, Dr. A. Ferguson, who retained to the last the most affectionate remembrance of his talents and virtues.'[24] Evidence of this affection is shown in Adam Ferguson's *Dialogue of a Highland Jaunt*, which was probably written in Ferguson's old age when his friends were dead, to recall the philosophical issues over which they had argued half a century earlier.[25]

Cleghorn was one of those who, along with Robert Adam, David Hume and William Wilkie, was persuaded, as Ferguson imagines with some amusement, to spend a day in the mountains above Blair Atholl, 'with nothing to see but heath and towering hills . . . and not a sound but of the whittering plover or moor cock when he springs from the heath.' So as not to be thought madmen, they were given guns and accompanied by a stalker. However, when 'Ghillie Whitefoot' sighted a stag and prepared to take a shot, it was Cleghorn whom Ferguson imagined crying out: 'For your life, do not shoot him. I would not forego the pleasure of seeing him pass for all the venison in your Duke's forest.' With the stalker going off in disgust, a discussion follows on the meaning of pleasure, the nature of beauty and freedom of choice. Ferguson gives Cleghorn a leading role in the discussion and together they are allies against Wilkie and Hume. Their first argument, over whether the stag acted by instinct or by thought, leads Cleghorn to set man apart from animals by his reason and on the 'distinguishing principle of right and wrong, honour and dishonour' (not merely interest and safety). In their discussion on beauty it is Cleghorn who argues for man's perception of Excellence, leading up to ideal perfection; while Hume claims that Utility is the criterion of beauty.

Thus Ferguson remembers Cleghorn and Hume as philosophically poles apart. The competition for the Chair of Moral Philosophy in 1745, between the two men, was between two genuinely different approaches in philosophy – and the choice had to be made in the year of the Jacobite Rising.[26] Cleghorn had already undertaken part of the work of the Chair when, 1742–4, with George Muirhead he stood in for Sir John Pringle. He was certainly anti-Jacobite, his mother was a Hamilton, whose family had provided a Principal of the University, ministers of the Kirk, and a forceful Bailie to the Town Council; and his philosophy was challenging to his students, over whom he is said to have had great influence. Whatever other factors swayed the minds of the electors on the Council, it was Cleghorn whom they chose in July of 1745, 'safely considering', as Chalmers said, 'that a deist might become a Christian but a Jacobite could not possibly become a Whig.'[27]

In September 1745 Cleghorn was one of those enlisting in the College Company of the Corps of Volunteers to defend Edinburgh against the advancing Highland army under Prince Charles.[28] When the civic authorities lost their nerve at the prospect of this inexperienced intellectual élite being slaughtered on the approaches to Edinburgh, and dismissed them in the College yards, Cleghorn was one of the dozen young men who went together to dinner, 'to a Mrs. Turnbull's, then next house to the Tron Church,' and discussed possible lines of action. It was in this discussion says Alexander Carlyle, that Cleghorn was 'very fiery', wanting to join Sir John Cope's army however few the volunteers from the University.

Out they went on foot – only William Robertson had provided himself with a horse – Cleghorn and a recruiting sergeant arguing vigorously whether the musket and bayonet or broadsword and target were the best weapons. At ten o'clock Robertson decided to stop at an inn where there were still beds available. 'Cleghorn's ardour and mine resisted the proposal,' says Carlyle, and they went on to the camp at Dunbar – only to find they were refused admittance, so they had to trail wearily back to a manse where, in the end, the minister allowed them in. 'We were hardly well asleep when, about six, Robertson came . . . quite stout and well-refreshed, while we were jaded and undone.' In all, twenty-five Edinburgh Volunteers asked Sir John Cope 'for arms and a station on the line', but he wanted them to scout the roads and bring back information on the Jacobite Army. So they went out in pairs – Alexander Carlyle going with William McGhie – and we hear no more of Cleghorn's role, except for the mention of his address after the Rebellion.

An amusing picture also survives of Cleghorn and William Wilkie, notorious for his absent-mindedness, spending a convivial Saturday evening out at Cramond with Gilbert Hamilton, Cleghorn's uncle. Gilbert at length realised the time and that he had no inclination to get down to preparing a sermon. Wilkie offered to preach for him in the morning and Cleghorn arranged that at the end of half an hour he would give Wilkie a signal to stop. Cleghorn duly hoisted the signal in church the next morning, but to no effect; at the end of an hour Cleghorn made another attempt and in addition held up a watch, almost touching Wilkie's nose; at the end of two hours Wilkie stopped, complaining that: 'an unaccountable feebleness of his limbs obliged him to give up though he had a great deal more to say!'

The most valuable record of Cleghorn's thought is a set of notes, in the possession of Edinburgh University Library, which were taken by a student at Cleghorn's lectures between December 1746 and April 1747. These, in Dr Nobb's estimation, 'show the originality of his mind and provide adequate vindication of the Town Council's choice.' His arguments here show too how truly Ferguson mirrored his thought in his imaginary debate written fifty years later. Cleghorn wanted to restore the link between politics and ethics and looked to Greece for his pattern. His concern was to define 'true social unions'. Only in such unions, Cleghorn believed, could men achieve their true fulfilment through the exercise of a positive benevolence. He was a republican: property and power were heritable but wisdom was not, and he advocated the drastic treatment of property either on the lines of More's *Utopia* or the agrarian law of Harrington's *Oceana*.[29] If Cleghorn's ethical theory led him to a political doctrine which was too idealistic for his time, this would perhaps explain why there is so little reference to his work by his contemporaries.

However, they enjoyed his company. According to his Uncle Gilbert, writing to his brother Alexander in Annapolis in 1749: 'William has the reputation of a fine scholar; he is a well bred man, keeps the best company in Town and as he is the Professor of Moral Philosophy in the College of Edinburgh, so he teaches it with deserved applause.' Hugh Cleghorn wrote in 1836 to Dr Lee about his uncle: 'I learned from many eminent men, most of them not unknown to you, particularly from the late Sir William Pulteney and from Andrew Stewart . . . that his lectures were universally esteemed and numerously attended by men of all ages and of the most liberal professions.' Hugh copied out at the end of his letter, the obituary notice on William's death which appeared in the *Edinburgh Evening Courant* of 26 August 1754, the author of which he was convinced was Adam Ferguson. The writer, whoever it was, said about Cleghorn: 'Esteemed as a philosopher, he was no less beloved as a man and a friend. Never did anyone possess a greater fund of innate worth and goodness. His whole character was a bright example of those moral virtues he taught others.'[30]

William never married. It was his younger brother, John, merchant and brewer, who carried on the line and was to be the father of Hugh Cleghorn. John married Jean Scott, the daughter of William Scott who had been Professor of Greek in Edinburgh for twenty-one years. Jean was a widow, whose first husband, Robert Hay, had died in 1742. He and his father had sold timber they did not in fact possess and when they died within thirteen months of each other, the bonds which they had signed were claimed by creditors. Jean Scott's husband 'appears to have been altogether insolvent and not having the wherewithal to pay the fourth part of his onerous debts'. She was in much quieter financial waters after her marriage, on 24 March 1751, in the south-west parish of Edinburgh, to John Cleghorn.[31]

Hugh Cleghorn's early years, 1752–72

A year after their marriage, Hugh, their first child and only son, was born on 21 March 1752, again in the south-west parish of Edinburgh.[32] His great-uncle, Gavin Hamilton, and his uncle, William Cleghorn, were the witnesses named when the birth was registered. Magdalene was the only other child of the marriage.

Of Cleghorn's education in Edinburgh we learn nothing from his own pen, but in Steven's *History of the High School of Edinburgh* his name appears in the list of distinguished pupils under the year 1762 as entering the class of Mr James French, one of the under-masters who would read the usual Latin books with the boys. In the next year Cleghorn had moved on to the Rector's class, where he spent only one year. Under this Rector, Alexander Matheson, the School was in a flourishing state – with the City Magistrates so pleased with the appearance made by the boys at the public examination, in 1762, that they added liberally to the boys' prize money and admitted the Rector and his staff as burgesses, even dispensing with the usual dues.[33]

Cleghorn kept in touch with many of his contemporaries at school: William Adam, distinguished lawyer and politician, remained a close and life-long friend;[34] General James Durham of Largo was dining at Stravithie in the 1830s as a member of their Octogenarians' Club;[35] William, Lord Robertson,[36] eldest son of Principal William Robertson, the historian, wrote to Cleghorn on his return from Ceylon recalling the 'days when we were wandering about Braid and Merchiston'.[37] Over fifty years later Cleghorn was writing to his son Peter in May of 1826 that he planned 'to attend our high school dinner which I believe to be the last time of its celebration'. Another was in fact held in 1827 with the comment from Cleghorn: 'Our members are reduced now to a few indeed and a few more years will annihilate all of us.'[38] This meeting, it seems, was the last.

That Cleghorn stayed only two years at the High School suggests that even before he went there he was already well grounded in Latin. In 1764 he went on to the College of Edinburgh and is recorded in 1766 as joining Robert Hunter's Greek class,[39] where he would be starting from scratch, since Greek was not taught at this time in the High School. He also joined the Logic class of Dr John Stevenson,[40] an experienced professor of whom many students spoke appreciatively, especially when he turned to Belles Lettres. Here his teaching made them aware of 'useful, practical rules of composition', of the nature and scope of literary criticism, the history of philosophy and much else in addition to Logic proper.[41] But he had been a professor for thirty-six years and his lectures did not satisfy the growing need for a more modern treatment of the English language, a need which first Adam Smith, before he transferred to a chair in Glasgow, then Robert Watson (before he transferred to the Chair of Logic and Rhetoric in St Andrews) started to fill. When Hugh Blair was made Regius Professor of Rhetoric and Belles Lettres, his course was widely praised and although Cleghorn did not officially register to attend Blair's class, he would be likely to sample all that was most distinguished in the teaching offered by the College at this time – and it was much. This awareness of questions of style can be seen in Cleghorn's own later lectures and letters and must owe much to Edinburgh's concern with the art of speaking.

The Edinburgh Matriculation Roll[42] shows that in 1768 Cleghorn registered for Adam Ferguson's Moral Philosophy course. Cleghorn's philosopher uncle, William, when he realised in 1754 that he was not going to recover from his illness, gave his 'dying voice' to Adam Ferguson, but in the event Ferguson had to wait ten years before entering his natural domain. One of the hurdles on the way was the time he had to devote to preparing his lectures as professor of natural philosophy. In these he showed his skill as a teacher but also that he was not to be diverted from his real goal. As he wrote in 1759: 'I like my situation very well and begin to admire Sir Isaac Newton as I did Homer and Montesquieu but it is on condition that he will let me go as soon as I become a tolerable Professor of Natural Philosophy.' It was in 1765 that the chief obstacle to Ferguson's promotion, James Balfour, whose class had 'dwindled to nothing', was transferred to the chair of Public Law so that Adam Ferguson could be elected to Moral Philosophy. Thus Cleghorn would be attending Ferguson's lectures at a time when he had 'won the lead in the university', when the Moral Philosophy class had over a hundred students who overflowed into the gallery and were frequently joined by 'gentlemen of rank'. Ferguson explained his approach to lecturing later in his *Principles of Moral and Political Science*:

'Conceiving that discussion and even information might come with more effect from a person that was making his own best efforts at disquisition and judgement than from one that might be languishing while he read or repeated a lecture previously composed, he determined while he bestowed his utmost diligence in studying his subject, in choosing the order in which it was to be treated, and in preparing himself for every successive step he was to make in his course, to have no more in writing than the heads or short notes from which he was to speak, preparing himself however very diligently for every particular day's work.'

That dedication, together with his concept of virtue as both the corrective and the goal of man, and the vigour and elegance of his style, gave Ferguson an authority which is reflected in his portrait by Raeburn and which led Alexander Carlyle to call him 'the Plato of Scotch philosophers'.

That Cleghorn valued Ferguson's teaching can be seen in the copy Cleghorn acquired in 1769 of Ferguson's *Institutes of Moral Philosophy*, which he had printed in that year specially 'for the students in the College of Edinburgh'.[43] Cleghorn's copy is still in the library at Nether Stravithie: on the back page he has tried out his signature – as seventeen-year-olds still tend to do – but he showed also that he had read the lectures thoroughly. Points are numbered, comments added; one way and another there is a good deal of ink splashed over the pages, but by an intelligent student. Certainly when Cleghorn himself came to prepare and deliver lectures he did his best to follow Ferguson's maxims and advice.

In 1770 Cleghorn joined the Speculative Society, which had been founded only six years earlier.[44] A fresh ballot still took place at the beginning of each session for admission to membership, which was limited to thirty after 1769 – it had at first been only twenty. Cockburn said of it: 'No better arena could possibly have been provided for the exercise of the remarkable young men it excited . . . the Speculative completed what the academical had begun; together they did more good than all the rest of my education.' Cleghorn remained a member even after he went to St Andrews, so he must have valued the contacts. He seems to have been eminently 'clubbable', this being the first of the societies we hear of him joining.

In a letter dated 1 December 1772, the Earl of Cassilis wrote to the Principal and Masters of the United College of St Andrews presenting Hugh Cleghorn 'to the office of the Professor of Civil History'.[45] He is described as Master of Arts in the letter, though the actual date of his graduation in the catalogue of Edinburgh graduates is 8 December 1772 – something of an afterthought, perhaps, after the eight years spent in an intellectual environment which was as stimulating and enriching as any to be found in Europe.

2

'The uniform, still life of St Andrews'
1773–88

A young professor

The contrast between Edinburgh and St Andrews in the 1770s was marked. In Edinburgh there was growth: its citizens were enjoying a lively awareness of their leading position in the capital city of Scotland, which had too the highest law courts of the land. In the University new chairs were being established amid a general assumption that theirs was the leading Scottish university; in the city, new and elegant building projects were developing and drama and the arts were flourishing in a way they had not done since Flodden. In St Andrews life was in more of a minor key, not melancholy (in spite of the ruins) but *quiet*. William Robertson, for instance, in a letter to Principal Joseph McCormick in 1785, spoke of the 'uniform, still life of St Andrews',[1] and Cleghorn himself, writing in his journal in 1790, was reminded of St Andrews when he and Lord Home visited Ferrara: 'There was scarce a person walking in the streets . . . and the grass was growing under our feet . . . it resembles St Andrews though on a much larger scale.'[2]

As far as the University was concerned, it continued its ordered way, drawing its students mainly from Fife, Perth and Forfar. But 'the turnpike road system and the later developments of the stage coach routes' in Scotland in the eighteenth century all passed St Andrews by and left it geographically isolated, which had its effect on student numbers.[3] The University had suffered a little too from the effects of the Hanoverian government's distrust of the students' Jacobite sympathies. The Masters had done something to banish that by electing the Duke of Cumberland as Chancellor of the University just *before* Culloden had been fought and won by him in 1746. In 1747 Principal Tullidelph had exerted his authority to achieve the uniting of St Salvator's and St Leonards colleges and the ending of the system of regenting, so that there would be more inducement to men of academic distinction to come on the staff of St Andrews – men such as Robert Watson, William Wilkie and George Hill. Thus the University was a valid place of learning and the number of students had increased from the exceptionally low average of fifty-six Arts students between 1738 and 1748 to a hundred in 1792.[4] Cleghorn never spoke unjustly of St Andrews. 'All that it professes to teach is well taught,' he wrote to Andrew Bell, but its range was narrow at this time, educating its students 'for none of the learned professions except the ministry'.[5] Cleghorn felt no inclination to conform to this pattern of clerical convention: he was of the generation which had been deeply influenced by the leaders of the Scottish enlightenment and delighted in the variety of approach and widening of intellectual horizons which they had achieved, as he was to show in his own lectures.

Certainly, 1773 marked the beginning of the next definite stage in Cleghorn's life. On 21 March he became twenty-one; on 30 March he was in St Andrews being examined on the qualifications for the chair of Civil History, and the Masters of the United College 'being perfectly satisfied therewith', he was admitted to their company on 1 April[6] and attended his first meeting of the Senate on 3 April. He threw himself with enthusiasm into working out a course of lectures on the 'Civil History of Man' but found his efforts nullified by the sheer force of the students' inertia. Civil History was not one of the compulsory subjects in the Arts curriculum and therefore students could cheerfully ignore it. The Chair had probably only been set up after the union of the Colleges, in 1747, to accommodate William Vilant, who had lost the Humanity professorship but refused to retire.[7] Indeed, the students had had every opportunity of ignoring the subject so far, as none of the three previous incumbents had given any lectures at all.

That Cleghorn was the first to do so and the shape these lectures took, can be seen from the thick pile of his notes that survive among the Cleghorn Papers. These are the result of a revision Cleghorn undertook in the 1780s. In the introduction to them Cleghorn says of his earlier versions: 'It was my fortune, at perhaps too early a period of life, to be appointed to an office whose object is to examine the Civil History of Men. And I entered into the spirit of my profession with youthful ardour, but having few motives to animate or interest me, my labours long remained unrevised.'[8]

Disappointed as Cleghorn must have been with his peripheral academic role in the University, he lost no time in coming to terms with the students: he wrote a glowing recommendation for Andrew Bell who was going to Virginia in 1774 to try his fortune there.[9] He supported Dr Flint at the examination of applicants for medical degrees and he played a part in college administration, inspecting accounts, attending meetings, serving four times as Inspector of Works: all the small beer of academic life, which gave him little scope for his energy and instinct for action.[10]

This was the time when his father died and he inherited the Society property in Edinburgh. The Instrument of Sasine which invested him with it was dated 4 May 1774,[11] followed by another instrument on 1 July 1774 establishing the right of Hugh's mother, Jean Scott, Mrs Cleghorn, to a £50 annuity for her lifetime, to be drawn from the rents of Society.[12]

Marriage

It was also the time of his own wedding: on 2 October 1774 he married Rachel McGill in the old Greyfriars Parish in Edinburgh.[13] It is frustrating that no letters from Rachel survive among the Cleghorn Papers, but, writing to Dundas over twenty years later about a pension for his wife, Cleghorn refers with pride to her connections.[14] In the Edinburgh Marriage Register (1751–1800) she is described as 'daughter of John McGill of Edinburgh deceased'. And in the Cess book of the valued rent of Edinburgh under 1771–2 both John McGill's name and those of his heirs appear, so presumably he died sometime within that year.[15] It seems likely that Rachel's father was a descendant of one of the younger sons of John McGill of Kemback.

This John McGill was himself a younger son to the laird of Nether Rankeillor. He had become a Presbyterian minister in 1646 but on the restoration of the Stuarts had refused to conform, had been deprived of his living and had gone abroad, where he had taken a medical degree. He had returned in 1667 and purchased the estate of Kemback. By his first wife he had had five sons and, by his second, another son, David – and other children before his death in 1673. His direct heirs kept the Kemback estate while the younger sons would have had to make their own way.[16] Certainly the Cleghorns kept up links with Kemback, judging by the messages which Cleghorn sent via Rachel when he was in India. On the other hand, the bookplate in Rachel's brother John's books, which are in the library of Nether Stravithie, has as his motto '*Sine fine*', which suggests that Rachel and John were of the line of the MacGills of Oxfuird, who also had that as their motto. On her mother's side she was related to the Douglases of Strathenry.

Adam Smith, whose mother was Margaret, daughter of Robert Douglas (who died in 1706), described Rachel in a letter to Edward Gibbon as 'a very near relation of mine',[17] and, on his death in 1790, he left Rachel and Hugh the reversion of the £400 which in the first place was to go to 'Mrs. Janet Douglas', for her life rent.[18] The link with the Douglas family is also brought out in a letter of introduction from Hugh Cleghorn to Adam Smith in 1777, on behalf of Dr Thorkelin of the University of Copenhagen. On a personal note, he ends this letter: 'Rachy and Miss Douglas join me in best wishes to you and Miss Douglas . . . '[19] Adam Smith's 'Miss Douglas' was his cousin Jean, a daughter of John Douglas of Strathenry. She kept house for Smith and died in 1788, doing her duty to the last and directing household affairs 'with her usual spirit and cheerfulness'. Rachel Cleghorn's Janet Douglas is described in her will as 'resident in St Andrews' and as a daughter of John Douglas of Strathenry, and she died in 1790 having already made over her interest in the use of Adam

Smith's £400 to the Cleghorns in 1788.[20] (Since the salaries of professors at St Andrews were still meagre, the knowledge that his wife and her companion had this sum to keep them going must have relieved Cleghorn's mind when he set off on his travels with Lord Home in 1788.)

General Patrick Ross, the second son of Susannah Douglas and Patrick Ross of Innernethie was also a relation of Rachel. Susannah was yet another daughter of John Douglas of Strathenry. There is a letter from the General to Hugh and Rachel proposing to visit them when they were living in St Leonards, St Andrews, and more family letters about his sudden death and the effect of this on his daughters.[21] There are references later on in the letters of Peter Cleghorn, Hugh's son, to suggest that the family was also connected with the Queensberry Douglases.[22]

Where the Cleghorns lived in St Andrews, during this period, is not clear. They did not buy a house, for their name does not appear in the stent rolls or Register of Sasines for Fife. Between their marriage in 1774 and his embarking on his travels in 1788, they had seven surviving children born to them, two sons and five daughters. (None of them emerges as an individual until after Hugh's return from his Ceylon adventures in 1800.)

Friends and colleagues in St Andrews

From among the somewhat meagre personal references of this time to Cleghorn, a picture can be built up of his circle of friends. Chief among these was William Adam, from his Edinburgh school days. Indeed, so concerned was Cleghorn to persuade the Principal and Masters of the College to look favourably on Adam's request to purchase the superiority of Riley in Kinross-shire, that he assumed the compliance of his wife's connection, Colonel Douglas, and assured the Masters of this – which proved to be a grave error on Cleghorn's part. The Masters felt they were honour-bound to offer the superiority first to Col. Douglas, who was the existing holder, and they were justifiably annoyed with Cleghorn for prodding them so vigorously into serving Adam's interest. They had, however, gone too far to draw back, so Col. Douglas was no doubt left feeling 'affronted and ill-used', and probably with no very kindly opinion of Rachel's husband.[23]

Another of Cleghorn's friends at this time was Robert Beatson (1742–1818). A letter from him written from Dysart – on the back of which Cleghorn scribbled some questions to put to his students on limited monarchy – is undated but must have been written in 1786.[24] Beatson had been an officer in the Engineers, had served in France but in 1766 had retired on half pay, and at Vicars Grange in Fife had become an agriculturist. He had also set about compiling a *Political Index*, which he dedicated to Adam Smith and first published in 1786. It comprises lists of the holders of important offices over the centuries and was obviously nearly ready for publication when he wrote to Cleghorn, for he tells him: 'My list of subscribers augments apace and I doubt not but your letter to Lord Torphichen and others your friends in my favour, will be attended with the greatest success.' The immediate purpose of the letter was to: 'present my respectful compliments to Mrs. Cleghorn and request she will be so kind as accept a couple of Russian tongues which I send along with this epistle and tell her that, agreeable to the St Andrews fashion, *they eat best cold.*' The phrase 'the St Andrews fashion' confirms the impression which Boswell's account of Dr Johnson's visit to the city in 1773 gives: that life in St Andrews for the university people, the gentry and the well-to-do townspeople was 'agreeable', that their houses were 'comfortable and commodious',[25] and that social life was conducted in accordance with well-ordered conventions.

Another point of interest in Beatson's letter is his reminder to Cleghorn of 'your promise to come along with your worthy friend Patton to pass your Xmas with me'. When Cleghorn was about to set out on his travels in 1788, it was Patton he asked to help Rachel with the family's financial affairs, and when he was in Sicily in 1790 he showed his regard for Patton when, commending the wine of Syracuse, he writes in his journal: 'It is an extremely rich and strong wine and I flatter myself I shall be able to share some of it with my friends in Scotland . . . the wine shall be drunk by Captain Patton and me, unmixed and pure as our friendship . . . '[26] Patton's name also crops up in the University Library Professors' Borrowers Book under Cleghorn's entries. This Captain Charles Patton (1741–1837) served in the Royal Navy and, judging by two of his publications, would enjoy discussions with Cleghorn on political issues and would probably have many opinions in common with him. The first was *An Attempt to establish the bases of Freedom on Simple and Unerring Principles*, and the other he called *The Effects of Property upon Society and Government investigated – a plea for the basis of representation upon Property*. Moreover, in the 1780s and '90s, Patton had property in St Andrews – in 1779 on the south side of Market Street, next to Dr Forrest, and then from 1782 a much larger house on the south side of South Street next to Lady Gibliston.[27]

Among Cleghorn's fellow professors, his closest allies seem to have been Dr Flint and John Hunter. Dr Flint lined him up on at least six occasions to be an examiner of applicants for medical degrees. This examination may have been something of a formality but it created a sufficient sense of obligation in Flint for him to agree to carry out Cleghorn's supervisory duties in 1788 when he set out with Lord Home on his tour of Europe. John Hunter, who became Professor of Humanity two years after Cleghorn's appointment, was his ally as Inspector of Works and Keeper of the Charter Chest.[28] As the two youngest Masters, they probably had more than their share of supervisory duties pushed their way. From 1778 to 1790, John Hunter was given a rent-free house on condition that he undertook all supervisory duties such as presiding at meals and inspecting the students' rooms, mornings and evenings. Cleghorn, by contrast, rented the United College garden![29] That Cleghorn had valued the sense of companionship which being a senior member of the United College had given him is shown by his expressing his regrets at the professors 'breaking off all personal correspondence' when he had cut himself off from them by an absence of four years.[30] That they valued him is shown by their readiness to have him back even after so long a time.

Cleghorn was also a member of the Masons, though he may have originally joined an Edinburgh lodge rather than the St Andrews one. When he was in Sicily he wrote, of a festive and hard-drinking party with the Governor of Syracuse: 'For the first time in my life I found it of advantage to be a Mason. In arbitrary governments, this institution forms a bond of union, and admittance to it is solicited by persons the most enlightened and with an ardour of which we have no conception.'[31] Rather suggesting that he hardly found the Scottish Masons the height of good fellowship!

The other group he joined, as his 'Diploma' dated 11 May 1788 shows, was the Beggars' Benison of Anstruther.[32] This Diploma is full of double entendres – a take-off of a ship's licence – creating the new member 'a Knight Companion of the Most Ancient and Most Puissant Order of the Beggars' Benison and Merryland . . . with our full powers and privileges of Ingress, Egress and Regress from and to and to and from all Harbours, Creeks and Havens and Commodious Inlets upon the Coasts of our extensive territories at his pleasure . . . '[33] Membership of the club was restricted to thirty-two and on the title page of its Bible were fixed many coats of arms of members – among them those of Gordon, Selkirk, Glasgow, Torphichen, Kellie, Balcarres, Elgin and Crawford, but it also drew its members from Anstruther worthies and local lairds. They met twice a year on St Andrews Day and Candlemas at Dreel Castle and the principal purpose of this pseudo-knightly order was phallic exhibitionism. Since Cleghorn was only issued with his Diploma after he had set off from St Andrews not to return for twelve years, the Beggars could not have mattered much in his scale of values. His only comment on them is in a letter to Peter in January of 1825, when he says: 'General Durham at the last meeting of the Beggars at Anstruther, unknown to me, proposed you and John to be members of the Club. Your Diplomas cost me six guineas – keep them out of female sight.'[34]

Cleghorn also probably played golf – if he was skilled enough to win the Medal only two years after his return from Ceylon and become Captain of the Company of Golfers of St Andrews, he was no novice at the game.

Academic background

On the academic side Cleghorn certainly took students for coaching privately. In 1785 he was writing to Andrew Bell in answer to his request for advice on suitable reading on principles of government and 'great nations of antiquity', and mentioning books he had recommended to two young men to whom he had been giving tuition during the vacation. He suggested Adam Smith's *Enquiry* (into the Causes of the Wealth of Nations) with the comment: 'upon commerce and political economy there is no writer equal to Smith; and if your pupil is intended for political life, he cannot too closely study the works of this author.' Inevitably he recommended Montesquieu – 'and the corresponding parts of Ferguson's *Essay* may be read at the same time. This book, though not well connected, nor remarkable for illustrating what it intends, abounds with many noble sentiments which cannot fail to make proper impression on a young mind.' Cleghorn thinks highly of John Millar's *Distinction of Ranks* but Locke's 'Civil Liberty' is dismissed as a 'tedious answer to the absurd writings of Filmer'. The French 'Economists' – particularly Quesnay – are recommended, but not so the Abbé de Condillac's *Cours d'Étude*. 'The book is in vogue but the learning of the author is that of a fop and his politics those of a pedant.' There is a good deal more both of advice and recommended reading – Cleghorn was employing an amanuensis that summer so his thoughts could run on unchecked.[35] If there is perhaps an element of showing off to a man only one year his junior in age, there are also discrimination and a real relish for ideas and their practical application.

This is also shown in the books he presented to the University Library from authors of his acquaintance, in his suggestions of books which he thought the Library should purchase, and in the multiplicity of his interests as shown in the Professors' Borrowers Book. One would expect a Professor of Civil History to be reading Montesquieu and Hume and even Francis Hutcheson, Adam Smith and John Millar, but Buffon's *Histoire Naturelle*, Hawkesmith's *Voyages*, five volumes of the transactions of the Royal Society, Priestley on *Vision*, Muller's *Mathematics*, Hogarth's *Anatomy of Beauty* – all show a genuinely wide range of interests. He was even enthusiastic enough in 1777 to volunteer to put the Old College Library – described as 'at present in great confusion' – in order, which he found took him much longer than he expected, a labour spreading over two years and earning him £45 for his extra work.[36]

That Cleghorn had given his mind to the preparation of his lectures is shown when he was, later on, writing to the Duke of Leeds about the need for a closer understanding between the Swiss cantons and Britain. He wrote:

'I had myself occasion to discuss the General Subject of political Oeconomy in the Lectures of my Professorship at St Andrews and the Labours of some years have given me, if not the ability to judge, at least the habit of directing my attention to those circumstances which commonly determine the Connection of Nations.'[37]

It is perhaps hardly fair to compare a student's notes which were taken at Professor Robert Watson's lectures on Rhetoric (themselves an innovation in 1758) with Cleghorn's own lecture notes but, injustice aside, the comparison is quite revealing. What the student took from Watson amounted to a series of pretty elementary definitions of figures of speech (metaphor, oxymoron, etc) with formal examples from the Classics. The tone is that of the schoolmaster, the contents cut and dried.[38] What Cleghorn's lectures show is an awareness that he is addressing those about to take a responsible place in society, that there is more to be cultivated at university than sensitivity to classical syntax, that there are new fields being opened up, knowledge of which will enrich the young men's understanding of their future role as

citizens. The conclusion of his introduction to his revised course
of lectures throws light on his approach:

'Such, gentlemen, are the objects to which your attention will
be directed . . . they lead to many important enquiries which do
not naturally belong to those branches of science which are the
common topics of academical lectures . . . When I address you
as men of independence and of active life, I describe in some
measure those scenes in which Providence may call upon you
to act. When I address you as Britons, as active members of the
government of your country, I consider it as your indispensable
duty to understand the Science of Politics. When I address you
as Scholars, I feel I present to your curiosity, liberal objects of
contemplation . . . '[39]

There is a confidence about this approach which suggests that
Cleghorn had been doing some effective empire-building on
behalf of his subject since his arrival, and there are signs of
this in the United College Minutes and University Register. From
1778 onwards a prize for Civil History is included among the
annual awards (Lord Elgin winning it in 1784). In 1783 thirteen
students enrolled for the Civil History class, and in 1784 the
College ruled that all bursars were in future obliged to go to
this class either in their third or fourth year. Once these classes
were launched they attracted interest and support. On a verso
page about halfway through his lecture notes, he had prepared an
announcement: 'Before I enter upon the business of the evening, I
beg to inform those gentlemen that have lately become students of
this class that upon Monday next I shall begin an abridged course
of my Lectures. Any person may avail himself of this. And I only
beg that he would inform me of his intention that I may hit upon
the hour most convenient for all. Ten in the morning would be the
most convenient hour for me, and if it does not interfere with the
business of your class, I could wish to adopt it.'

That he had a synopsis of his lectures printed for distribution to
his classes is shown by his reference to it, but unfortunately none
has been discovered among the Cleghorn Papers.

Cleghorn's lectures on government

The general title of his course is 'National Institutions – Origin and Progress of Government'. Originally he planned a most ambitious survey: first the political section was to consider 'the Government of Nature'; then the 'progress and principles of particular governments', and, last in this section, an analysis of the government of Great Britain.

The second part of the course was to be 'on the progress and principles of commerce – an immense field of curiosity'. More fully: 'A curiosity not merely speculative, but whose well directed researches might lead to the establishment of principles which might materially affect the political happiness of the world.'

He proposed to conclude with a third part: 'a history of Philosophy with an account of the various causes which have promoted or retarded in different ages the progress of Science.' He goes on confidently:

'I shall trace it from its first dawnings in Egypt and its full appearance in Greece, to the era of our celebrated countryman Lord Bacon of Verulam. I shall give an account of the improvements and new arrangements which this celebrated nobleman introduced into Science . . . the history of Science which I propose to investigate will not be merely a detail of opinions. The state of philosophy will be explained by or will itself be brought to explain some of the most important transactions that have happened in civil society.'

Cleghorn is too ambitious here: only the notes for Part I of the course survive, and even in those there are indications that he ran out of time. (That he had in fact read a good deal of Bacon is attested by the Library Borrowers Book.)

'Governments of Nature'

Cleghorn begins his lectures with the origins of authority among men. Here he follows John Millar, to whom he owes far more than he acknowledges.[40] And, like Millar, Cleghorn does not pretend to originality: he wants to make his students aware of the importance of the achievements of pioneers such as David Hume, Adam Ferguson and Adam Smith in understanding the evolutionary nature of society. He uses Millar's categories, as set out in *Distinction of Ranks*, of physical strength as a source of authority; superiority of mental qualities, the authority which age gives in the first stages of society, especially to the authority of a father. Even some of his examples Cleghorn draws from Millar. Others are his own, less historical than Millar's but reflecting his own relish for poetry – as when he cites the lament from Milton's *Samson Agonistes*:

> God, when he gave me strength, to show withal
> How slight the gift was, hung it in my hair.

Then comes a discussion of wealth and birth as sources of authority over others. He adopts Adam Smith's division of society into four periods with regard to property – that is: hunters, shepherds, husbandmen, and the commercial state.[41] He rounds off this section with his conclusion that: 'the adventitious effects of birth and fortune are strongly felt and continue to be the two principal circumstances which set one man above another: the Scots expect courage from a Douglas; the English boast the hereditary virtue of the house of Cavendish.' Perhaps it was Adam Ferguson who had made him especially aware of the inner bonds of loyalty among Highlanders to the clan and to the chief: 'The influence of a Cameron of Lochiel – only a simple feuar under the Duke of Argyle by outward show – yet could take eight hundred of his men into the rebel army. The authority of an English Duke scarcely extends over his own menial servants.'

Cleghorn owed much to Adam Ferguson, more perhaps in the assumptions that were basic to his thought than in actual arguments. For instance, Cleghorn assumed like Ferguson that society progressed from 'rudeness to refinement' but that progress might be in a destructive direction such as was threatened by the new economic developments of the eighteenth century which might lead to the de-naturing of man. Perhaps it was from Ferguson that Cleghorn took his innate conservatism, his belief that a sound society did not need radical alterations in the social structure or forms of government – the fewer of those the better – but active benevolence, vigilance and a sense of justice among its citizens.

Evolution of governments: 'Rudeness to Refinement'

Supposing government has been established, Cleghorn asks upon what principles are we bound to submit to it? He gives the Tory view of the duty of passive obedience because of the divine origin of kingship and the Whig idea, as shown in the systems of Sydney and Locke, that only the usefulness of government to men makes obedience acceptable. He concludes that: 'these two principles ["admiration" and "utility"] being conjoined and not giving too much to either, may be esteemed the foundation of government.' He lists his arguments vigorously against the idea that any government was ever founded upon an 'Original Contract'.

He then traces the formation of village confederacies, leading to 'aristocratical government' based on land holding. From this, royal power developed by stages. Again Cleghorn turns to Millar to question whether financial self-interest and the 'lucrative arts' create or undermine political despotism. On the one hand both monarch and people found the demands of the feudal levy so tiresome that both were ready to commute service into taxes. This led to the forming of mercenary standing armies – the chief tool of the despot (echoes here of the great debate in eighteenth-century Scotland on the role of a national militia). On the other hand:

'It is only by applying to the practice of commerce and the arts that the lower ranks of the people can hope to better their condition. According to their success in business they possess wealth and they aim at independence. Every man is able to earn a livelihood by his own labour . . . He behaves with civility indeed but not with servility.'

But once the people have a role of their own, conflict with the monarch becomes inevitable. Cleghorn concludes with Millar that 'in small states, the people commonly get the better of the prince', but 'great nations have developed in the opposite direction'. He then considers what are the other alterations 'which commerce and the arts have upon the government of a country and the manners and disposition of the people' and observes:

'I by no means join in opinion with those who exclaim against the depravity of the present age. The modes of virtue are changed: we may be less hospitable but more charitable; less valourous but more moderate; less courageous but more clement.'

He discusses (in a way which suggests his mind is full of his current reading rather than his own lecture themes) whether there are any connecting principles between the Elegant Arts and the Science of Morals. Then, claiming to have traced the progress of Society from Rudeness to Refinement, 'I propose therefore to stop here for a moment in order to make some reflection upon the present state and condition of the human race.' At this point comes his first set of prepared questions. This questioning continues to punctuate the rest of the course. He was obviously trying to check up on how well the students were absorbing his arguments.

Three tests of happiness: comparing past and present

Acting on his intention to consider the present state of man, he questions whether men are as happy now as in former ages and applies three tests. The first is to see if population is increasing. 'Men will multiply to the measure of their subsistence', and since agriculture is improving in so many ways, increased production will provide for more people's needs. He goes on to discuss the controversy between David Hume and Robert Wallace over whether ancient nations were *less* populous than ours and comes down on the side of Hume, that they were.

His second test is to examine the institution of slavery. He discusses at length and with feeling the origins of slavery and its evil effects, his indignation also being directed: 'against those authors who have coldly transmitted to us a detail of these execrable facts and who expatiate on the praises of the barbarous people [the Spartans] by whom they were committed. Hence I have been induced to think that history thus written may become too dangerous for the perusal of youth. It is high treason against humanity to describe actions so atrocious without invoking posterity to turn from them with horror.' He points out that at least in Europe slavery has been abolished and lists the factors which have led to this abolition.

That Cleghorn's lectures provoked argument is shown by some comments pencilled by another hand opposite Cleghorn's passage (which he has largely taken from Millar) on the role of the Church in helping to end slavery. He says that both Paul's letter to Philemon and the somewhat ambivalent attitude of churchmen towards their own villeins throw some doubt on how much the Church really helped to end slavery. His critic protests in the note that Cleghorn has gone back on his previous acceptance of the position of St Paul: 'We once conversed on the subject of this epistle and you seemed to me satisfied that you had not before understood it.' And opposite Cleghorn's use of the word 'casuistry', concerning the attitude of churchmen, is written the question: 'Was there anything like *prejudice* in the application of this term – which certainly is not an epithet of unqualified praise?' It is true that Cleghorn rarely misses an opportunity for a side-swipe at priests, and this had obviously been an old subject of debate with this particular colleague.

It is interesting too that Cleghorn follows Millar in making a plea on economic grounds for the ending of bondage among the colliers and salters of Scotland and cites Millar's figures to show how bondage distorts the level of wages.

When he looks at slavery in North America he shows how uneconomic it is as well as how immoral – and he underlines the irony behind the war which the slave-owning colonists had fought against Britain to defend their right to tax themselves. His sense of outrage against the continued existence of slavery in the West Indies and America is made abundantly clear. He describes the West Africans being driven:

' . . . for some hundred miles across the desert, chained in a ship, the first perhaps they ever saw, tossed for months on an element with which they are entirely unacquainted, exposed to uncertainty, the most cruel tormentor of the miserable and finally condemned in an unknown land to all the severities of servitude . . . Fortune never so capriciously exerted her empire over men than when she subjected those nations of heroes to the refuse of European jails; to men who possess the virtues of neither country – neither the humanity of that from which they go nor the simplicity of that in which they settle, but who by their levity, tyranny and baseness are just objects of contempt and indignation to their slaves.'

He refutes all the arguments put forward in defence of African slavery and asserts that if better tools and more scientific methods were introduced, slavery would not be needed. Here he quotes from Adam Smith's *Wealth of Nations* on the effect on the labour force of improvements in technology.

Coming back to his tests on whether 'the national happiness of man is as great during our times as it has been in former ages', the third one is applied to the practice and the art of war. He claims that it is less savage than in former times, that contending nations hardly feel any direct effects of war but 'in augmentation of their debts'. The effect of the prevalence of mercenary armies is discussed at some length, both good and bad effects. No automatic progress is assumed but a balance of loss and gain, showing Cleghorn again as very much the pupil of Adam Ferguson.

Feudal government

The next main section of the lectures is on the emergence and development of feudal government. He obviously feels some need to justify spending time on this. 'Let us enter into the house of the nearest lawyer and peruse the first deed, the first instrument of sale . . . and from the very mention of the words – "holds of the Crown"; "superior": "vassal"; "feu-duty" – we will be convinced that we are only the heirs of the Goths and the Lombards.' And again in justification:

'The principles of this government fall very properly to be explained in this part of the course because the Feudal System may be regarded either as a government of nature or of art, as a government which naturally arises from the situation of the shepherd and rude agricultural tribes or as moderated and improved by the northern tribes after they became masters of the provinces.'

Then he follows an historical approach and does his duty by Montesquieu, Hume and Robertson in picking out the main developments. From Hume he quotes the profound difference between money payments as reward and the assignment of lands: money payments can be stopped, 'but the attachment naturally formed to a fixed portion of land, gradually begets the idea of something like property and makes the possessor forget his dependent situation.' On the effects of entail he quotes Robertson: 'A great family in feudal times is not improperly compared by Dr. Robertson to a River which becomes considerable from the length of its course.' But politically the growth of power of the nobles was destructive of good government and during the 'feudal centuries': 'Uninteresting events and wars without notice and without consequence fill and disgrace the Annals of Europe' – and with that somewhat '1066 And All That' remark the section on Feudalism comes to an end.

'Governments of Positive Institutions'

He calls his next section 'Governments of positive institutions' but insists that they are not opposed to 'natural governments', because: 'every government which now exists or which ever existed in any former period was not the effect of sagacity and contrivance in the Legislator, was not a system formed on his abstraction but arose naturally and necessarily from the character, circumstances and situation of the People over whom any particular species of Government is established.' Nor, he hastens to add was there ever a Golden Age from which we fell.

So he classifies past and present forms of government very much on the lines laid down by Aristotle and elaborated by Montesquieu: democracy, aristocracy, monarchy; with their variations, their virtues and their weaknesses. His range of examples is wide: they include Cicero on the tyrant of Syracuse; the Medici of fifteenth century Florence; Boswell on Corsica under the French; the effect of the war of American Independence on the fortunes of the Irish. All well-trodden ground, but treated with some liveliness.

Theoretical, 'Ideal' governments

Cleghorn then turns briefly to Sir Thomas More's *Utopia* and James Harrington's *Oceana*. More gets short shrift for his description of the Utopians' attempt to make their people despise silver and gold while also using it for foreign trade, that is, trying to: 'render the same subject both an object of public concern and of private contempt.' Harrington's ideas on the method of choosing representatives, annual rotation of office-holding, the break-up of the big landed estates, the lack of checks on the power of the Senate, are all examined and severely criticised.

Suggested reading

To help those who 'incline to pursue this subject' of national institutions, Cleghorn gives a brief reading list consisting of: *Les esprits des lois* by Montesquieu; works on political laws by Pufendorf and Burlamaqui; on the people's rights by Vatel and *De jure belli et pacis* by Grotius. He then sums up what he has attempted so far in his analysis of political institutions, and concludes:

'The observations I have made on these subjects may perhaps be of use if you animate your attention and direct your judgement in examining the important questions which occur in Political Science – and surely if the study of Morals is deemed necessary because it teaches you what you ought to wish for yourselves, the study of Politics cannot be less so since it teaches you what you ought to wish for your country.'

The British Constitution

In tackling the subject of the British Constitution, he conveys his sense of its importance but warns there is some heavy ground ahead – which he promises to get over as lightly as possible: 'The various enquiries which this subject presents cannot all be rendered equally splendid or interesting. Parts and important parts too, must sometimes seem little calculated to excite our attention . . . ' And he is aware of this when he is listing the prerogatives of the Crown, the great offices attached to the Court, the terms of the Bill of Rights. Also, about a third of the way through this section of the notes, the neat copy ends and the rest is in Cleghorn's own hand and much more hurriedly put together – unlike Millar's notes on government, which are very thorough, even remorselessly so.

Balance of powers in the British Constitution

He begins by saying: 'You all know that the British Constitution is a mixed form of government consisting of Monarchial, Aristocratical and Democratical powers . . . It affords ample security for the enjoyment of Civil Liberty . . . The sovereign power is so constituted that the King is great and safe only when he maintains the Laws and the rights of his subjects.' The prerogatives and personal safety of the King are secured by the constitutional maxim that 'the King can do no wrong'. But the rights and privileges of the people are secured by the maxim that the King's express command shall not vindicate his ministers for acting contrary to the law, and also by their right to choose their members of Parliament. 'The equal distribution of Justice, prescribed by the Laws of Britain, which pay no personal regard to any man' is another source of security to the people.

His simile to describe the tensions within the British system is very much of his generation – they are like: 'three distinct powers in Mechanics that jointly impel the Machine of Government in a direction different from what either acting by itself could have done but at the same time in a direction, partaking of each and formed of all.'

The role of the MP

On the role of the MP in Parliament – whether he has respon-sible or delegated power – Cleghorn takes up the same position as Burke had taken with his Bristol voters. Cleghorn says on this issue:

'M.P.'s when assembled in Parliament do not represent their constituents only but the whole body of the people, for a member, though elected for a particular district, serves the whole realm; because the end for which he is sent into Parliament is not partial but general, is not barely for the advantage of his County or his Borough, but for the good of the Commonwealth and therefore an M.P. is not bound like a deputy of the United States of the Netherlands to obey the instructions of his constituents on every particular point unless he thinks it proper to do so.'

In pointing out that the hereditary title of the Hanoverians to the throne rests on an Act of Parliament he asserts: 'For I hold it to be the fundamental law of every state . . . that should the people assemble and with one accord or by a great majority agree to dissolve their present government, that such government would be very legally dissolved.'

The dangers of 'Influence'

Having listed the royal prerogatives, he points out that they are circumscribed by many limitations, which he lists. 'It is not now prerogative but Influence which is complained of . . . an influence which has been acquired by accident and confirmed by corrupt means.' He goes on to point out how both the First Lord of the Treasury and the Secretary of State for Southern Affairs have gradually by the multiplication of offices built up such wide patronage that one of the two is assured of a dominant position in Parliament and the administration. Cleghorn condemns in particular: 'the applying of public money to Secret Services for which no detailed account need be submitted to the Commons.' (There is an ironic slant to this in that Dundas about ten years later was financing Cleghorn's Ceylon expedition out of the funds of just that service.)

He then turns to Parliament, describing the composition of the House of Lords and saying that it is: 'a body of nobility peculiarly necessary in a mixed constitution in order to support the rights of both the Crown and the People, by forming a barrier to withstand the encroachments of both.' On the Commons he describes the process of electing the 558 members of the House. With regard to Scotland he says: 'A man must possess 400 pound valued rent, holding of the Crown, to entitle him to be elected for a county, and for a borough he must be a burgess. The same qualifications that are requisite to enable a man to be elected are requisite to entitle him to be an elector.' He gives penalties for corruption or the buying of votes during elections but does not say how often these were enforced.

He is distinctly woolly on the stages of a bill through Parliament except for his description of the Royal Assent. He *is* clear on the process of impeachment.

On the revenues of the King, he promises to speak at greater length: 'under the head of National Resources . . . I shall therefore confine myself at present to a few observations.' These comprise a description of the annual taxes on land and malt which yield about £3,500,000 yearly; and the perpetual taxes: Customs; Excise; Salt Tax; Post Office; stamp duties; house and window light tax; taxes upon men servants, Hackney carriages, which yield about £17,000,000 a year.

The importance of the Bill of Rights

In the last part of Cleghorn's lectures that survive he begins with the Bill of Rights and Act of Settlement, 'since no mixed form of Government can be free, permanent and peaceable but where the jurisdiction of its several powers are clearly described. We may venture to pronounce that the political freedom of Great Britain did not arrive at any degree of perfection till the Bill of Rights was admitted and further limitations to the Crown were made by the Act of Settlement . . . ' He gives the Bill of Rights in full and then stresses that: 'the whole plan of Civil and Religious liberty in Britain depends entirely upon the freedom of elections;

if this is violated either by the Crown or by the People, the balance of our Constitution is completely overturned. That freedom of elections has been frequently violated since the Revolution, partly in the latter part of the reign of Queen Anne and since that time by the ministerial power of the Crown is beyond a doubt. But the basest and worst subversion of the Right most frequently occurs on the part of the people who bestow their votes on unworthy persons either through selfish or partial principles.'

The duties of the subject

He goes on: 'Let us then fairly state some of the duties which British subjects owe to their King and Country.' The people should support the legal prerogatives of the Crown; should not publish wanton accusations against the Sovereign and his ministers (for 'the Pen of a party writer in Great Britian may prove a dagger to his country'); should not speak 'disrespectfully or indecently of their Sovereign . . . or ridicule his foibles'; should provide against any abuse of the ministerial power of the Crown by bringing ministers to justice if necessary. British subjects should also choose proper representatives to: 'exercise the power of the people, for the good of the people . . . and not for their own particular advantage. But as men are apt to be blinded and misled by this private advantage, nay, as there will always be a great number of men in every society who will knowingly sacrifice the public to their private interest no members should have any private advantage or emolument to get or lose, by his being for or against either side of the question.'

He points out the danger of a First Lord of the Treasury using his powers of patronage to such good effect that he will always have a working majority in the Commons. This brings him back to the vital need for voters to exercise their right of choice with responsibility, not like those who: 'dispose of their votes by bribery or promises, for party purposes or court favours – a feast or a drunken carousel.'

Cleghorn also asserts that honest subjects should refuse offices for which they know themselves unsuited; should not accept unmerited places or pensions nor 'hold more public employments than it is possible for any man to fulfil with honour'. He has a high idea of office-holding: 'There is scarce an office in this free government but demands the utmost application, exactness and fidelity and to which a man of honour and integrity may not devote every hour of his life that can be spared from private concerns and the relaxation necessary to invigorate his powers.'

The lecture notes peter out here with more lists of questions and half sheets of points about British Law, but there is no systematic conclusion or rounding off of Cleghorn's main themes. However, these have emerged clearly from his course: that the development of all societies is a natural process, the evidence for which can be studied by accepted rules of observation; that all stages of development bring with them their own dangers and opportunities which responsible citizens should make it their business to study and be aware of; that this awareness, honestly acted upon, is the best safeguard of healthy political development, which, with men's proneness to corruption, does not take place automatically. He does not quote Burke but what he says chimes exactly with Burke, that: 'the price of liberty is eternal vigilance.'

Thus Cleghorn's lectures may be said to throw a little light on his character, and add something to our knowledge of university teaching in St Andrews in the 1770s and '80s. They show him as an enthusiast; if he was not an original scholar in his own right, his reading and the use he made of it show a vigorous and resourceful mind at work, and a certain generosity which would appeal to the young. When he was in India at the beginning of his Ceylon adventure, one of the young officers asked him if he knew the Cleghorn of St Andrews, of whom his brother, who had been a student there, had spoken enthusiastically. This clearly gratified Cleghorn and does suggest that he had awoken a genuine response among St Andrews students. The lectures also establish that St Andrews, for all its seeming remoteness, was aware of the advances in political science which had been made in this period.

It is easy enough, nevertheless, to understand how, after fifteen years of the ordered academic round and the 'uniform still life of St Andrews', Cleghorn was ready to seize the chance of travel that came his way in 1788. Thirty-six years later his friend William Adam said of Cleghorn when, after the death of his wife, he was thinking of moving into St Andrews: 'No man is worse calculated to sit down in a country town and live on capital without occupation.'[42] If that was true of Cleghorn at the age of seventy-two, how much more applicable must it have been when he was only thirty-six.

The Grand Tour Begins
May 1788 – June 1789

The opportunity to see the world outside Scotland – and to see it in some style too – came in 1788 when Alexander, tenth Earl of Home, needed a travelling tutor for a tour of Europe. Cleghorn was recommended to the Homes by Lord Elphinstone,[1] on the suggestion of William Adam, who had married an Elphinstone. Lord Home had been a student at St Andrews for a couple of years – in 1787 he had enrolled in Cleghorn's Civil History course[2] – he was nineteen years old and as Mrs Cleghorn, Hugh's mother, pertinently remarked in a letter to Andrew Bell, he was 'now among the richest of our nobility'.[3] In this she was referring to the fortune which Lord Home's mother, Abigail, had brought to the family as the daughter and co-heir of John Ramey of Yarmouth, a fabulously rich barrister-at-law and West Indian merchant.

Cleghorn kept diaries of these next two years of his European travels but he did not do this on a daily basis till he started his second volume in May of 1789. It was not till he realised how quickly events could become blurred in his own mind that in October 1788 he began to write up his assessment of what had been happening in France since April. 'The imperfect accounts which I have received', he wrote, 'are almost forgotten during the interval that has elapsed since they were collected, I shall shortly relate what my memory has been able to retain.'[4] However, he does also include some rather sparse references to his and Lord Home's movements during this first stage of their Grand Tour.

Cleghorn himself left St Andrews on 15 May 1788. He was asking Rachel to stay behind and take responsibility for their seven children while he satisfied his ardent desire to travel. He had at least asked his friend Captain Patton to look after his business affairs for him and Rachel while he was away, which Patton did 'with a knowledge and attention of which I am incapable', as Cleghorn wrote later with disarming self-knowledge on receiving 'comfortable accounts' of how things were going in St Andrews in his absence.[5] Before he joined Lord Home at the Hirsel, he had obtained letters of introduction from Adam Smith to those Physiocrats in Paris with whom Smith was still in touch,[6] and to Edward Gibbon in Lausanne – a letter in which Smith describes Cleghorn as 'my particular and intimate friend'.[7]

From the Hirsel Lord Home and Cleghorn travelled to London, where they stayed for about a month, making arrangements for their tour to the continent. Home House, Number 20 Portman Square (until 1989 the home of the Courtauld Institute of Art) had been built by Robert Adam between 1773 and 1776 for the Countess of Home, as a house designed for entertaining – with a dramatically elegant staircase and each room opening into the next, with walls that were curved or inset with niches or broken up with columns, and painted with colour schemes which showed Adam's subtlety as well as his daring and originality. But what Cleghorn noted down about this month in London was the opportunity it gave him of going often to Westminster Hall during the impeachment of Warren Hastings, in which William Adam was playing a leading role as Counsel for the Commons. Cleghorn was enormously impressed by 'the solemnity of the proceedings and the pageantry of the Courts'.

In France – Paris and Soissons

Once they had set off on their travels, Cleghorn made a note of their stay at Douai in Flanders as standing out in his memory. It was here that Lord Home met up with his friend Ramsey, in the monastery in which he was staying, while Cleghorn renewed his acquaintance with Principal Farquharson of the Scots College, and found Professor Dugald Stewart also on a visit to Douai. With him, Cleghorn called on Principal Gibson of the English College[8] and for the first time was 'present at the celebration of the Mass, a ceremony which till then I had never had an opportunity of seeing'. But it was the tremendous thunderstorm of the next day, Sunday 13 July (1788), which left such a deep mark on Cleghorn's memory and which had a political impact too, since the trail of destruction it left through Northen France helped to ruin the harvest and added actual food shortages to the rising tide of discontent. Cleghorn described the sudden darkness and veering of the wind and the lightning as 'one long uninterrupted sheet' and the rain accompanied with pieces of ice, 'the smallest of which were larger than pigeon eggs.' Very soon there was not a whole window pane left in the town: 'houses were unroofed, trees torn up by the roots . . . ' and apples and pears perforated by the hail as if they had been struck by gunshot. 'I have read of such storms,' Cleghorn wrote, 'but never thought they visited European climes.'

Cleghorn and Home arrived in Paris in the middle of July, 'during the turbulent administration of M. Brienne,' but stayed there only until the middle of August, when 'a variety of reasons then induced me to leave it'. Cleghorn chose Soissons for what proved to be a five-month stay and he: 'had no occasion to regret the choice I had made. The town is healthy and the country beautiful, the company agreeable and accessible and there were no extravagant Englishmen nor expensive amusements . . . and the French language is here spoken in its best Dialect.' For company they had a Mr Markham, son to the Archbishop of York, a Mrs Stainforth, who as well as being hospitable was a good conversationalist, and two Sheldon brothers: 'gentlemen of high birth and most agreeable manners.' So here Lord Home had to settle down to learn to talk French and Cleghorn too presumably improved his accent.

In October 1788 Cleghorn, at any rate, was in Paris, and it seems to have been then that he resolved to record his impressions of developments in France from April to October. As a piece of political analysis it showed both shrewdness and a pretty accurate understanding of French politics. He began at the point when the Parlement of Paris had launched on its resistance to royal authority and the King's ministers prepared to reply with edicts – setting up a *cour plénière* to register royal acts (in place of the Paris Parlement) and enlarging the jurisdiction of the Bailliages, 'to supersede the judicial power of the Parlements.' Cleghorn then gives an account of how Espréménil warned Parlement of the nature of these edicts and 'prevailed upon every member to sign a paper and declare on his honour that he would not act in that court'.

In Cleghorn's account of the army being sent to arrest Espréménil, he obviously thought it rather poor-spirited of the lawyers to permit their doors to be opened to the soldiers: 'They should have allowed them to beat them to pieces and they ought to have received the soldiers with silence and gravity of the Roman Senate on the invasion of the Gauls.' However, his penchant for drama apart, Cleghorn brought out well the impasse in which the government found itself: 'The future of the Cour Plénière and the Inaction of the Bailliages suspended almost . . . everywhere in France the execution . . . of Justice.' The national expenditure had for some time exceeded the Revenue by near three million a year . . . 'the Pays d'État are the most troublesome . . . ' but the only example he gave was Brittany (he did not mention the Vizelle Assembly).

Cleghorn attributed the dismissal of Brienne and Lamoignon to court intrigue, and went on to describe the reaction of the Parisians – burning effigies of the ministers, lighting bonfires at the Pont Neuf, killing the Guards who were sent to put them down and throwing their bodies into the Seine. 'The slaughter was so considerable that Government, it is said, to prevent the people knowing the extent of their victory, ordered the net at the bridge of St Lô to be drawn up that the bodies of the drowned might float incognito to the Ocean . . . ' The fixing of a date for the summoning of the Estates General and the recall of Necker excited too much hope, in Cleghorn's view. 'I have read Necker's *Discourse* and heard his system explained by men who have the best opportunity of knowing it . . . ' Perhaps he was thinking here of the discussions he had had with Adam Smith's friends, the Physiocrats – through whom: 'I had access to information concerning the schemes which were then agitated, relative to the government and finances of France . . . '9 as he explained later to the Duke of Leeds.

Certainly his reaction to the exaggerated expectations of what Necker could achieve were set down soberly enough in October 1788: 'I am disposed at present to consider it as Ideal . . . ' On Necker's proposal to recall the Assembly of Notables to decide whether the Estates General were to vote by heads or by order, he observed: 'The États Generaux are to be indebted for their existence and their form to the Assembly of the Notables. To an assembly in which the people have not one Representative and before which they have always acquiesced in the idea of their own insignificance. To expect the great will divide their political right with the people without a struggle is to expect an event neither warranted by History nor by a knowledge of the human heart . . . '

His final note is dated May 1789: 'The Notables did nothing and after a long delay the King was obliged to issue an Edict for the assembling of the Estates. France, I think, is yet very far from being soon in possession of a Regular Constitution . . . Before any general laws or an Equal System of Imposts can be established France must be consolidated into one great Monarchy, instead of being divided as at present into various little states which claim separate privileges and exemptions.'

How long Cleghorn was in Paris in the autumn of 1788 is not clear, but he was back in Soissons in December for on the 19th he was writing – and not before time, it might be thought – to the Principal of St Andrews University, asking for: 'your permission and that of my brethren to pass this winter on the continent. The uncertainty of my situation prevented me from applying earlier on this subject to the College . . . '10 (Perhaps he and Lord Home had decided on a six-month trial run to see how compatible they found each other.) Cleghorn went on to mention how his predecessor had been given a similar indulgence and explained that: 'Dr. Flint has been so friendly as to undertake my official duty at College Table.' Principal McCormick wrote back giving him permission, 'because in the circumstances of his case, they do not find his attendance absolutely necessary.'

Switzerland

The first volume of Cleghorn's journals ended at this point, and the second found the two of them settled at Neuchâtel.[11] Before the winter of 1788–9 really set in, they had presumably made their way there from Soissons via Besançon and Geneva. (There is a note at the end of the second volume of how much it cost to bring the carriage from Besançon at the end of March over the snow.) Cleghorn certainly felt at home in Neuchâtel and formed friendships that were to alter the pattern of his life.

Neuchâtel was known as the 'royal canton'; it was outside the Swiss Confederation and under the rule of the King of Prussia. The city of Neuchâtel was a small, flourishing one of about four thousand inhabitants, still almost wholly confined within its medieval walls, while the slopes round it were covered with vineyards. Built amid these were two splendid residences, the Hôtel du Peyrou and Grand Rochette. The owners of these, Madame Du Peyrou and the Comte de Meuron, gave not only their hospitality but also their friendship to Cleghorn. Henriette-Dorothée was the wife of Pierre Alexandre Du Peyrou, a millionaire of Dutch descent from Surinam who had become a citizen of Neuchâtel. A man of some intellectual calibre, he had won the confidence of Jean-Jacques Rousseau, who wrote freely to him and made him one of his literary executors. He had aged early, was deaf, and somewhat given to hypocondria, and was twenty-one years older than his wife. She had been a pupil of Rousseau, was vivacious, good-looking and loved to entertain lavishly, with dinners, balls and fêtes on the lake. She enjoyed acting and shone as the leading figure among the social élite who took part in plays such as Beaumarchais' *Barber of Seville*. She gathered round her a group of admirers, and of these Cleghorn must have been one.[12] There is a note among his papers of a copy of Helvetius sent to Mme Du Peyrou and he wrote to her from Egypt and India in terms of warm and teasing friendship.

Cleghorn's second volume began with his resolving on 9 May 1789 to pay a second visit to Geneva because he had been sent letters from England for different gentlemen there. Lord Home and Col. O'Dunne of the Irish Brigade went with him as far as Yverdon at the western end of the lake of Neuchâtel. Col. O'Dunne had seen service in the French army, had a small pension from France, but financially was none too secure. He and Lord Home however shared a passion for sport – fishing, riding, shooting – and as these were not of interest to Cleghorn, he was only too happy to leave Home in Col. O'Dunne's company at Yverdon, to watch the exhibitions of horsemanship taking place there.

The next morning (Sunday, 10 May 1789) Cleghorn went on by himself, finding: 'it is almost impossible to weary on the roads of Switzerland. The chestnuts and the almond trees were everywhere in blossom, the meadows were covered with the most lively green,' and in the distance the snowy peaks of the Alps. He dined in the middle of the day at a small village where the company of the Neuchâtel diligence had also stopped, among whom were Mr and Mrs Chandler. 'We made an agreeable party', he goes on. 'Mrs. Chandler was young and handsome. She had travelled a good deal and her curiosity, despising the danger . . . had led her to ascend to the burning top of Vesuvius and the snowy glaciers of the Alps.' Having thoroughly enjoyed the Chandlers' company and conversation, Cleghorn was vexed with himself – after they had all gone their separate ways – that he had not realised that it was Richard Chandler, the classical antiquarian, whose work he knew, to whom he had been talking. 'How much I regret my ignorance of this circumstance; our conversation might have been more particular and instructive.'

He lodged at Rolle that night and for the first time saw the waltz danced. The people of the village had gathered: 'under the shade of the trees; and to the music of the fiddle the youth were dancing the Valses of Switzerland. The movements of this Dance are rapid and uniform. The Parties encircle each other . . . they move and twirl with amazing velocity; they direct their course from one corner of the room or field to another; many parties are engaged at the same time and it requires no small dexterity to steer clear of each other . . . '

He arrived at Geneva on 11 May and stayed a week there, thoroughly relishing his meetings with the scientists and philosophers, some of whom were on the frontiers in their own fields, as Hutton, Black and Smith were in theirs. Jean Senebier, whom Cleghorn describes as 'a most respectable clergyman', contributed to our knowledge of the influence of light on vegetation and was the first to give a connected view of the whole process of vegetable nutrition in strictly chemical terms. Jean Charles Trembley, who took Cleghorn under his wing, was descended from an old family driven out of France for their Protestantism in the sixteenth century, was a member of the Great Council and also the intimate friend of a nephew of Necker who gave Cleghorn insights into what was happening in France. He took Cleghorn out to see Charles Bonnet and his wife at Genthod, where he also met Horace de Saussure, their nephew, whom they had brought up as their son. Bonnet had made many discoveries in the course of his studies of insectology and botany and, when his eyesight began to fail, turned his mind to the speculative side of physical science.

Saussure had for the last fifteen years been studying the geology and physics of the Alps – in 1788 he had spent seventeen days in making observations on the crest of the Col du Géant. It had been he who, in 1760, had offered a reward to the man who first reached the top of Mont Blanc. In 1785 he himself made an unsuccessful attempt, while in the following year two men from Chamonix succeeded, and in 1787 Saussure did it too. Both Bonnet and Saussure had been made Fellows of the Royal Society in England. Cleghorn certainly appreciated meeting them: 'I was much pleased with the company of this day and hope to have an opportunity of renewing acquaintances I but faintly formed.' He did ride out to M. Bonnet's again, 'and found his Lady who is one of the most agreeable women I ever saw. She constantly speaks of Mr. Smith (who had been in Geneva with the Duke of Buccleuch) with most affectionate remembrance. She drew his character most inimitably well. She said he was *"un homme sensé, de beaucoup d'esprit et dans sa conduite, La Vertue personnifiée".*'

In the Comte de Pictet, to whom M. Du Peyrou had particularly recommended Cleghorn, he found a congenial spirit, as interested as he was in political developments and very knowledgeable about the politics of both England and France. Cleghorn was again sorry that his meeting with the Comte had been so brief: 'I regret my departure from Geneva obliged me to refuse an invitation for passing an evening with the Comte. We promised to meet in September and I expect much pleasure from the conversation of a gentleman who is at once a man of knowledge and a man of the world.' He was determined to get a grasp of the political set-up in Geneva and found M. Trembley a mine of information – 'but I must have another conversation with him before I put it in writing' – and he does note down a good deal of information – (as a disciple of John Millar) – on the occupations of the Genevese and the relative balance of numbers of men and women and so on.

Another of his days in Geneva he spent with his Neuchâtel acquaintance Madame la Chanoinesse du Pyrou, who was accompanying two ladies of the same order on their way to France. Here Cleghorn's attitude was much more ambivalent: 'I could not observe where her allegiance was due.' She had servants and a carriage; Cleghorn had gone shopping with her and he had observed no awareness by her of any vow of poverty. She 'lived exempted from the authority of a husband or of an Abbess' but, when taxed with this, 'she only replied: *"Monsieur, vous vous plaisantez."*'

On Sunday 17 May he left Geneva at five o'clock in the evening and made his way along the Savoy bank of Lake Leman, staying the night at a small noisy inn. He was up at four next morning and rode through walnut trees to breakfast in Thonon, which he thought very poorly of. His next stop was Evian, where the innkeeper talked about a certain: 'Milord Beckford whose expenses in this contemptible village . . . commonly amounted to £50 a day. But he surely exaggerates even the licentiousness of English extravagance.' Cleghorn was to meet William Beckford later on in his travels in Florence, when his first impression would no doubt be confirmed, for Beckford's own journal of his travels showed an arrogant young man who had the wealth to cultivate his own Romantic sensibilities without consideration for others.[13]

The road from Evian to Meillerie beside the lake was beautiful but so sheer down to the water that: 'I was obliged to walk and could thus contemplate with safety and pleasure the grandeur of the scene.' He found that his evening walk from Meillerie to St Gingolph was far more hair-raising; there were stones and trees on the road, 'left till they are collected in sufficient quantity to be thrown into vessels that carry them to Geneva.' There was a great boulder 'blocking the road to within a foot of the precipice'; and a wooden bridge so rotten it broke under the weight of his horse. He did in the end reach St Gingolph by nine and over supper he had a good talk with the landlord about the government of the canton. 'All the Swiss have political Intelligence,' Cleghorn noted, and then with some satisfaction: 'I shall soon know more of this country . . . I had an excellent bed.'

He started at six the next morning; not only were the glimpses through the trees beautiful, but he heard singing from many parts of the woods. When he caught up with the singers he found they were girls and youths in white mantles accompanied by a priest going on their Rogation-tide processions to the crucifixes and little chapels along the highway.

He next had to cross the Rhône where it joined the lake. He was tickled to be ferried across by the 'Governor' of the fort there, accompanied by another who was styled 'Le Colonel des Chèvres'. Cleghorn arrived at Vevey in time for dinner and spent the rest of the day there, finding much to admire. 'This town is one of the most beautiful in points of situation that can be conceived. It commands a noble view of Savoy and the mountains of Valais. It has a fine walk on the side of the Lake. The church is upon a rising ground behind the town and from the burial ground is seen the greater part of the Lake, innumerable towns and villages and the boldest aspects of the background of St Gingolph.' He left Vevay at four the next morning and arrived at Lausanne at seven in the evening, where he found letters from his family and Captain Patton, which set his mind at rest. He stayed at Lausanne from 20 to 25 May (1789), the main purpose of his visit being to meet the great historian, Edward Gibbon, to whom he had been given letters of introduction by Adam Smith – letters which 'instantly secured his attentions and his confidence'.

Cleghorn's account of his meeting with Gibbon went on: 'He was indeed much flattered by the compliments paid him by Mr. Smith and very candidly said that he would have thought Mr. Smith had said more of his merits, had he said less. He thought Mr. Smith neglected by the Government and said it was a shame to deprive the country and the world of his literary and political ingenuity by absorbing his time in an office which the merest subaltern could discharge. He seemed sincerely to feel the loss Mr. Smith had sustained by the loss of Miss D. He talked a great deal and with great affection of Dr Robertson; he said his *History of Scotland* had got justice; that of Charles V perhaps ample justice and that of America less than justice. He told me that the Dr. meant to have wrote the "History of Britain" from the Revolution to the Hanover Succession but that McPherson had wrote him that every work of that kind was superseded by his labours and that he would consider every such attempt as a personal insult. The aversion to a dispute with such a man induced the Dr. to drop his design. He told me that McPherson and Whitaker after their reconciliation dined with him and he was surprised to observe the authenticity of Fingal supported by the latter and almost given up by the former. He received the compliments I presumed to pay him on his history very well. He said he regretted but he was obliged to answer Davies. He was an antagonist from whom no honour could be obtained even by victory . . . '

Three days later Cleghorn, dining at Launcelot Brown's,[14] found Gibbon to be a fellow guest. Perhaps it was then that Gibbon advised Cleghorn that if he had 'twelve months to stay in Italy, he ought to pass eight of them in Rome'.[15] Cleghorn thought that Gibbon's house in Lausanne was one of the best: 'It commands a most extensive view of the Lake, has fine gardens laid out with great taste and an adjoining vineyard of considerable extent. It is situated in a spot where formerly lived an eminent saint. But the present occupier vies with his predecessor neither in Faith nor in Mortification. St. Bernard founded a convent on the banks of the Lake and he made a covenant with his eyes never to contemplate its beauties nor the sublimity of the opposite shore; one must see the morning sun reflected from the waters and shining on the surrounding hills to form an idea of the Piety or Insensibility of this singular Saint.'

Cleghorn also made the acquaintance in Lausanne of Comte Catuelan, 'who engaged to meet me at Neuchâtel and make a tour of the mountains.'

Back in Neuchâtel on 26 May, Cleghorn found that Lord Home and Col. O'Dunne had been involved, through no fault of their own, in the death by drowning of a foolish young soldier of the city named Jacobil. He would attach himself to them on their shooting expeditions though they, only the evening before, had obliged him to return home. His father tried to keep him in the house but he eluded him and joined them the next morning. Cleghorn's account of this event went on:

'His presence made them resolve to leave the river but a wild duck was unfortunately killed and this young man instantly leaped into a little corracle to follow it . . . but by bad management it overset; he was in great coats and though an excellent swimmer and close to the side of the river, he was unfortunately drowned. A French gentleman stripped and attempted to save him; he received from Jacobil a kick in the groin which instantly swelled and the pain made him faint and sink to the bottom.

Lord Home got hold of him and saved him but Jacobil's body was not found till next day.'

All involved were very distressed, though Lord Home had in fact acquitted himself well both in the way he tried to choke off the foolish young man from continuing to pester them, then in taking action to save the Frenchman and finally in writing a hasty note to Cleghorn at Lausanne because the word had got round that it was Home himself who had been drowned.

The Comte Catuelan arrived at Neuchâtel and on 3 June their party of seven (Lord Home, the Comte, Col. O'Dunne, Gouldsberry, Hare, Denny and Cleghorn) set off for La Chaux-de-Fonds up in the Neuchâtel Mountains to the north. Three of them rode and four went in a charabanc – Cleghorn noting that: 'the ease with which you mount and descend is another reason for employing this conveyance in a country where you are frequently obliged to walk.' The party also took their umbrellas with them: 'We were sheltered by parapluits and suffered little inconvenience' from the rain. (Umbrellas were in use – in England since 1756 – but they were bulky and clumsy, with whalebone frames and canopies of oil-cloth.)

Cleghorn was vastly impressed with the inventiveness and enterprise of these people of the mountains in the way they had developed watchmaking: 'It is not above three centuries ago since this beautiful and industrious country was inhabited only by wolves and boars,' – and he went on to describe what Droz and Richard had achieved. The party had dinner with one of the master craftsmen – Huquenin Kadry – 'who has perfected a most complicated machine which in a few minutes enables him to emboss with various figures the cases of his watches and which answers the purposes of the engraver or the printer; he formed in our presence and in a few minutes, a beautiful urn on a silver case, which he gave me and which I presented to Lord Home.' And indeed Lord Home had again by his presence of mind given the party cause to feel in his debt – especially the Comte – when they inspected the mill at La Chaux de Fonds. To see the falls they had had to cross a narrow plank bridge:

'I followed the guide and arrived in safety, but the Comte who came next, unluckily stepped upon a board which was rotten' . . . Cleghorn shouted a warning but the board broke and there was the Comte, 'suspended by the shoulders between the rock and the remaining board till Lord Home with evident hazard to himself, seized him and enabled him to regain the side of the cavern.'

They went on to Le Locle and then the next morning on towards France to see the Doubs waterfall. Crossing the Doubs also provided its hazards but the falls proved to be very impressive: 'The rains of the preceding days had augmented the volume of water and we saw it in its glory. An immense river perpendicularly fell upon the rocks below; the force of the fall and weight of the water excited a noise which was heard long before our approach and the spray ascended and met the spectators upon the high mountains above.'

Returned from this expedition, Lord Home went fishing for trout in the Areuse, in the Val de Travers, for some days and Cleghorn joined him to explore the valley and visit the village of St Sulpice, in which was 'the house of my friend Colonel de Meuron who has collected an excellent Cabinet of Natural History'. At Motiers Cleghorn by chance met with Mr Durham, his wife and Miss Hare. This gave them a chance to discuss their plans for joining up for the 'great tour of Switzerland' which they proposed to embark on at the end of June.

On 17 June they made up quite a large party (three cabrioles and one on horseback) to visit St Peter's Island in the Lake of Bienne. The expedition was a success: 'We spent the whole day traversing the isle; under the shades of oak and walnut were contemplated at leisure the beauty and riches of this happy country. Our company was numerous; we had mothers and their children; the sports of the nursery were renewed and blind man's buff and running round the trees became at length the pastime of all.' Of course they went over the house which Rousseau had used as his retreat – in his room: 'near the stove is a trap door thro' which he used to descend and conceal himself when company intruded during his peevish or melancholy hours.'

Home, Cleghorn and Gouldsberry decided on one other expedition to try out how fit they were for the 'greater tour of Switzerland' they were planning.[16] This time they went southwards to Fribourg. Their 'rehearsal tour' was not in fact too strenuous. Their sail across first Lake Neuchâtel and then Lake Morat took four hours; they visited the site of the Battle of Morat (1476) and were disconcerted by the ossuary in which the bones of the defeated Burgundians had been piled; they tried the waters at Bonne, which Cleghorn compared to those of St Bernard's Well in Edinburgh; they were shown over the Hermitage of Madeleine by the hermit who lived there, whom Cleghorn found disappointingly dull; they toiled up and down the 'fatiguingly steep' streets of Fribourg and watched the city worthies take their annual oath of allegiance in the Church of the Cordeliers; they were impressed by the sheer extent of the walls of the old Roman city of Avenches.

Of Cleghorn's relish for travel there can be no doubt. It was heightened by his sense of history, but its essential element was interest in his fellow men whether they were farmers, soldiers, scholars, lawyers or innkeepers. He also enjoyed trying out the wines of the region he was in – and its food. No one could call Cleghorn a Romantic, but the sensitiveness to landscape which Wordsworth showed in his Swiss tour of 1790 was heralded in Cleghorn's reactions to the grandeur of Swiss scenery – though he was equally likely to be noting with interest 'a field of turnips in seed, which I am told owes its introduction into Switzerland to Sir Jas. Hall'.[17]

Whether Lord Home's enthusiasm was equal to that of his tutor's we simply cannot tell. His health was not as good, his passion for sport much greater. They may have had different interests, but found each other's company congenial enough to spend two years travelling together.

The second volume of Cleghorn's journal ended with a note about Lord Home and expenses: 'Lord Home is by no means wantonly expensive . . . there never has been money thrown away in an improper or immoral manner – Lord Home has remained here for three months with patience and good humour. It is an excellent situation but has no amusements for a young man that lead to extravagance. To induce him to remain in this situation it was necessary to indulge him in riding, in hiring charabancs and in parties upon the lake.' As Home's chief satisfaction lay in all forms of sport, it was probably no hardship to him to miss some opportunities of seeing more pictures and libraries and ancient monuments.

4

The 'Great Tour of Switzerland'
June – August 1789

Through the Swiss Jura to Basle

Their 'great tour of Switzerland' began on Sunday 28 June, at five o'clock in the morning, and lasted a month. There were six in their party: Home, Gouldsberry, Cleghorn, Col. O'Dunne, Mr Durham and Mr Denny. They had servants with them and, for some stages at any rate, horses to carry their luggage. So big a party made for difficulties in some places, but they were ready, if necessary, 'to sleep on mattresses on the floor or straw in the stable.'

The first stage of their journey took them north from Neuchâtel up into the spectacular scenery of the Swiss Jura. They stayed the first night at Courtelary[1] and here Cleghorn obviously had the opportunity for conversation which enabled him to find out how nearly all peasants owned their own land and what their rights were on grazing and cutting wood for 'firing and building'; how they had to pay 'Disme' to the Bishop as well as 'Corvé'; and 'gabelles'.[2] He noted how green and quiet their churchyards were, with no boastful funerary monuments. He learned how those who became soldiers much preferred French service to Dutch, 'because in France a soldier learns to dance and to fence and he returns "*comme il faut*".'

The next day Cleghorn was fairly bowled over by the country they went through: the drama of the River Birse, bursting out from the rocks on the floor of the valley; the arch of rock under which the road passed; the way in which the mountains pressed in on them. In the end he gives up: 'In this country the eye ever sees new beauty but language cannot vary its terms of admiration.' Their stopping place that night was Delémont, where they had 'a good supper and excellent beds'. Another bonus was to be:

'served by three fair maidens, and one of them sat up all night to wash and dry our stockings. In the morning she was clean and even elegantly dressed, her hair powdered, some of which stuck on the noses of a few of the company.' They were now in Roman Catholic country and Cleghorn went off to visit the summer palace of the Prince-Bishop of Basle. No one was there and he saw no priests, 'but it was after eight and [impossible for him to resist the dig] they were either at Vespers or the Bottle.'

Tuesday 30 June was a long day on foot. They started at five in the morning and arrived at Basle at six in the evening, 'but the clocks here are always advanced an hour before those of any other country.' They stayed at the Hôtel des Trois Roys on the right bank of the Rhine where: 'from the Balcony there is a commanding view [as there still is from the same hotel] of the River, the largest and most rapid I have ever seen.'

The following morning was dedicated to 'doing' Basle. Cleghorn had a thoroughly satisfactory visit to Mr Hass, the printer, 'who carried me [Lord Home not on the scene here] thro' his printing office and showed me the proof sheets of Necker's works which they are now preparing upon paper and a type that rivals that of the Foulis.' This was high praise indeed for Robert Foulis (1707–76), bookseller and printer, had produced for Glasgow University a number of remarkably fine editions, including their first Greek book and an 'immaculate Horace'.

Cleghorn was not nearly so sure that he knew where he was with Holbein, many of whose paintings and drawings were in the Hall of the public library, which they were 'most politely shown by Professor Rihiner'. Cleghorn calls Holbein 'this interesting and eccentric artist', and speaks of the 'whymsical genius' shown in his 'Dance of Death'. Cleghorn paid tribute in the Cathedral at the tomb of Erasmus, the 'mildest and most Enlightened of Reformers'. Here again he runs true to form: from Voltaire onwards, Erasmus had been regarded as one whose pleas for reason, though overwhelmed by religious strife in his own day, yet earned him a place in the pantheon of the Enlightenment.

In the afternoon the party went out to Birschem to see the

grounds and gardens of the Grand Chapter of Basle. The actual proprietor of the grounds was Madame d'Andlau and it was her cousin, Henri Ligerty (one of the canons) who had planned it all. He must have enjoyed himself, using the caves and waterfalls and natural viewpoints to enhance what were already beautiful grounds. In one cave was an urn 'sacred to the memory of Gessner', poet and painter, whose widow and son they were to meet later in Zurich.[3] Higher up was the Hermitage, where Cleghorn was deceived by the realism of the figure of the hermit, sitting 'gently saluting visitors with his head'; so when they, continuing on their tour, came to an elegant pavilion with two ladies sitting there, Cleghorn hung back – but: 'I was twice disappointed, having mistaken wood for a Man and Ladies for wood.' After some polite conversation, they went on to a ruined castle, then a 'Temple de la Mort', then a 'Grotto of the Resurrection'. But at least after all that they were revived with various liqueurs and 'excellent beer which we drank out of cups of Beech, covered with rough bark'.

Along the Upper Rhine

The next day, 2 July, they left Basle at six o'clock, by carriage this time, with 'German postillions in red livery with the Eagle of Austria and horns hung on their shoulders' (necessary to warn carriages of each other's approach). Although the land should have been good enough – 'resembling our carses' – Cleghorn was critical of the growing crops: 'I suspect they neither fallow nor manure.'

On this day's drive they were following the left bank of the Rhine until they reached Laufenburg, where they had intended to cross by the bridge there. But the river was so rapid that the bridge had been carried away (at this spot, only four years later, Lord Montagu and his tutor were drowned, trying to swim the Rhine for a bet). With no bridge they had a longer drive and, at half past nine at night, stopped at Lauchringen, where there was only a 'miserable auberge'.

On 3 July they left Germany after a bad breakfast at Neuhausen, and back in Switzerland they found Schaffhausen to be much cleaner. The rest of the day was spent at the Rhine Falls. These certainly impressed Cleghorn – they are, after all, the widest and most powerful in Europe, plunging down seventy feet or so. He and the others saw them from one viewpoint as 'one large and extended shield of troubled foam'. From above they saw the river glinting white or blue or green as it slid over the rock; they crossed in a boat to Lauffen and saw the whole panorama 'with ease and safety'. But the best view of all was when they went down steps cut in the bank and saw the falls forming rainbows and throwing up spray till it appeared to mix with the clouds and 'the houses on the opposite bank seemed suspended in air'.

The next day – a Sunday – they walked from Schaffhausen to Constance, a distance of about thirty miles, which proved too much for the feet of some of the party. After this they put stag's grease on their feet every night, 'and some cover them with fine old linen. These precautions prevent blisters – but they ought to be carefully washed at night.' Their exhaustion meant that they spent longer in Constance than they had planned, 'when all that we have seen might have been viewed in an hour.' Constance was still subject to Habsburg rule and Cleghorn picked up some gossip about the Emperor, Joseph II ('that he was dying of the pox'), and saw the effects of some of his secularising policies in the Convent of the Dominicans, which Joseph had given to refugees from Geneva. 'The cells of the monks are occupied by weavers; the gardens are bleach-fields and the Chapel is a drying apartment for muslin. Industry has succeeded to Idleness.'

Cleghorn, at any rate, seems to have been fully mobile. He paid tribute to the shade of John Hus, in the Town Hall, the Prison and the Armoury; he climbed the tower of the Cathedral and in the evening went to a German puppet show. 'As Punch's wit consists in the language of action, we have some chance to understand it.' But in the event it proved 'the dullest of all entertainments'. Punch had 'neither wit nor profaneness'. However, the inn was good and they met up with a Count Antonelli Romain, who asked them to call on him in Florence.

St Gall and the Appenzell

The party divided the next day and each thought his own route had been the best. They met up again at Rorschach at southern end of Lake Constance but the inn proved: 'barely tolerable with the beds too short for our feet and the price too high.' For the rest of the journey, apart from a little sailing on two of the lakes, Cleghorn at any rate walked all the way – some of it formidably mountainous. At St Gall he was vastly impressed both with the Abbey Library, with its ancient manuscripts, and with the Librarian. Latin was their only common language, and Cleghorn admired the 'ease and classical purity' with which the Librarian spoke and the patience with which he 'listened to my jargon'. They were both in agreement in wishing 'the progress of toleration to extend', and Cleghorn goes on: 'It is the only Religion of Enlightened Minds and it begins to display its influence in a convent!'

On their next day's walk between St Gall and Appenzell they went through the village of Tuffein, where: 'we saw a toyshop well supplied with all the little articles for children . . . and we were attracted by its noise to visit a school for which we procured a holiday and made the children happy by leaving money to purchase strawberries.' Appenzell won his approval for its practice of toleration for more than a century, after a time of religious discord when they had learnt at each other's expense that: 'the Hangman is never a Reformer and men when they cannot reason, cannot be convinced.'

Herisau too proved very much to his liking: 'compact, well-built and elegant' – and it gave him an evening to remember. 'After dinner, I ascended a hill above the town with a very polite citizen I met at the Inn; . . . my conductor stopped every moment to speak with uncles and cousins and, though unknown and most miserably dressed, I met from every eye looks of complacence and philanthropy. Below us were mills and bleachfields. There was summer in all its beauty to the south and behind, winter in eternal snows in the Alps. Little verdant hills displayed their crops, their trees, their houses. Every object was delightful; but the mind feels more than language can express,' . . . he manages to convey, however, even in these commonplace phrases, something of the delight – the exaltation even – which is the lure of the traveller.

The next day after a twenty-five mile walk, they were refused shelter at the inn where they had expected to stay, but they had a good night's sleep in two haylofts in the village and congratulated themselves on the money they had saved. The following night, at Elgg, there was no stream near the town, so they could not enjoy: 'the comfort and pleasure of bathing – a circumstance we have rarely omitted when we could find an opportunity.' They were finding the middle of the day increasingly hot so they set out at four o'clock next morning – Cleghorn and Durham walking, 'the rest were in a coach or following more slowly on foot.' It was a day of lightning and heavy showers and hail, 'with pieces of ice as large as half crowns; the leaves cut from the trees as if struck by pistol shots.'

Zurich – introductions taken up

They arrived at Zurich from the north-east, through suburbs where: 'the gardens are in the old taste – fountains playing and the box and yew cut into a thousand fantastic shapes.' Obviously for Cleghorn the perception of landscape, not as a stage where nature is drilled, but as a scene of unforced adaptation of natural features to a pleasing harmony, was so much part of his experience that he dubbed the Zurich gardens old-fashioned without reflection – so much had the English proved to be the 'makers of fashion' through their gardens created by William Kent, 'Capability Brown' and William Chambers.

They had introductions to J K Lavater,[4] to M. Hass and to Madame Gessner, widow of the poet, and in the end they stayed there three days. Johann Kaspar Lavater was a Zurich pastor with a great reputation as a preacher, a mystic and a poet, who also claimed through his studies to have developed a high degree of skill at judging character from a person's face, the art of 'Phisyognomy', as Cleghorn engagingly spells it in his journal. He found the Pastor rather trying: 'I had not been five minutes in his company when he insisted I was an excellent judge of pictures . . . I assured him I had never seen any collection of merit, that I was ignorant of the chef d'oeuvres of the principal masters, knew so little of the arts that I could not even apply to any given piece the language of applause. All was in vain: I had, he said, "the eyes of Nature" – a gift', Cleghorn wrote with some exasperation, 'I possess in common with all two and four footed animals in Creation.' Nevertheless, next day he took Lord Home to call on Lavater, who insisted they should write their names in a visitors' book – 'an affectation he might just as well avoid. He is much flattered and I believe he knows when and to whom to give it.' So much for the Pastor!

The orphans' hospital drew unqualified praise from Cleghorn. His visit was obviously very thorough for he notes down much detail on it, even to the children being given two clean shirts a week. He paid his respects to Huldrich Zwingli, the sixteenth-century protestant reformer, and William Tell, whose famous crossbow was displayed in the Arsenal, though Cleghorn viewed it with a historian's scepticism.

When he had been in Basle he had been given a letter of introduction by the printer there to M. Hass, a painter by inclination and a butcher by trade. When Cleghorn visited him he had only a small collection of his work, mostly landscapes and heads of animals, the sketches for which he made when he went up to the mountains to purchase cattle. Cleghorn found the painter/butcher 'modest and intelligent, gentle and polite'. His friend and companion was the son of Soloman Gessner, who had died the previous year. Cleghorn knew his 'Idylls' and when he visited his widow was shown 'the small cabinet of paintings which Gessner had finished a short time before his death'. Cleghorn remembered the tribute paid to Gessner by Henri de Ligerty in the gardens at Birschem and looked back in his journal (which was in his pocket) to what he had written about the cave with its urn in Gessner's memory. Madame Gessner was very moved by this, Cleghorn's interest and concern giving him the ability to get through to people.

The volume of the journal to which Cleghorn referred had in fact been lost when his greatcoat was missing on their arrival at Zurich (this must have had the capacious pockets of that time because the journal is about seven inches by nine and quite thick as well). However, the landlord of their excellent Zurich inn, who was also a magistrate, 'dispatched a servant on horseback with an order to stop all strangers and in a few hours the servant returned with my coat.' Cleghorn often expressed his appreciation of the honesty and the 'cordiality and ease which characterises the manners of the Swiss'.

The cradle of Swiss democracy:
Schwyz and Lake Lucerne

Their journey the day they left Zurich was southwards along the east shore of the lake and then by boat to Rapperswil and across to the west shore – to Lachen (twelve miles by land and then nine by water). Wednesday 15 July saw them making for the Hacken Pass. They stopped at the famous pilgrimage town of Einsiedeln for some hours to visit the church with the most prized of its relics, the tenth-century statue of the Virgin, of which Cleghorn remarks: 'Both she and Our Saviour whom she carries in her arms have the complexion of negroes.' He did not have time for a proper look at the library and his tolerance was strained by the clutter, round the church, of small shops selling: 'crucifixes, beads and other trumpery of Catholic superstition to the pilgrims who come here some hundreds of leagues from all the corners of Switzerland and Germany.' It was hard climbing after that, both up to the pass and down to Schwyz, Cleghorn finding, what many others would agree with, 'that the descent of the mountain took much time and was much more fatiguing than the mounting.'

He was interested in the 'democratical' system of government he found in Schwyz: how everyone over sixteen had the right to vote for magistrates; how the executive consisted of a Council of Sixty; how in criminal matters, each of the Sixty had to carry with him to the assembly two citizens who had an equal right with the Councillors to deliberate and vote. His informant seems to have been a Swiss mercenary colonel in the service of Piedmont. The Canton of Schwyz also had regiments in the service of Spain and Naples, as well as always being able to raise seventeen thousand men in arms for their own defence.

After breakfast the next day they dropped down to Brunnen and took a boat on Lake Uri to Altdorf. Opposite Brunnen they saw the Field of Rutli where the thirty patriots of Schwyz, Uri and Unterwalden swore to act together against Austrian despotism. On the eastern shore of the lake they landed to look at the Chapel of Tell, with its paintings of scenes from the life of 'this real or imaginary hero'. Cleghorn goes on, rather crossly: 'Had he been a pretended Saint, his miracles however disputable would have been recorded and preserved by better kept festivals.' (It should, perhaps be remembered that Schiller's *William Tell*, which really enshrined this whole legendary cycle, was not written till 1804.) They landed at Fluelen and walked on to Altdorf, the key to the St Gotthard Pass on the north side of the Alps, where Cleghorn noticed the beginnings of the Italian influence.

On the way back to the lake he and two others in the party wanted to visit a convent of Benedictine nuns at Seedorf – a diversion of about two miles from the road to Fluelen. 'The singularly romantick situation, wild, covered with wood and overhung by the Alps, irresistibly led me to this peaceable retreat.' Cleghorn found the nun who opened the door to them a real charmer, and when she played the organ and led them to a window to view the garden, and 'when unobserved, she gave us her hand,' he felt: 'tho' old, almost the instincts of chivalry . . . anxious to deliver the captive.' They had wine with the Abbess and bought some trifles. Cleghorn enjoyed his visit and was no doubt right about the sisters when he wrote to round off his account that: 'those who see strangers seldom always see them with pleasure.' Less pleasurable was the two-hour wait which this delicate flirtation caused the rest of the party: the boatmen were angry and the villagers backed them. Cleghorn, the chief cause of the trouble, had no German. But matters were arranged in the end for the return sail, though it was nine o'clock before they arrived back at Schwyz.

Cleghorn was again with the energetic group when the party divided the next day, the less strenuous making their way to Zug directly. Lord Home and Cleghorn wanted to go up to the 'island mountain' of Rigi, which has Lake Lucerne to the south and west and lakes Zug and Lauerz on the other sides. It was hard going and they were often in the clouds but, 'after a walk which even the weather could not rob of its beauty,' they arrived at the hamlet of Rigi Kulm and lodged at the sign of 'The Ox', where they heard all about the summer migration and the making of cheese, and butter which was not salted but heated over a slow fire so that it would keep all the year round. After dinner they went to the top of the mountain and Cleghorn counted twelve lakes that he could see and the Aare flowing north-eastward. 'Behind were the Alps which mock description.'

The next morning they again went up their mountain but had no luck with the view, though they did see lightning flashing below them as they looked down on the clouds – as Cleghorn remembered reading Ulua had done in the Andes in the sixteenth century. In descending, they saw an immensely deep fissure and, throwing stones down it, drove out a fox. Their guide told them that these foxes never killed lambs but lived mostly on large black snails. The cows they saw were mouse-coloured (presumably the Schwyz breed) and like the sheep were remarkably tame, following the party 'till they were drove back by our guide'. The descent, though long and fatiguing, was made in the end and at Arth they got a boat up the lake to Zug. Maybe it was the boiled butter, or perhaps he had bathed when he was too hot, but during the night Lord Home was taken extremely ill and Cleghorn was so worried he sent for a physician. The doctor gave Home: 'A few grains of rhubarb till the stomach was fortified.' And then Cleghorn insisted that he be given laudanum. The doctor said he had heard that the English were addicted to it and duly administered thirty drops. He himself did not use it as a medicine, he said. He had heard that: 'it was taken by the Arabs when they went to war and by the Turks when they went to their women, but in neither of these respects was it useful to the Swiss.' Lord Home was sufficiently recovered to go to Lucerne by carriage the next day with Mr Denny, while Cleghorn and Durham crossed Lake Zug in a boat and then walked.

Lucerne – 'Aristocratical Government' and Society

Back in civilisation, they changed and dressed for one of Lucerne's 'conversatione'. There was a beautiful Roman princess there and Cleghorn found M. Balthazar,[5] to whom he had a letter of introduction, and made the acquaintance of another member of the Council of Lucerne, M. Mayer, 'a most agreeable and polite young man.' From them Cleghorn learned that, unlike the democratic mountain cantons, Lucerne's government was 'aristocratical'. He was interested that M. Balthazar had travelled in England to study English criminal jurisprudence and to buy books on it for the Lucerne Council. He wanted to reform his city's laws so that torture could not be used any more. He was also worried that those who held *his* office on the Council could 'materially change the nature of the evidence adduced' by witnesses, when he 'reduced their depositions to writing in his own home'.

Another of the notables of Lucerne they met was 'Old General Phiffers',[6] who invited them to come to his house to see his great model of the map of Switzerland – about thirty feet by fifteen – showing towns, lakes, villages, 'the cascades represented by little chains of silver, the glaciers by wax painted white at the top.' He also had a fine collection of fossils and inspection of this led to a discussion on the age of the earth, and from there to how the Alps were formed. Cleghorn suggested that they must partly have come into existence by the 'agency of fire', showing he was familiar with Hutton's theory of subterranean heat. There is in fact a reminder at the end of the journal to send to the Chevalier de Dolomieu a copy of Dr Hutton's *Essays*. (Sylvian Dolomieu, 1750–1802, was an eminent French mineralogist.) The General would have none of all this, but it does illustrate Cleghorn's interest in every aspect of the achievements of the Scottish Enlightenment. The General ended the discussion by quoting Voltaire: 'That our globe resembled an old coquette who wished to be thought a great deal younger than she really was.'

It proved difficult to find anyone who would cash their letters of credit in Lucerne and they were running short of money, so they set off on Tuesday 21 July for Berne. They got as far as Escholzmatt – a walk of about twenty-five miles – and though the beds promised to be very indifferent, Cleghorn at least had the prospect of some good conversation with 'an agreeable clergyman of the Canton of Berne'. There was some concern about Lord Home having lost his watch and a servant was sent back. In fact he retraced their footsteps almost two-thirds of the way and then he found the watch (by the light of a lantern) lying within a foot or two of the high road.

The next evening saw their arrival in Berne after going through pleasant, fruitful country. At Langnau, on the way, there was a fair in full-swing – 'the favourite dance is the valse and they very good-humouredly allowed some of us to join in their party.' Cleghorn notes that it was near this village that the famous 'Physician of the Mountains', Michael Schuppach, lived – 'who pretended to know all the diseases by inspecting the urine, and whose fame at last brought to his cottage persons of all ranks and of both sexes from every country in Europe.' Certainly Pierre Alexandre Du Peyrou, husband of Cleghorn's admired Madame Du Peyrou, had visited him twice and changed his plans to follow Schuppach's advice.[7]

They decided to stay for two days in Berne, 'to rest before

we return to Neuchâtel.' Cleghorn comments that: 'We have travelled near 600 miles; our next tour will be to the valley – but a fortnight in Neuchâtel is necessary to arrange our little affairs – after which we must bid farewell to a city which I shall remember with affection and gratitude as long as I have a heart to feel.' Cleghorn was to visit Neuchâtel again six years later in a very different role from his present one of interested observer.

Haute Savoie and the glaciers of Mont Blanc: August 1789

The record of their tour to the glaciers and the Canton of Valais is not in Cleghorn's journal but in a report from Maxime Effrancey, the schoolmaster of Sallanches who acted as their guide and courier.[8] In his covering letter addressed to 'M. Cleghorn presently at Lausanne', he asks to be remembered *'à toute l'illustre compagnie, au doux prince surtout'* – perhaps a noteworthy choice of adjective for Lord Home. It is not clear who made up the party for their tour of Haute Savoie, but what they wanted was to have a closer look at the High Alps, to get above the snowline and to see glaciers and the birthplace of rivers.

It was in August that they left from Geneva, went up the valley of the Arve to Sallanches, where *'la chaine de Mont Blanc se présente'*. The next day they went so far by 'char-a-banc' and then climbed past a remarkable waterfall to the Lake of Chedde – *'cet endroit enchanteur – cet veritable jardin Anglais.'* The party then divided, the more energetic going up with guides to the beautiful 'Glacier des Bossons', which they crossed – and then on to Chamonix. There half the party at any rate spent the next day climbing up to the glaciers on the Massif of Mont Blanc. The first stage of their ascent was on muleback – an alarming experience, but the only thing to do was to rely on the sure-footedness of their mules. After that they depended on their guides to point out safe footholds and they did reach a height where they viewed a whole panorama of peaks while they picnicked.

The descent was hair-raising and their guides would point out to them where climbers before them had fallen to their deaths, but '*en marchons ni timidement ni temerairement*' they returned to Chamonix very much set up in their own esteem. Their last day in the high mountains took them north from Chamonix to view the Chaine du Bravent and then back to Sallanches. They then returned through the Canton of Valais (no record of this stage, except that they went by the Gemmi pass) to Neuchâtel, to prepare for their descent on Italy.

To Rome and the Cities of Italy
October 1789 – June 1790

Crossing the Alps: October 1789

For the crossing of the Alps to Italy, Lord Home and Cleghorn joined the Elchos[1] and their family, along with a Mr John and a Mr Batt. The party was thought to be too large for the inns of Savoy so Cleghorn stayed behind a day with Mr Batt. They had arranged to pay a lump sum down for the hire of the horses, carriages and inn charges from Geneva to Turin. Cleghorn chafed at the time the journey was to take – seven days for only a hundred and seventy-seven miles, but the arrangement proved a wise one because it saved all the squabbling at inns, and those whom they met travelling post found it was not always easy to hire horses.

The journey – starting on 11 October 1789, via Frangy, Rumilly to Chambéry – was uneventful.[2] At Chambéry, in addition to his interest in the law courts and the castle as the residence of the prince of Piedmont, Cleghorn remembered Rousseau's somewhat high-flown description of the welcome given to him at Les Charmettes by Madame de Warens, 'whose character Rousseau has defamed in attempting to exalt. Her house at a little distance from the town is now demolished to make way for a better. The spot derives an interest with many who admire the confessions of Rousseau.' Again Cleghorn shows he was not among their number.

From Chambéry, they went south-east to Montmelian, turning into the valley of the Isère. They climbed to the ruins of the castle there which had belonged to the Counts of Savoy and which had been the scene of much fighting with the French. As they came down from the castle an old soldier stopped them and demanded to see their permit, but when he heard they were English he waved them on: 'The English have permission to see what they please' – and a few pence, Cleghorn found, made the veteran perfectly happy. Their stop that night was at Aiguebelle, where Cleghorn noted how many of the people had goitres – but at least over supper he had the company of 'some agreeable Sardinian officers'.

The next day they made their way up the valley of the Arc, 'with the air of the West Indies and the scenery of Greenland.' They only travelled twenty-five miles to St. Michel, where: 'the wind blows a hurricane. If it does not abate I dread we may find difficulty in passing Mt. Cenis.' But his fears were premature and they spent the next day travelling partly by carriage and partly on foot, ascending the whole time. They had their mid-day meal at Modane, 'only distinguished by the superiority of filth which abounds in its streets.' In fact, Cleghorn wrote: 'Since leaving Chambéry, we have not seen a town in Savoy a single house of which bespoke either the affluence or the taste of the proprietor. All is one scene of poverty and nastiness [and] in the winter much harassed by the ravages of wolves and bears.'

It was pouring so hard with rain when they reached Lanslebourg that they stayed the night there and made an early start for Mont Cenis the next day. Cleghorn found: 'there is nothing dreadful in the ascent which can be accomplished in an hour.' This, plus crossing the plateau and the descent, was altogether a distance of fifteen miles – 'not fatiguing for a man in health.' The whole way was practicable, and: 'we met many hundreds of mules, carriages and chairs passing from Piedmont to Savoy.' And as it took 'nineteen mules to transport ourselves, two servants and two carriages across', the claim to have seen so many mules was not perhaps exaggerated. Cleghorn's general comment on this crossing of the Alps was that: 'I found the crossing of the Gemmi more dreadful in appearance and much more fatiguing in fact than that of Mt. Cenis.'

The journey to Rome: 25 October – December 1789

At Turin they rejoined the rest of the party and spent over a week there but Cleghorn was 'so occupied with company that I had no time to make particular remarks'. When they did resume their journey to Rome they had to wait once again at Alessandria, 'for the arrival of Lord Elcho's family as Lord Home who was with them had been taken ill.' After they reached Genoa on 29 October there is a blank in the journal until, for the second half of December, there are some very impersonal notes on the classical monuments and papal and other palaces they were visiting in Rome.

However, when Arthur Young was in Florence in 1789 he noted under 22 November:[3] 'Dine with His Majesty's envoy extraordinary Lord Hervey, with a great party of English among whom were Lord and Lady Elcho, Mr. and Miss Charteris, Lord Home, Mr. and Mrs. Seckford, Mr. Digby, Mr. Tempest, Dr. Cleghorn, professor of history at St. Andrews, who travels with Lord Home, with ten or a dozen others.' The next day Young dined with Lord Elcho at Meggot's Hotel. 'Lord Home, Mr. Tempest, Mr. Tyrrhit as well as Lord Elcho's family and Dr. Cleghorn present. Some agreeable conversation,' in the course of which Arthur Young gave Cleghorn a recipe for making Parmesan cheese – which Cleghorn duly noted at the back of his journal had been given him in Florence by Mr Young, 'a great farmer in Suffolk.' Young assured Cleghorn that he had made a special journey to Lodi, 'to examine the soil and the grasses and to attend to the manner in which the cheese is made there,' and he was quite sure there was nothing special about the soil – it all lay in the mode of making the cheese; and Cleghorn notes down practical and detailed instructions.

Also at that dinner the young people 'engaged in sport to walk on foot to Rome', and Young adds the comment: 'Right – I like that. If the Italians are curious in novelty of character, the passing English are well framed to give it.' Cleghorn with his relish for exercise would presumably join in this: the distance was only about a hundred and fifty miles and would not be formidable to anyone who had covered between five and six hundred miles on his 'great tour of Switzerland'. It would also explain the gap in the journal if he had forgotten to put the volume in his pocket and it had gone on with the luggage to Rome.

That they were in Rome over the winter of 1789–90 the journal makes clear, though with nothing but the flattest mention of places and sites visited: the Forum; the Colosseum, the Borghese Gardens and Villa; the palace of the Constable Colonna. On 16 December the day was bad so they went to the Vatican. Cleghorn noted that in the Library there were 40,000 manuscripts and books in presses six feet high – but there was no good catalogue. He also remarked on the top of the presses many Etruscan vases and ornaments, among which the most striking was the carved head of a negro; it led him to speculate on the Etruscans as navigators – 'or had they got their knowledge from the Carthaginians?'

In the spring of 1790 Cardinal Erskine, writing to his kinsman Lord Buchan, remarks that among visitors from Britain he had only met Lord Home and Mr Cleghorn, and Mr and Mrs Coutts and their daughters.[4] The Cardinal adds that Mr Coutts had offered to be the bearer of his letter as he and his family were leaving Rome on 1 May. The banker, his mistress and trio of daughters do seem to come in as something of a 'leit-motiv' during this spring of 1790,[5] especially for Lord Home – culminating in the apparently unfounded notice in the Scots Magazine in 1790 of the marriage of Miss Coutts and Lord Home in Italy. But there is not the faintest whisper or hint of anything more than acquaintanceship in Cleghorn's diary, which bears out the fact that the notice was just plain wrong.

The brief notes on Rome come at the end of Volume 3. Volume 4 begins on 13 March 1790, halfway through a tour of Sicily. Cleghorn's companion on this journey was not Lord Home (who stayed in Rome) but a Mr Innes, who knew St Andrews – and the two take it in turns to write up an account of their travels, though Cleghorn's part is by far the greater.

Sicilian journal, Agrigento to Messina: March 1790

This time it was not arable crops and turnips they were commenting on but apricots, almonds and 'branches of oranges loaded with fruit'.[6] They had with them Pierre, Cleghorn's Swiss servant, invaluable sometimes in dealing with refractory guides and mule drivers. Crossing a river, for instance, 'if Pierre had not pushed the mule on which he rode to the opposite bank, we should have been obliged to make a circle of some miles. The courage of Pierre obliged the Guard to follow and we all got safe over.'

They had come over from Palermo to Agrigento, with its wealth of classical ruins and 'perfectly entire' Temple of Concord. Their next main goal was Syracuse and they had certain tentative plans but very little confidence in them. As Cleghorn remarked: 'The uncertainty of human schemes is no better illustrated than in the course of a Sicilian journey.' On a practical level, they had by this time discovered the value of macaroni, which, with grated cheese, 'will always afford us a light, nourishing and agreeable meal,' and they laid in other provisions and always carried with them their 'tea equipage'. 'Upon the whole, I believe,' Cleghorn wrote, 'we travel cheaper in Sicily than we could live at Naples or Rome.'

Their route was at first along the southern coast and Innes notes that: 'the sand from the beach is encroaching on this flat promontory and the sea with its rocks and small tower representing a windmill forcibly recalled to my mind the Links of St. Andrews.' When they arrived at Licata (Cleghorn with his hand full of prickles from a hedge of aloes which he had clutched to save himself from slipping) they could find no lodging. They had however been given the name of a Signor Angelo Caseino and he rallied round nobly, requisitioning an empty house and sending along to it 'mattresses, chairs, table, wine and all from his own house'. And there was a little boy who attached himself to them, 'who has gone on errands and who has most contentedly laid himself on the floor covered only with his greatcoat to sleep with us,' and who would take nothing except bread because it was Lent.

The next day they continued along the coast to Terra Nuova (Gela today). Their main hazard was a number of rivers swollen from recent rains – and in spite of Pierre they decided they must have a guide. Even so, crossing the 'Manumura' in a litter, they, and more particularly some of their luggage, got a dousing. Then, 'on a fine strand by the seaside we mounted the horses of the Guard and servant and rode along the shore for about six miles,' on an extremely pleasant afternoon. They were able to cross the River Dirillo by 'a tottering and crazy timber bridge'. Their lodging-place that night in Biscaris was another empty house, this time: 'the grandest house in the town, adorned on one side with the King and Queen of Sicily and on the other with that of the Prince of Biscaris, the proprietor of the town and its neighbourhood. The green cloth was sent for and spread on the long table and all our wants have been amply supplied. The name of our host is Antonio De Christopho and if we see the Prince at Catania we shall mention our obligations to his delegate.'

And Cleghorn goes on: 'From the adventures of this day and yesterday, we have every reason to join the praises which all travellers have bestowed on Sicilian hospitality.' They lost their way on the mountains on 18 March, but: 'at last found a shepherd who accompanied us as guide. We gave him about a shilling (English) and by his gratitude and his looks, he seemed to be in possession of the greatest sum he had ever commanded.' The day's journey to Palazzolo proved to be much further than they had been led to expect and when they did arrive there were more problems over where they were to put up. They were offered vaults (into which they would have had to be lowered like sacks of grain) or spare cells in the prison, 'but the rooms of the felons who were gazing at us from the windows were adjoining to ours – impossible to be happy in the neighbourhood of misery.'

They would have been content with the stable, but at that point a Dominican, returning to his house, opened the cells of the convent, 'and offered to provide us with everything.' Once the problem of where the visitors were to stay had been settled, everyone was free to enjoy their presence: 'Numberless are the visits we have received and the questions that have been put to us. Visitors from the other world could hardly have excited more curiosity – but it is tempered by a natural politeness and dictated by benevolence.' They were asked about the name and character of the British King, about what was happening in France, 'about Lunardi and the nature of his balloon . . . Our names were asked and often repeated but mine stuck in the throat of a Father who attempted to pronounce it . . . My portable ink case was much admired and as we have another with us, I was happy to give it to one of the monks.'

Though they rose at 4.30 a.m., there was no getting away so early. They had to hang about for another hour or so – and then: 'no superlative can express the badness of our road . . . We arrived at Floridia after travelling five and a half hours – only fourteen miles.' The road from Floridia to Syracuse was much better and they arrived there in the afternoon. Their contacts here were the Chevalier Landolini and his son and the Commandant, the Marquis di Gregorio. Upon Cleghorn delivering his letter of introduction from the Baron de Salis, the Landolinis, father and son put themselves at the disposal of their visitors.

Here at Syracuse, more than anywhere else in Sicily, feeling for the classical past wells up in Cleghorn: the cathedral whose immense pillars were first carved for a temple to Minerva; the red wine of Syracuse, mentioned by Theocritus and made in the same manner as of old; the papyrus plants growing in the marshes, which Chevalier Landolini had discovered through his careful reading of Pliny, and made up to 'equal the ancient mode of preparing it'; the Ear of Dionysius with its extraordinary echo, which recalled the cruelty of past tyrants; the fields of Ancient Syracuse – a city 'which rivalled Rome in army and Greece in arts, now converted into vine and cornfields'; above all perhaps the fountain of Arethusa, source of poetic inspiration; though seeing a girl – one of the Nereids – beating linen there reminded Cleghorn that he must get his shirts washed – preferably not there, 'because the water of the Fountain is brackish and close to the sea.'

They were royally entertained by the Commandant and the Governor as well as the Landolinis. They were 'very decently lodged in a furnished house at the Hotel of St. Joseph', and they spent their first evening at the Commandant's. 'His lady sat at the end of a large room opposite to a chaldron placed near her feet; there was a long row of gentlemen on each side and we marched between the lines in great form to make our bows.' Among the guests that Cleghorn met was 'a Major in the Russian service of the name of O'Hara'. He was of the Catholic branch of the Tyrawley family, was a Knight of Malta and a loyal Jacobite, and he showed Cleghorn 'letters of attachment and friendship which he had received from the Prince Cardinal of York'. Cleghorn found him congenial company.

The following evening, after a day among the classical remains, they: 'supped with the Governor, a most pleasant party – a great deal of wine. We were near twenty at table; besides the wine during the time of supper, the health of every person was drunk in his turn in a bumper, his country, his friends and his possessions; infinite was the gayity and numberless the songs that were sung . . . The Sicilians drink hard and we got home about two in the morning. We slept regardless of a most dreadful storm of thunder and a slight shock of an earthquake. It was, on the whole, one of the happiest evenings I have passed since I left Scotland.' It confirmed what Cleghorn had observed earlier in the journal: 'I own I am extremely fond of the Sicilian character nor did I ever in my life experience such hospitality as in this Island.' This even extended to the Governor calling on them the next morning, 'having got from the country, fresh butter for our use which is one of the greatest luxuries this country affords.'

They did get away on 21 March, rather apprehensive about the height of the rivers. But the first part of the journey presented no great problems and the air was heavy with the scent of hawthorns and other flowering shrubs. They stopped that night at Lentini, where they were assured it would be impossible to cross the river the next day. But they decided that: 'at all events we will go to its banks and trust to no authority. Everything is an enterprise to the people of the warm climate of Sicily and we have often been told of dangers and inconveniences in our route which we never experienced.'

Innes takes up the account of their anxieties in crossing the River Simeto: in the first place, meeting all those turning back; then the long wait while the drivers paddled a boat across in order to fix a cable by which the ferry could be hauled over. They also had to spread dry sedges and sand to enable the mules to land in the shallows and mount the opposite bank. They took two and a half hours. Then having set all this in motion, Cleghorn and Innes were in danger of being swept aside by the waiting crowd and their mules, 'but Pierre with his sword in his hand asserted our right to prior admission as we had been first by the river.' Then, as they were congratulating themselves that the crossing had been achieved, 'our baggage mule sank in a deep morass which was full of water.' It took half an hour to get the poor creature out and they then found that all their bed linen, their changes of clothes and Mr Innes' *sac de nuit* were dripping wet and his notebooks absolutely illegible. 'All this', he goes on severely, 'has been owing to the obstinacy of the Drivers who have preferred this to a better road to save half a mile.'

From now on Mount Etna dominated the scene. Cleghorn wrote: 'It is beyond all comparison superior to Vesuvius . . . The last is ascended in two hours but it requires two days to get to the top of Etna . . . which carries its destructive power to the very objects around its throne . . . The hills under Etna are very beautiful and well cultivated, full of villages and country houses. But the mountain itself is inaccessible from the snow.'

Arrived at Catania, they found that the city had been destroyed in the 'last dreadful irruption of 1693' and rebuilt out of volcanic rock from Etna. They put up at the Elephant, 'by much the best inn we have seen in Sicily and there are few superior to it in Italy.' The place was clean and they did not need their bed linen, which was washed and dried for them. At supper they drank the white wine of Catania, grown on Etna and greatly superior in Cleghorn's opinion to sherry or even Madeira; he was sure it would particularly suit the market of Scotland. (He had already sent home some of the wine of Syracuse.) They were again well looked after: by the Vice Consul and his son; by the librarian who acted as guide to the classical ruins; by the brother of the Prince of Biscari, Don Francisco, a secular abbot (who did not wear clerical dress, except for his purple stockings) who: 'received us with that kindness and hospitality which characterize this elegant and well-informed family.'

Cleghorn was impressed with the museum built by the Biscari: 'It was the Father who began and this Son continues to augment their splendid collection of antiquities and Natural History, including a complete assembly of rattles, whistles and all the playthings of the children of old . . . and ancient strings of beads exactly resembling those which the Catholics use when repeating their prayers and the Abbé di Biscari said that in ancient times they were applied in the same manner – "You see," he said with a smile, "there is nothing new."' The Abbé was also interested in fossils and he and Cleghorn indulged in speculation on 'the theory of the earth'.

They were also given an opportunity here to see how justice worked – somewhat to Cleghorn's dismay. On the previous day, when they arrived in Catania, they had asked a 'peruquier' to direct them to the Elephant Inn. A rival innkeeper had then fallen on the unfortunate hairdresser, beaten him and brought witnesses to swear that he had decoyed the visitors away. Cleghorn and Innes told the Vice-Consul what had happened and offered to go to the Judge. 'He told us this was impossible for we were cavalieri, but that he and our servant would go to Court and in our name give evidence for the Peruquier.' The Judge accepted their evidence, acquitted the hairdresser and ordered the innkeeper to apologize to the visitors: 'This part of the sentence we have with difficulty prevailed on the Judge to dispense with.' Cleghorn goes on: 'The Judge came here and told us that the testimony of one Englishman was more to be depended on than a hundred such witnesses as produced by the innkeeper. But Justice is strangely administered when Evidence only appears when of the same rank with the parties.'

Their next day's journey (29 March by now) was to Taormina and was without incident and very beautiful, with Etna on their left and the Calabrian Mountains in the distance. (Cleghorn had had to accept defeat over his desire to climb Etna: 'No money can at present bribe a guide to go up. Snow still falls and the attempt is impracticable.') Arrived at Taormina, they lodged with the warmly hospitable Capuchins and went with an antiquary to view the ruins. These are fully described but the Theatre takes the crown: 'Time has destroyed much of the artificial but it can never destroy the natural grandeur of the situation of this superb theatre.'

The journey from Taormina to Messina was a long one but not difficult. Twenty miles of it was along 'a firm and agreeable sea beach' and for the last eight there was a 'tolerable made road'. They put up at an inn called the St. Phillipa whose windows had no glass and whose ceiling was of wooden planks with gaps between. This was just one sign of the 1783 earthquake which Messina and lower Calabria across the Straits had suffered. The Vice-Consul, whom they sought out, had been there during the earthquake and had had his house destroyed, and: 'he and his family for a fortnight had no shelter against the weather but what two hogsheads afforded.' The visitors had no antiquities to look at in Messina: 'It is a mass of modern and mournful ruins.' However they called on the Governor and found him, 'a most polite old gentleman who invited us to dinner and is to carry us afterwards to the best points of view for seeing the Town.' (This was General Danero who was to live to be over a hundred and see stirring days after the French invasion of Naples in 1798). They explained to the Governor that they planned to sail to Naples so he sent for the Captain of a ship due to sail there and 'gave him in the hearing of our Consul the most strict commands to treat us with the utmost civility'. So they booked their passage, but a strong northerly wind prevented them sailing. Instead they hired 'a boat with five stout hands' to take them across the Straits to Reggio, which they found still completely in ruins. They walked a couple of miles up a valley to an orange garden where the sheer opulence of nature in a Mediterranean spring overwhelmed them. It was a hot day and they sat in the shade with the scent of lemon blossom from the enclosing hedge in the air and ate oranges 'in their greatest perfection'. It all 'gave to a Northen Eye, the appearance of Paradise' – a paradise which even had members from the animal kingdom as well, when the guard dogs came and sat at their feet to eat the peel from the perfect oranges. To get back across the Straits they were dragged by two oxen for more than two hours close by the coast, almost to the rocks of Scylla; they could then set sail back to Messina.

The wind was still against them the next day so they went shopping for clothes made from Sicilian silk. Cleghorn had already noticed on their way to Messina many of the black mulberries on which the silk worms feed. He bought six pairs of white silk stockings, 'a dozen heavy silk napkins for the pocket, two silk cinctures and two black silk manteaux.'

Voyage to Naples: 28 March – 1 April 1790

The wind had veered the next day – Palm Sunday – so they settled their bills, bought provisions and went aboard, where they had to wait for a female passenger, so they did not get off till three. Cleghorn and Innes had in the meantime chosen their sleeping places, one each side of the helm, where they hoped they would enjoy fresh air and be free of vermin. Just before midnight they sailed past Stromboli, 'which emitted great quantities of smoke and some flame.'

In the morning Cleghorn tried to find out from one of the hands who had been a prisoner in Algiers for two or three years how the Moslems treated their Christian slaves, and this questioning involved everyone in the discussion. 'All aboard agreed in saying that the mildest slavery was in Tunis.' It made Cleghorn regretful that they did not have the time to go to Malta and so on to Tunis and the ruins of ancient Carthage.

Then the wind dropped and so did their spirits, 'which were not raised by the chanting of vespers which is now going on. A dish of tea may have a better effect.' The discovery that their ship was not in fact going to Naples may have added to their depression. Their destination was to be Sorrento, eighteen miles from Naples, and that meant hiring a felucca or going by mule for the additional distance. Rain then set in all night and members of the crew tried to share Cleghorn's partial shelter, curling up at his head and his feet. But they spent so much time scratching and searching for lice that Cleghorn 'obliged both my visitors to remove'. Another wearisome, dawdling day followed and they finally reached Sorrento on Tuesday 30 March.

They then discovered that the Health Laws enforced yet another twenty-four hour wait while the ship's returns were sent to the Health office in Naples and the necessary permit came back. It meant another night of cold and vermin on board ship or the Lazarretto on shore, 'perhaps more dirty and disagreeable than the ship.' But it was not twenty-four but getting on for forty-eight hours they had to wait and then were forced to hire a felucca for five crowns, 'when the regular boat would not have cost two shillings.' (Obviously collusion between the authorities and the local boatmen.) They finally sailed at 1.30 a.m., with a bright moon and a fair wind and reached Naples at six o'clock. Four hours in bed and then at ten o'clock Mr Clarke,[7] the 'circerone' in Naples, was at Cleghorn's bedside to rouse him for their expedition to Portici.

Antiquities around Naples: 1–5 April 1790

They went there because: 'it contains all the Antiquities that have been found in Herculaneum, Stabia and Pompei.' Innes took over the journal with a careful detailed description of what they saw in each room of the Museum – all sixteen of them. In the tenth, for instance, Innes notes that: 'one side of the Room was fitted with provisions found in the houses in Pompei – fruits of various kinds . . . several loaves of bread with the maker's name . . . eggs, become perfectly solid.' And, in the sixteenth room, 'iron stocks for the soldiers found in the guard room . . . made for fourteen prisoners and the skeletons of four were found in them.'

On Friday 2 April they visited Herculaneum, where Innes was 'surprised that the King of Naples should have done so much rather than disposed to censure him for doing so little'. Then they went on to Pompei, where they were thorough in looking at the barracks, the theatre, the Temple of Isis; then to the streets – where the description peters out in an exhausted 'etc'.

On the Saturday they went again by boat, this time westward from Naples past the island of Nisida, where Brutus had had a villa, then to Pozzuoli (where Sulla died – they had certainly done their prep), then across by boat to Miseno, the port where the galleys of Pliny lay when the irruption of Vesuvius destroyed Herculaneum. 'And it was from hence he sailed to Stabia where he was killed at the irruption of the Mountain.' They found the view from Miseno enchanting.

Cleghorn then takes up the writing of the journal to describe how the port consists of three basins, all of which communicate by a narrow strait, 'and the last of these is the Styx; it is a circular lake about two miles in circumference and around it are a continued line of sepulchres. This circumstance might have suggested the idea of its being the passage to the other world.' They went past the Lucrian Lake, 'now three quarters swallowed up by the sudden formation of Monte Nuovo,' and remembered that: 'it was from this lake that the Romans had fed the oysters that came from Britain.'

They then walked on to the Lake of Avernus, which they found: 'extremely picturesque: it does not now kill birds that fly over it. The air is much purified. Earthquakes may have dried up and destroyed the channels of sulphurous vapour . . . ' In the grotto of the Cumaean Sibyl, they: 'got into a passage and were carried on the backs of the boatman through deep water for a great way . . . they had flambeaux in their hands . . . '

This obviously intrigued them because on the Sunday they went back to Pozzuoli and inspected: 'an ancient crater whose lava is decomposed by vitriolic acid. Smoke everywhere issues around and a stone thrown with violence on the ground caused a trembling like the slight shock of an earthquake.' They walked on three miles or so along the ancient Via Campania to Cumae, where they were delighted by the immense and noble views and where they again explored the Grotto of the Sibyl.

On Monday morning they made preparations for their return to Rome. Cleghorn, who was feeling anxious about Lord Home's health because of letters from him waiting at Naples, met a Dr Bates from Rome who relieved his mind of its worst fears but could not wholly dispel them.

Before their departure they went to look at Sir William Hamilton's[8] collection – the only sightseeing they did in Naples itself. Cleghorn commented on the Etruscan vases particularly – and was intrigued by the history of what he considered the best picture of the Collection – the Venus of Corregio. 'It was part of King Charles I of England's collection and was sold originally for £300 to the Royal Family of Spain. It fell into the possession of one of their Neopolitan Viceroys and after passing into different hands, it came to Sir William's. He offered it to his present Majesty [i.e. George III] for the price it had been sold for when it was carried from England but our Sovereign neither wished to possess nor would look at a naked woman.' (This seems to do less than justice to a monarch who added nobly to the Royal Collection.)

Their journey from Naples to Gaeta took six hours. Though

they left the next day at 8.15 a.m., they had before this visited what had been another of Cicero's villas, the one where he died. The upper part of it had been converted into a garden – another beautiful Italian garden. 'It commands the prospect of the whole bay; it was planted with lemon trees, now pendant with fruit. It is hardly possible to conceive any appearance more beautiful . . . '

They covered about a hundred miles that day from Gaeta to Albani and so returned to a Rome which would probably be very thin of company, 'the functions of Holy Week and the splendid nothings that accompany it being now finished.' This rather sour note had its origin partly perhaps in meeting some of their Rome friends going south – 'Among these Mr. Lancelot Brown and his lady, a family with whom I have lived in great friendship since the commencement of our acquaintance about twelve months ago in Lausanne. It is', Cleghorn goes on, 'the severest tax on travelling to be perpetually separated from those places and persons whom we love and esteem.'

The return journey: 20 May – 21 June 1790

At the end of May Lord Home and Cleghorn began their homeward journey. They were now much more seasoned travellers. One evening when they were at Loretto, for instance, Cleghorn asked their guide to show them some viewpoint from which they could see the sunset and its afterglow: 'This – I never omit,' Cleghorn wrote. 'And without often having observed it in Italy, it is impossible to judge of that beautiful and lively blush which shines in the landscapes of Domenico Morone . . . ' A far cry from his desperate disclaimers of any knowledge of pictures made to Pastor Lavater at Zurich.

They were making for Venice and the great cities of the Lombard plain before recrossing the Alps for Neuchâtel and back to England. They stopped at Terni to look at a three-hundred-foot waterfall nearby and were surprised to hear that Mr Coutts before them had safely climbed down a difficult path to see the falls from below. Count Antonelli Romain, whom they had met at Schaffhausen and Constance, turned up to give them wine and take them to see the paintings of a friend of his, the Count de Sperola, 'who follows the pencil for pleasure rather than for bread.' At Loretto they visited – as far as they could for the crush of pilgrims – the church within which stands the 'Santa Casa' (Holy House) reputed by the faithful to be the house of the Holy Family miraculously transported there from Nazareth in 1294. All this inevitably failed to appeal to Cleghorn, as he shows in his final comment: 'I never expected much gratification from this spectacle but I have been disappointed both in the outward appearance of the Cathedral and the quantity of riches it contains.'

After Loretto they descended to the Adriatic coast, and at Senigallia Cleghorn inspected the town while Lord Home bathed in the sea. It was getting very hot – in the middle of the day – 'impossible to bear the weight of our coats in the carriage.' All along this coast they were 'serenaded night and day by the nightingale'. They duly noted their crossing of the Rubicon, 'an inconsiderable brook', and arrived at Bologna to find the Coutts family there and a Mrs O'Grady and her four daughters, 'than whom better never left the Kingdom of Ireland.'

In spite of all this throng Cleghorn made a thorough inspection of the Public Academy – 'a very noble institution,' he called it, with some rooms devoted to plans of architecture, others to paintings by young prize-winners, 'with laboratories for Chemistry, Cabinets of Natural History . . . models of Land and Marine tactics and a very complete apparatus for experiments in natural philosophy.'

At Ferrara Cleghorn was pleased to see the house where Ariosto had lived ('not so large as mine in St. Andrews'); also the university where they prized his manuscripts and displayed his chair and his 'curious, silver ink holder' – and his tomb in the Church of the Benedictines, with its simple inscription. But Cleghorn was 'greatly fatigued having had scarcely any sleep last night' – and the impression left by Ferrara was that it was something of a ghost city.

At Padua they hired a gondola; the journey to Venice was supposed to take seven hours – in fact it took nine, and for a good part of the way down the Brenta Canal: 'We are considerably below the level of the country and cannot enjoy its prospect.' By contrast, out in the sea, 'Nothing can be more singular than the view we now have of Venice. The city with its churches, palaces and public buildings . . . trees apparently growing in the midst of the ocean; innumerable little islands full of houses and seemingly floating like cork upon water.' Once arrived in Venice, Cleghorn sent to the posts, 'in anxious expectation of letters which I am almost afraid to receive.' He already knew that Adam Smith was ill, with no hope of recovery, and Cleghorn's distress over this is a measure of the affection he felt for Smith. The post was shut: 'I still have an hour and a half of reprieve but I do not know whether I feel it as a blessing or misfortune.' His letters, when the post was open, 'contain nothing decisive: Mr. S. alive but still very bad.'

Home and Cleghorn stayed six days in Venice. On 4 June, 'All the English, of whom there are now few here, dine this day with Mr. Coutts to drink the King's health.' Cleghorn's description of what he saw reflects his interest but he did not really find the Most Serene City congenial. Passing Venetian galleys, for instance, as he sailed on the canals, he commented: 'It requires custom to reconcile me to the rattling of chains on human feet.' He disliked the many gaping stone 'lions' mouths' with their encouragement of 'Denunzie Secrete'. He found the water 'extremely bad' in its effects on him. ('It acts sometimes as a strong Physic and sometimes as a Vomit – I was cured by drinking nothing but Cyprus wine.') Above all he missed exercise. In Venice none could be taken 'either on foot or on horseback'.

After Venice they pushed on to Vicenza and Verona, and then up the Valley of the Adige to Trent. As they left Italy Cleghorn commented on how extraordinarily kind the Italians were to foreigners, but he was quite glad to be free of the beggars – 'these all over Italy are most troublesome and importunate' – and the children were the worst, whereas: 'in the Tyrol, the peasants are well fed and clothed and the houses are uniformly good and clean.'

On the way to the Brenner pass 'the road was so very steep that we are obliged to put six horses to the carriage.' There followed the descent to Innsbruck,[9] where they dismissed Lord Home's carrier, who was perpetually drunk. Then it was up again among the snow-capped mountains, Cleghorn tormented by toothache which he attributed to the change of climate. The rest of the journey (via Lermoos, Fussen, Lindau on Lake Constance, St. Gall, Zurich and Baden) was accomplished without incident. The only two references to the revolutionary fever which was spreading out from France during 1790 came on this return journey: in Zurich they heard of peasant riots in Schaffhausen against the extortions of their Bailiff. There was also unrest within the canton of Zurich itself against the abuse of their commercial monopoly by the merchants of Zurich, who kept the prices they paid the peasants for their textile goods unfairly low. Cleghorn felt sufficiently familiar with the Swiss political scene to generalize confidently:

'The government of Berne as well as that of Zurich is strictly aristocratical. But Berne is a farmer, who without speculation, manages the affairs of the country and the people with justice, economy and order; Zurich is a merchant whose temporary and short-sighted interest, leads the government to prefer the fleeting advantage of the governors to the lasting and real happiness of the people. All aristocracies are bad but mercantile aristocracies are in their nature diabolical.'

The other reference to the effect of events in France was made at Soleure, where there were many French refugees, 'among others the Baron de Breteuil, lately at the head of the War Department of France. He has just passed the window on foot adorned with many ribbons; he is a stout, well-looking man, past the prime of life.'

There is more than a hint of travel weariness in Cleghorn's reaction to the cleanliness and comfort of the Swiss way of life: his enjoyment, for instance, of a warm bath, 'which is the most pleasant and refreshing of all luxuries, after the great fatigue which for some months I have been obliged to undergo.' There is no doubt he was glad to be back in Switzerland and was even beginning to think of home:

'I am extremely happy to visit once more a country I so love and admire. Its natural beauties have ever given me a pleasure I am unable to express, and the impression of these beauties has neither been effaced or forgotten amidst all the scenes of nature or art which I have since seen. I now consider this happy country as a resting place for my heart before I reach that other which contains all the objects for which I wish to live.'

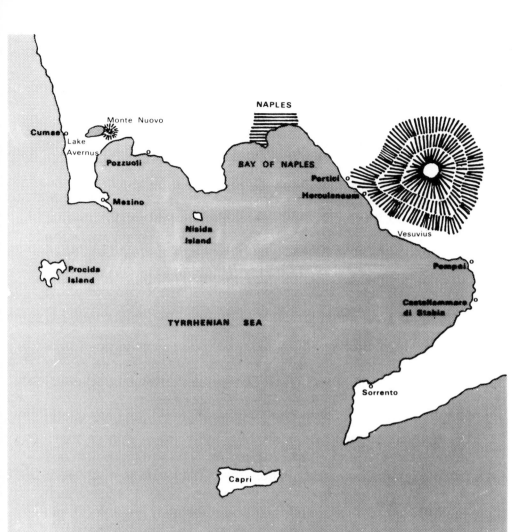

Places round Naples visited
by Cleghorn and Innes
April 1 st — 5 th, 1790

6

'Persons who hang about office'[1]
October 1790 – March 1795

After nearly two and a half years' travelling in Europe, Cleghorn returned in 1790[2] to England, his perspectives altered, his appetite for politics whetted and his instinct for action, especially action at some centre of power, heightened. His fertile mind was busy with wide-ranging schemes for his country to adapt its policies to the changing power patterns brought about by the collapse of the French monarchy. Without doubt, his duty should have taken him north to St Andrews, where the new university session would just be beginning and where his wife, with the responsibility of their children on her hands, must have been feeling this more keenly with the death in 1790 of her relation, Janet Douglas, who had over many years helped her with her young family.

Yet to return to the academic life of St Andrews would seem to be embracing an intolerable narrowing of opportunities, convinced as Cleghorn had become that: 'Learned retirement and secluded leisure for study is nonsense. The world is a school of letters as well as of business;' while universities: 'educate men most profoundly learned and most consummately ignorant.'[3] And if ever he was to break out of academic circles – and the salary he was paid as a professor would never enable him to provide adequately for his seven children – it had to be at this point. So he lingered in London, hoping to find some way to bring himself and his ideas to the notice of those in power, and for the next two years he seems to have been one of those to whom his own rather disparaging phrase in the chapter title would apply.

During November 1790 he drew up a clear analysis of the factors which led to a change in the attitude of the Swiss cantons towards their ally, France: the coming to an end of the 'public subsidies and private pensions, paid by France to the Governing powers and Individuals of the Cantons',[4] with the 'total change in the French constitution', the exposure of Swiss mercenary soldiers in the French service to many insults and much unjust treatment, the reluctance of the Swiss to invest their capital in the uncertain French funds any longer. In this changed situation, Cleghorn urged the British government to fill the vacuum left by France. He pointed out the advantages this would bring in defence: the long-term possibility of striking a blow at the heart of France from the only part of the French frontier which they could not easily defend. Moreover, 'seventeen Marching Regiments of Swiss and several Regiments of Swiss Guards are at present in the service of Foreign powers,' and: 'all would prefer, on Account of the Superiority of the pay, the British Foreign Service, to that of any other power.'

In finance, a Swiss alliance would: 'open to our Funds an extensive Capital which its possessors would at all times willingly lend upon annuities.' Cleghorn also pointed out what great advantages the Swiss enjoyed as Intelligence gatherers: 'As soldiers or merchants, the Swiss are settled in every country in Europe . . . A system of general Intelligence might here be more easily formed than elsewhere which coming in aid of information from other quarters, might be peculiarly serviceable to Ministers.'

It is quite a persuasive exercise and ends with the suggestion that an agent from Great Britain, properly authorised and really knowledgeable on the situation in the cantons, should be sent to Switzerland to see what could be built up between the British and the Swiss. Cleghorn sent this policy document of his to the Duke of Leeds, Foreign Secretary till 1791, in Pitt the Younger's first ministry. He made no effort to bolster it with personal recommendations – he would do that if the plan met with any favourable reaction. That it provoked some response is shown by a letter from Cleghorn to Henry Dundas,[5] dated 16 December 1790, following an interview between the two 'at Wimbleton' (one of those shots in the dark at spelling place names which did not quite – as so often with Cleghorn – hit the target). This was the first of a number of visits which Cleghorn paid to Dundas in his villa at Wimbledon and it evidently raised his hopes, for his letter ends: 'I have no claims from personal pretensions to employment; yet should I be honoured with any commission, I would endeavour to act so as not to disgrace it. And I am confident that, sent into that country, I could be of use to my own.' But his hopes were premature. In 1791 Lord Grenville became Foreign Secretary and chose his friend and fellow student at Christchurch, William Wickham,[6] to be the main two-way source of information on Switzerland for the British Government. Grenville, however, seems to have regarded the information from Wickham as being for his own use and kept Wickham's letters from the knowledge of the diplomatic service generally.

Dundas, a tough and able Scots lawyer, though not yet in the cabinet, was an increasingly powerful figure. He had won the complete confidence of the Prime Minister because he could deliver to Pitt the reliable support of the Scottish MPs in the Commons. He also had an extraordinarily detailed knowledge of the affairs of the East India Company, a knowledge which brought power and patronage – and, in 1793, the Presidency of the Board of Control. Since 1784 he had been treasurer of the Navy, and in the summer of 1792 he was brought into the Cabinet as Home Secretary. He evidently judged that Cleghorn had qualities of initiative and political perception which might be useful to him.

Dundas seems to have put Cleghorn to work at once drawing up reports, because at the beginning of 1791 Cleghorn wrote to Lady Home that: 'I am at this moment very much occupied and have therefore to entreat you would forgive the shortness of this letter.' (The import of the letter suggests that Lady Home was trying to pin her son down to write to Mr Dundas – perhaps about a family claim, for Cleghorn suggests that Lord Home should write a short letter, 'stating the attachment of the family to the Government, the high military offices held by Earl William – and the loss which his private affairs sustained by his being constantly abroad on the affairs of the public . . . If a petition to the King is necessary,' Cleghorn added, 'I will certainly hear and write one accordingly for Lord Home to sign.'[7] Cleghorn does not seem to have had much confidence that his former charge would get down to dealing with business matters.)

In March 1791 Cleghorn was writing to Principal McCormick of the College to excuse his continued absence from St Andrews: 'A variety of circumstances which I could not foresee have detained me and are still likely to detain me here for some time.' But he had every intention of performing: 'the duties of my office next session. I shall not therefore be under the necessity of soliciting from the Society a continuance of that indulgence which they have hitherto had the goodness to grant me.'[8]

The Principal replied that: 'the Society can dispense with his attendance no longer than the sitting down of the College in October next.' But October came in St. Andrews without the return of their professor of Civil History and the tone of the Masters' letters began to harden towards him. The minutes of the United College record on 19 November 1791 that: 'the Principal shall write a letter in the name of the Society requiring Mr. Cleghorn to return to his charge in the College on or before Tuesday, 3 January next . . . if he fails to comply with his requisition, they will consider him as having Deserted and vacate his office.'[9]

What probably kept Cleghorn in London, balancing the hope of landing some permanent position in the administration against the growing necessity of returning to St Andrews if he was to keep his job there, was the arrival of the Comte de Meuron in England in the autumn of 1791.

Charles-Daniel, Comte de Meuron, was one of that circle of leading figures in Neuchâtel whom Cleghorn had found so stimulating and congenial when he stayed there with Lord Home. That the feeling of friendship between the two men was genuine can be seen in the Comte's affectionate references to Cleghorn in his letters written to his family during their voyage to India in 1795. But what concerned both of them on the Comte's 1791 visit to London was the future of the regiment of which he was the 'Colonel Propriétaire' and his brother, Pierre-Frédéric, the 'Colonel-Commandant'. Charles-Daniel de Meuron had first seen service in the Swiss Régiment de Hallwyl, made up of foot soldiers in the French Royal Navy. Then from 1765–81 he had been in the Swiss Guards and had come to look on the Duke de Choiseul as his patron. Choiseul acted to some effect in 1781, when the Dutch East India Company asked the French government to procure for it a new regiment to re-enforce the defence of its eastern possessions. He put forward the Comte de Meuron, who in May 1781 signed a Capitulation with the Dutch Company which defined the commitments of the two sides.

From 1783 to 1788 the Régiment Meuron served at the Dutch base in the Cape of Good Hope. Military duties there gave the Comte no joy and in 1785 discontent in the regiment reached its climax. As a result the Comte announced that he had remitted command to his brother, Pierre-Frédéric, and that he himself was returning to Europe. Back there, he brought all the pressure he could to bear on the Dutch East India Company to make them pay the arrears owing to the regiment – but to no avail. In 1788 the Régiment Meuron was sent to Ceylon and to Dutch bases in India. In 1790 the Comte was in Paris, actually applying for service in the French army. (It was also the Countess Duhamel who drew him to Paris: '*L'amie dont je revère de plus en plus les qualités.*' She had since 1773 lent him money for his various enterprises. His first fortune had come from his wife's dowry, but the marriage had broken down and a divorce was in process of being arranged and was completed in 1792.[10])

The Comte's purpose on this somewhat mysterious London visit was to test reaction, unofficially, in government circles to the possibility of the British instead of the Dutch becoming his regiment's paymaster. He wrote of this visit: '*Je dois chercher à sortir de l'oppression d'une manière ou d'une autre; il y a quelques possibilités à la réussite de mes vues, quoique la Chose soit encore bien peu avancée. Tu conçois toute la circonspection que je dois mettre.*'[11]

Cleghorn was more forthcoming to Dundas. In a letter dated 28 October 1791 he explained how the Comte de Meuron was disposed to quit the Dutch East India Company and to put his regiment at the disposal of the King of England or the English East India Company. He added that the Régiment consisted of 1,200 men, that they were seasoned troops and used to service in a tropical climate.[12] But all those interested were aware the time was not yet ripe for action. The ferment of revolution in France had yet to provoke war with Austria and Prussia, and England was to cling to her neutrality till the beginning of 1793. So the Comte went back to the Continent and Dundas set Cleghorn to write his reports – whether or not on this subject is not known.

What is certain is that Cleghorn did not write to the United College before 3 January 1792, when he was due to return, because in the minutes of 28 January the Masters: 'being fully sensible of the propriety of proceeding with the utmost caution in a matter which involves in it not only the Interest of the Society and publick, but the rights of one of their own body . . . resolve that, before taking further steps towards declaring the said office (i.e. the chair of Civil History) is vacated, they will consult Learned Council.'[13] There was in fact no precedent that could be cited and a letter from Cleghorn in February of 1792 gave them a breathing space before they need take the final decision.

He wrote from London, telling his colleagues: 'how sensible I am of the indulgence I have received from them in their acquiescence to my absence from the duties of my office for so long a time, especially when I am so particularly situated as to be restrained from giving them that satisfactory information on this subject which they have a right to expect.'[14] (A reference to his intelligence work, on which he maintained a permanent silence.) He went on to ask the Masters if they would agree to appoint a deputy to teach his class and to allot him that proportion of Cleghorn's salary which they thought adequate and proper. The College Statutes did not allow the Masters to make any such arrangement, but they had no sooner decided this than they received a letter dated 17 February 1792 from Robert

Hepburn, private secretary to Dundas, who, among his many other offices, was also Chancellor of St Andrews University. The letter contained a request for leave of absence for Cleghorn for the remainder of the session. There must have been some quite specific intelligence task that Cleghorn had been set, 'in consequence of a very late Conversation Lord Grenville has had with Mr. Dundas.'[15] The letter went into no more detail than that, except to say that the information Cleghorn was to work on would be useful to the government. The Masters, no doubt feeling that they had for the time being been let off the hook, wrote back that 'they were happy in complying with the wishes of the Lord Chancellor'.[16]

It is possible that Cleghorn's work may have been concerned with the visit of Talleyrand to England from January to March 1792 because this seems to have been the only occasion when Cleghorn would have had 'more than ordinary opportunity of being acquainted with Talleyrand', as he mentioned much later in a letter to William Adam.[17] Cleghorn's fluent spoken and written French would be useful in such work. Dundas would perhaps set him to deal with information coming out of France and Switzerland.

As a consequence of the important administrative revolution in the British government in 1782, the Home Office dealt with the business which had previously been covered by the old Southern Department, which had taken in the Mediterranean and France, together with influence in naval matters. (The Under Secretary at the Home Office at this time was Evan Nepean – and he was certainly paying a number of naval officers who were engaged on intelligence work in France.[18])

Evidence that one side of Cleghorn's business was to gather intelligence can also be seen in an order from Nepean on 25 March 1793, which Cleghorn signed as witness, authorising the payment to him of £20 for 'Monsieur de Bertrand, S.S.' and £9/16 shillings for: 'Ferade S.S.'[19] It is possible that these expenses were incurred in the course of Cleghorn's being sent on government business to Switzerland, because the Comte de

Meuron, writing to his brother Pierre-Frédéric in Ceylon, to introduce Cleghorn, implies this in his letter of 1795:

'Mr. Cleghorn is an English gentleman who for a number of years has been my friend and who lived in Switzerland, particularly at Neuchâtel where he won the esteem and confidance of all our governors by the uprightness and honesty which he showed in all the commissions entrusted to his charge by the English government.'[20]

There is another note that he was given £400 over two years by Nepean out of the 'extraordinaries of the Police', but there is no more evidence as to whom he gave it to or what it was spent on; though it was certainly not regarded by Cleghorn as his salary. This is shown in Cleghorn's letter of 25 November 1794 to Evan Nepean, in which Cleghorn reminds him of: 'the considerable arrears of salary which are owing to me. I was during more than two years attached to or at least attending your office . . . More than a year's salary is of course due to me.'[21]

The somewhat haphazard financial arrangements of the Home Office under Dundas are very well illustrated by a letter from a Home Office official, J Reeves, to his senior, Evan Nepean, trying to check up on the moneys which Cleghorn had received: 'I believe the first letter was sent in to the Treasury as a voucher – and I have never had it back – or had *you* got it and kept it, saying you wished it not to appear and you would get a letter signed by Mr. Dundas in its place – *you who forget nothing*, assist me in this.'[22] Cleghorn had in fact to borrow £200 from Nepean because he had had 'very considerable accounts, contracted for my son on his going to India'; he wanted to repay Nepean and asked 'where I may apply for payments'.

It was at the beginning of 1793 that Cleghorn became a government servant, because matters had come to a head by then with the United College over the chair that he still held. That he did actually tender his letter of resignation to the Earl of Cassilis before the Masters formally declared his place vacant, is clear. On 24 November 1792 they wrote requiring him: 'peremptorily to return to his duty . . . on or before the 5th January next, with certification if he does not, they will immediately proceed to take legal steps for vacating his office.'[23] When Cleghorn received this, he sent a copy of it to Dundas and wrote explaining to the Masters that he had continued in London by the desire of 'Mr. Dundas intimated to me by Mr. Pulteney and therefore I submit myself entirely to his direction'. With a letter ten days later, he sent two eminent doctors'[24] certificates, stating that in his present state of health 'a journey north may be attended with material hazard to his constitution'; otherwise, he assured the Masters, he would have come. They seem to have received this in the spirit in which it was no doubt written because on 30 January 1793, they were telling the Earl of Cassilis: 'We have till this day been constantly amused by assurances from him that he was to return to his duty.'[25]

From Cleghorn's point of view, he would not willingly – with a wife and seven children – give up his professorship, until he was promised an alternative source of income. Such a promise was obtained in December and, on 31 January 1793, payment of £100 was made to him (though from the list in the William R Perkins Library, it is not clear whether this was salary or expenses for his work). Anyway, that same January, Cleghorn wrote to the Masters that: 'the gentlemen of the College may give themselves no further trouble respecting my absence. Lord Cassilis, who is in London, has fixed upon a gentleman of talents to be my successor and I shall resign into his Lordship's hands the office which I hold in St. Andrews.'[26]

Under Pitt's reforming impetus, the days were passing when a patron could declare roundly: 'Since the post is a sinecure, what matter whether a man is paid here or in London?' Still, the College had been generous, and Cleghorn had been given a good run for his unearned university salary.

The other work Cleghorn did in the Home department was in what he called 'the Précis Office'.[27] The task of summarising the main points of government papers under separate heads would be work for which he was very well fitted. This can be seen in the reports on Ceylon that he later sent to Dundas. That his friends knew of his work in the Home Office can be seen in a letter that Cleghorn kept among his papers from Mlle D'Éon, who had been commended to him by General Melville of Strathkinness. Mlle D'Éon was a singular character who had come to England in 1762 as a high-powered diplomat for Louis XV, to negotiate peace with the English government. Fortune had turned against him at the French court and he had stayed in England, adopted woman's dress and styled himself Charlotte-Geneviève-Louise-Auguste-Chimothée D'Éon de Beaumont, to the consternation of polite society, so that he was obliged to retreat to Scotland, where friends such as Melville stood by him. In March 1793 he was writing to Cleghorn to thank him for what he had done at the Home Office to enable him/her to obtain passports from the Secretary of State to go to France, because of the recent death of his/her mother at Tonnerre, and giving the particulars Cleghorn had asked for, about the two other French men who were to accompany him/her to France. (Under 'Declaration d'Armes', Mlle D'Éon proposed to take '*mon ancien sabre, mon epée, deux anciennes carbine Turques par tirer ou prix et un seul pistolet Turc*'.[28])

While the outbreak of war between England and France in February of 1793 in the end prevented Mlle D'Eon's journey, it opened up more lines of action which in Cleghorn's view ministers should pursue. In June 1793 he was writing to Lord Fitzgerald, minister at Berne, about England's future military needs in India and how valuable the Régiment Meuron would be there, if their transfer could be arranged.[29] As Cleghorn was aware from de Meuron of how resentful the Dutch were in the East, of Britain's overbearing attitude (for example, over the use of Trincomalee in Ceylon), he felt prompt action was all the more necessary.

In the Netherlands there was a strong enough pro-French Patriot Party to ensure the success of the French revolutionary armies when they invaded Dutch territory in January 1795. This was followed by the establishment of the Batavian Republic and the flight of the Stadholder, William V of Orange, to England, where he was installed in Kew Palace. The chief fear of the British, at this point, was that Dutch overseas possessions would follow the Patriot Party at home and set up pro-French revolutionary governments which would threaten British possessions, especially in the East, where places like the Carnatic would be vulnerable to attack if the French were invited in by the Dutch in Ceylon. The Stadholder was therefore persuaded in his capacity as Captain-General and Admiral of Holland to sign, on 7 February 1795, a directive – which came to be known as the Kew Letter – ordering all Governors of Dutch colonies and commanders of Dutch forces to hand over the forts and installations under their command to the British. The British on their side promised that these would be restored to the Dutch on the return of independence and of the country's ancient constitution and established forms of government.

The Kew Letter was used by the British during 1795 to demand the submission of the Dutch who held the coastlands of Ceylon. Lord Hobart, governor of Madras, made it the basis of his ultimatum to the Dutch there, who were in fact split in their reactions to the British demands. There was sufficient Dutch resistance, however, for Madras to claim that the British were no longer under an obligation to treat the Dutch possessions in Ceylon as protectorates taken on trust, as had been promised in the Stadholder's Letter. At the same time Madras sent a mission under Robert Andrews to the King of Kandy in the interior, to forestall independent action on his part. But, while all this diplomatic and military machinery went slowly into action, it had taken Cleghorn less than a week after the Kew Letter to realize that this was the moment for action.

Lord Spencer and Dundas had been planning to send Cleghorn to France as Commissary for prisoners, 'on account of the Information they expected from me.'[30] But the chance of weakening Dutch resistance in Ceylon and of gaining the services of a disciplined, seasoned regiment for the British in India was not an opportunity to be missed, and they had Cleghorn to prompt them to action. On 14 February 1795 he had written to Dundas urging on him the need for swift and secret negotiations with the Comte de Meuron, to set in train the transfer of his regiment in Ceylon from Dutch to British allegiance. By 17 February Cleghorn's formal instructions had been worked out, largely by himself; these were approved and returned to him on 24 February.[31] He set off that very afternoon but was held up at Yarmouth for four days by contrary winds. Finally, on 1 March 1795, he sailed for Cuxhaven, thus launching himself on a five-year adventure which gave him more in the way of action, decision-making and crisis than even he had reckoned on.

Eastward Bound
1 March – 12 September 1795

The launching of the mission

The mission on which Cleghorn was now sent had been explained to the King, who had given his approval. It had the backing of the Prime Minister and the Cabinet; most important of all, it had the active support of Henry Dundas, now Secretary of War. The idea for it had originated from Cleghorn himself, with his appreciation of the strategic value of Ceylon to the British position in India in general and in the Carnatic in particular. He saw Ceylon (in the last resort, if the British were for the time being eclipsed by the French in India) as 'a long boat to a ship in flames'.[1] He had swiftly seized the right time for action – action for which he had already prepared Dundas. He gave confidence to Dundas that the Comte de Meuron would co-operate in his plan because of the genuine friendship between the two men. He had shown initiative in making decisions.

All these factors make this first journey to India and Ceylon very much Cleghorn's adventure. The fact that he had been entrusted with it was a sort of vindication of his instinct not to go back to Scotland in 1790. His own ambition was to prove himself through this opportunity, but he needed some assurance from Dundas that provision would be made for his family and that he himself might be recommended to the government of Madras. He ends this request: 'but I have the most perfect reliance on your generosity and I hope my conduct has evinced my sentiments when I made no terms whatever for myself before my departure.'[2] In answer to this letter, Dundas wrote back: 'By the existing Acts of Parliament, you cannot (as you are not a servant of the Company) be appointed to any situation under the government of India, but you cannot entertain any doubt that your services will be duly rewarded by pecuniary compensation. As soon therefore as the objects of your mission are fully completed, you will return to Great Britain and no delay shall take place after your return in making a liberal compensation to you and your family for the services you have performed. I do not therefore think you need entertain any anxiety on that head.'

Cleghorn's own sense of personal obligation overrode what he must have learned in government circles since 1790 – that the promises of politicians were more easily made than carried out. That he had some doubts is shown by a number of references to his family in his letters to Andrew Stuart, who was going to deal with his correspondence home.[3] For example, he writes from Venice on 13 May 1793: 'I hinted to Mr. Dundas to allow Mrs. C. £300 instead of £200 a year out of any allowances which may be granted to me. She has seven children to maintain and they are at an expensive time of life. She deserves all I can do for her or them and it is for their sakes only I have undertaken the present expedition.' And again he reminds Stuart to check with Dundas about these matters: 'I have the most perfect confidence in his warmth of heart: I have not the same in those employed in office under him.' Judging by the receipts which Rachel signed – during the years from 1795–9 when Cleghorn was away – she received £150 a year from the War Office; except in 1798, when £200 was paid. But as in three of the years' records there are no October receipts, she probably was paid the £200 promised.[4] (Incidentally, her signature on these receipts is the only written record of hers which survived.)

However, all Cleghorn's energies were now focused on the carrying out of his mission. 'The only wish in my head is to execute my business with advantage to the Country,'[5] he wrote to Rachel after reasuring her about the pension. He had sufficient government resources for the European stage and the promise that he could draw on 'the respective Presidencies in India to whom you may have occasion to resort'.

The crossing of the North Sea to Cuxhaven took three days and though he had 'wretched quarters'[6] there, he was lucky: 'in meeting with an American gentleman who came with me and who understands the language and money well; he has been most capable and civil to me.' This meant that Cleghorn had a companion on a ninety-mile journey in an open cart through rain 'accompanied by snow' from Cuxhaven to Hamburg.

His crossing of the Elbe was 'partly by water, partly by a sledge drawn on the ice and mostly on foot'. In Hamburg he provided himself with a carriage tough enough 'to resist the rough movement of the German Roads'.[7] The British Resident in Hamburg, Mr Frazer, also helped him to engage a Polish servant, Michael Mirowsky, 'who speaks German and French remarkably well,' and who accompanied Cleghorn all the way to India. His honesty in dealing with day-to-day business was valuable as Cleghorn had found that: 'the money of the country puzzles me confoundedly as it differs in name and value in almost every Town and Village, thro' which you pass.'

Cleghorn's letter to Rachel went on: 'I have no more of the German language than is barely necessary for eating or drinking, tho' from my perfect knowledge of broad Scotch, I can make shift to understand a great deal of what is said.' And he pictured himself 'in the room of my German landlady surrounded with her children and maids', smiling at each other in mutual incomprehension. Though he always sought in his letters to reassure Rachel about his health and to minimize possible danger, odd phrases reflected his moods. In Hamburg he was exhausted by two nights and a day of rough travelling, and very conscious of his responsibilities in the hazards ahead. After telling Rachel that her letters to him should be sent through Andrew Stuart, he added: 'I beseech you, do not write to me in low spirits.' By contrast, six days later, rested and better equipped, he was writing cheerfully: 'I always agree with travelling.'[8]

From Hamburg he went to Hanover, 'as I have a commision to Lord Malmesbury and there I shall see our new Princess who has got that length from Brunswick.' From Hanover to Neuchâtel the travelling was trying: 'I have been this day, twelve hours in a carriage and am now stopped for want of horses, tho' I have in fact sown the roads with gold. I have crossed the great Prussian army consisting of 60,000 men going to Westphalia. Their artillery required fifteen days to march twenty-five miles; hundreds of their horses are lying dead on the road and I everywhere met their mangled carcases half devoured by wolves and ravens . . .

'All Germany is in motion and nothing but soldiers to be seen in the cities and on the roads' (17 March 1795).[9] Slow as his progress was, it was better than the time taken by the post – though Cleghorn did write ahead from Cassell to warn the Comte de Meuron of his impending arrival. Finally, on 25 March, the two men met in the Comte's summer residence – La Petite Rochette on the shores of Lake Neuchâtel.

It took five days of negotiations – and some hard bargaining by the Comte – to draw up the new Capitulation. Cleghorn began by translating for de Meuron the instructions which Dundas had given him (omitting what Cleghorn was to do if the Comte refused to go to India). He also produced copies of the Kew Letter and the general orders of the Stadholder to the governors of the Dutch colonies in India and Ceylon, telling them to open their ports, etc, to the British Navy. The bases of their negotiation were the articles (drawn up by Cleghorn himself and approved by Dundas) of which the most important were the promises that the Régiment Meuron should receive British pay from the time they left the Dutch service and that the British would pay such arrears as were due from the Dutch East India Company. But Cleghorn knew that the most difficult hurdle would be to persuade the Comte that he himself should go out to India to give authority to the change of allegiance. For this purpose he had, in reserve, permission to offer a 'douceur' of £15,000 to de Meuron, if this would persuade him, as a man of fifty-seven with a broken leg only half healed, to go.

Cleghorn marshalled his battery of arguments: that the regiment had at this point no practical line of retreat – it was isolated in Ceylon; that if Ceylon fell to the British, without the Comte accepting the terms now offered, he would be depriving his regiment of the advantages of British pay and condemning them to the status of prisoners of war; that he need not feel any longer bound by the terms of his former agreement with the Dutch East India Company because for the last three years they had reneged on their promises by paying the regiment in the Cape with paper money and in Ceylon with copper coin. In addition, the Dutch Company was so changed from that with which he had negotiated that it was simply a puppet of French revolutionary forces. Moreover, his residual obligations to the Stadholder would be fulfilled rather than broken by the transference of the allegiance of the Régiment as was shown by the orders of Stadholder to the governors of the Dutch colonies.

Since they had talked this over when the Comte was in London, he was ready to agree on the principles; the bargaining came over his detailed demands. The results were set out in fifteen points (which, following Cleghorn's own practice when writing reports for Dundas: 'I have thrown into an appendix'). The two men signed these on 30 March 1795. Some of the articles had not been authorised by the British government – chiefly the promises that the Comte should be given the rank of Major General in the British Army and his brother, Pierre-Frédéric, Brigadier General; also that the Comte should be allowed to take Captain Bolle with him as aide-de-camp with all his expenses paid by the British. To obtain government approval, Cleghorn set off the next day for Berne, where he had arranged with William Wickham to have a courier ready to take his letters to London and return with the government answers to Venice as soon as possible.

The Comte had already had second thoughts about going to India. That night he wrote to Cleghorn: 'I find your eloquence has somewhat taken advantage of the esteem and friendship which has bound us together for so long, for it is foolish at my age, after establishing a delightful little retreat where I meant to live in peace, to embark on the stormy sea of business . . . I tell you again, my dear friend, nothing less than the opinion I have of your character, of your mind and, Mr. Cleghorn, most particularly of your affection, makes me decide to go to Venice to wait the return of your courier and ratification of the Articles you have made me sign . . . ' No doubt there on to whose shoulders responsibility was firmly fastened!

Cleghorn also had the idea that it might be possible while the Comte was settling his affairs, for himself to slip over to Stuttgart to reach a similar agreement with the Duke of Wurttemburg, who also had a regiment in the service of the Dutch East India Company. However, he decided that what he had definitely achieved in Neuchâtel might be put at risk by failure at Stuttgart, so he gave up the idea. There was no doubt that if Cleghorn and the Comte could keep the existence of their mission secret, so that no hint of it reached Ceylon before the arrival of the Comte himself, then the strategic effect of the transfer of the regiment would have maximum impact on undermining the Dutch position there. Cleghorn had arranged a sort of cypher with Andrew Stuart to keep the secret even if his letters from Europe fell into unfriendly hands: he would refer to himself as Andrew Johnstone; de Meuron he would call 'one of the partners'; the British government should be Horton and Co., etc. In fact only one letter survives in which he used this code to Stuart and the secret of the mission did not leak out in Neuchâtel.

There is also an interesting glimpse of two professional intelligence gatherers at work in the brief correspondence between Cleghorn and Wickham, the British chargé-d'affaires in Switzerland. He was deeply involved at this time in building up a French royalist and anti-revolutionary movement which extended to include Lyons, the Vendée, the south of France, the Austrian court, the Rhineland centres of the French princes and even General Pichegru in the French army itself. Negotiations were at a delicate stage and Wickham was alarmed at Cleghorn's appearance on his beat. 'Will you please excuse me,' he writes, 'as I am ignorant of the object of your mission, if I request, if it in any way relates to the new levées, that you will be pleased to observe as much precaution as possible . . . '

Cleghorn was able to reassure him by return of post in a note in which he told of his intention to come to Berne with letters for the courier, whom he asked Wickham to hold for him. At their meeting Wickham evidently asked Cleghorn for information on Neuchâtel. Cleghorn's reply was as detailed and factual as he could make it: on the Neuchâtel counsellors who were buying arms for the defence of their Canton – and, by contrast, on a Neuchâtel merchant who, under cover of a commission from the Austrian Emperor, had requisitioned materials in the Habsburg territories and was finding the means of sending: 'through the Valle de Travers to Besançon . . . copper in plates for the French ships of war and brass for casting their cannon.'

Cleghorn also took the opportunity to write to Rachel from Berne, a letter full of elation at the success of his negotiations with the Comte. With time now for his affection for Switzerland to re-surface, he was wanting his family to share it. 'Will you spare me my two eldest daughters? I will board them in Switzerland where they will be most carefully attended to, learn French and every accomplishment joined to the example of great moderation of mind. Think of it – we will all come home together! . . . ' (20 April 1795).[10] But in the next letter, written from St Gall, he realised: 'they can nowhere be or make you so happy as by remaining with you.' He did not give up the idea, though, but began planning for Peter to come out to Neuchâtel to stay with: 'my worthy friend Captain Dunbar who is married to a lady of that place . . . in that Country he will meet with many of his father's friends who will treat him as they have always done me, with a kindness and respect far beyond what I deserve.'[11]

31 March to 8 May 1795 was a time of underlying anxiety for Cleghorn: he had committed the Government to more than he had been authorised to do, but he had to act as if he had received that authorisation. In particular, he had to keep the Comte up to scratch. There had been, in the event, no need to offer him the 'douceur' at all but he had demanded a loan of £4,000 to settle his debts in Neuchâtel so that no one could spread the rumour that he had left the city to escape them. In addition, there was the complication that the Dutch Company had suddenly conferred on the Comte the rank of Brigadier General,

a rank which they had consistently refused him over the last ten years.[12]

The Comte had not been beguiled by this sudden move but it underlined the need for the British to give in to his request for the brevet rank of Major General. Cleghorn was finding his anxiety very undermining. On 8 April he was writing home to Andrew Stuart that if the planned expedition to India was *not* approved by the government, 'instead of being called home under circumstances which must be extremely disagreeable, I must earnestly entreat your good offices and those of Sir William Pulteney that I may be allowed to remain for some time at least Chargé D'Affaires for the Circle of Swabia.'[13]

Still there was nothing Cleghorn could do but make his preparations *as if* he had government approval, since speed was just as essential as secrecy. He wrote to Admiral Hotham asking that the frigate which the government had ordered for him and the Comte at Leghorn should be cancelled, as it was better for them to leave from Venice. He wrote to Sir Richard Worsley, British resident in Venice, asking him to charter a ship if there were no British frigates in the Adriatic. He wrote to his family and friends in England and Switzerland and later received in reply from Anna Ross (a relation of Rachel Cleghorn) the assurance that: 'Mrs. Cleghorn and the bairns are all in perfect health – Mrs. C. much supported by so frequently hearing from you.'[14] William Duff Dunbar, his friend in Neuchâtel, promised to carry out Cleghorn's requests, including possible plans for his son to study in Neuchâtel, 'upon the most economical plan possible.'[15]

From Venice to Suez

On 20 April 1795 Cleghorn set off for Venice with his Polish servant, Michael Mirowsky. The next day Captain Bolle followed and a few days later again, the Comte – so as not to arouse suspicions of collusion. On 8 May they reached Venice to find that the dispatches from Dundas had arrived and that Cleghorn's

arrangements had been given official approval. The conferring of
the brevet ranks of Major General and Brigadier General on the
de Meurons would have to wait until India was reached and the
purpose of the mission had become public.

In the dispatches Huskisson had enclosed the necessary letters
of credit on the house of Sir Robert Herries and Co. – though
rather tiresomely, at Leghorn. From Venice Cleghorn wrote to
Rachel that: 'I have remitted £800 to Col. MacGill by way of
Switzerland. I have no object on earth but to perform my duty to
the public as the only means of providing for you, and for God's
sake, use what I can send you and keep up your spirits if you wish
to preserve my life . . . '[16]

Passages had been booked for the party and provisions laid in,
on board the Venetian ship 'Inocenza' under Captain Zannie,[17]
and on 18 May they set sail for Alexandria. When they inspected
their provisions they found them ample except for 'garden stuff'.
Cleghorn was also pleased that: 'No English ship can be more
attentive to cleanliness; every part of the vessel is regularly
washed and swept.' On 4 June, the King's official birthday, they
rustled up some sort of meal for the rest of the passengers and
drank the King's health – 'Our Venetian Captain, by a private
signal, ordered his guns to be fired, having previously, though
unknown to us, caused them to be charged for that purpose.'
Cleghorn himself was 'reduced to broth made of fowl and rice'.
However, an Armenian surgeon on board bled him and provided
him with medicines – as he wryly remarked, it was the only part
of his journeying so far when he had had nothing to do. On
leaving Venice they had decided not to shave, so that when they
arrived in Egypt they would be ready to wear their Turkish dress
(which all Europeans there adopted).

The Comte did not think much of his moustache: '*Elle est
toute blanche et mal garnie, de sorte que je n'ai pas l'espoir
de faire conquêtes en Egypte.*'[18] Cleghorn's beard was 'black and
formidable as any Turk'.[19]

There was a slight awkwardness between the two men over
the position of M. Choppin, whom the Comte had brought with

him as secretary and whose expenses he expected the British government to pay. Cleghorn pointed out that no mention of this had been included in the Capitulation and while he had accepted Captain Bolle as the Comte's aide-de-camp – since every British General had one – he could not support the need for the government to pay for secretarial services for the Comte.[20]

On 10 June they arrived in Alexandria and Cleghorn found the British consul there, Mr Baldwin,[21] a most valuable ally. Between them they put up a smokescreen of gossip on the peaceful purpose of their journey to India – since the Comte was so constantly referred to by his real name and title that it was impossible to conceal his identity. Secretly, Cleghorn, having learnt that the Dutch had sent dispatches to their bases in India, asked Baldwin to use all means, short of murder, to obtain them when he heard of their passage through Egypt.[22]

They went by boat to Raschid (Rossetta in the Journal) where Cleghorn, never one to miss an opportunity, had the first Turkish bath – from which he felt 'the most sensible benefit'. From Raschid they took a boat with the shallowest of draughts up to Cairo, yet, even so, 'we were constantly touching ground.' It took four days to reach Cairo, days of pure enjoyment for Cleghorn, except that he could not sleep at night because of mosquitoes. At any rate, as he recalled them in his letter to Madame Du Peyrou: '*Le voyage est le plus riant et agréeable qu' on peut concevoir.*'[23] They made their way past dovecots and minarets, palm trees and villages, enjoying the music which M. Choppin played on his violin and Mustapha, their escorting Janissary, 'sang with his songs of a plaintive melancholy.' Cleghorn was touched that Mustapha had expressed to the Armenian doctor his deep regret that Cleghorn, who he felt was his friend, should as an infidel be shut out of the delights of Paradise.

In Cairo they stayed in Mr Baldwin's house and were entertained to dinner and greatly helped by the Imperial Consul, Mr Rosetti – most vitally in the procuring of a Moorish vessel at Suez to take them down the Red Sea as no English ships were available there.

Cleghorn was also instructed by Rosetti on the importance of giving presents to Arab rulers if they were ever to act upon promises.[24] Cleghorn wrote to Dundas on this subject and gave as an example, to prove the point, a treaty which Baldwin had made with the rulers of Egypt in 1794 to help protect English shipping and commerce between Suez and India.[25] Because the treaty had not been accompanied by presents from the British government, it was a dead letter. Cleghorn put in a plea for greater support to be given to Baldwin,[26] seeing how important it was strategically for Britain to be on good terms with Egypt (a point which Napoleon's Egyptian campaign three years later must have rammed home). Helped by an Italian from Smyrna, Marquetti, a member of Mr Rosetti's household, they ordered Turkish dress and bought mosquito nets, thus ensuring some sleep for the night, though when new clothes arrived Cleghorn found them very inconvenient.

He was mainly involved with writing his dispatches and letters, in receiving and returning visits from the European community, and in making preparations for their crossing of the desert to Suez. They did pay an official visit to the Castle, whose defences were in very poor shape because the Pasha nominated by the Porte: 'prefers in general to pocket the revenue rather than to employ any part of it in the public service.' They were entertained to coffee by the Lieutenant of the Pasha, who then: 'handed to me his long pipe as a mark of respect and as such I took two or three mouthfuls of smoke. Water mixed with perfumed sugar was then presented – given to us by slaves on their knees.' By 22 June Cleghorn felt free enough to go out to Giza to see the Pyramids. They spent a night there at the house of the governor of the province, where they had: 'an elegant and plentiful supper in the Turkish style. It was placed on a large round platter while the guests placed their plates on their knees.' At three o'clock the next morning they went to view the Pyramids. Cleghorn was astonished by their sheer mass and, of course, wanted to enter the Great Pyramid. He took off his outer clothes, put a candle between his teeth and followed his Arab guides *'ventre à terre'*.

All except three of the party gave up the attempt but Cleghorn and the other two reached the largest chamber in the centre, with its granite sarcophus, and commented on:

' . . . the slabs of granite and marble finely polished in some of the passages, and the way footholds in the stone had been cut [by a modern chisel; also] the air was disagreable and in many places we fancied that we felt a cadaverous smell . . . I returned more astonished than satisfied from these wonderful works; we were all in the most profuse perspiration and were much refreshed by regaining the light. Close by the Pyramids is an immense stone much covered with sand and called the Sphinx but it has not at present, being indeed much worn and defaced, the least resemblance of that imaginary animal.'

Back in Cairo Cleghorn met, at Mr Rosetti's, 'the Chief of the Arabs who conducts us to Suez and, according to report, is the most determined villain in these parts and connected with all the robbers of the Desert. As they never attack those with whom they have connection, we were assured he was the best protector we could find.' Their preparations were all made and letters of introduction procured but they had to wait first until after a Moslem festival and then for a courier of the Bey's who wanted to take advantage of their caravan. Cleghorn found that all the presents he had to give for the various services they had received, and all those he had to buy for the Arab governors at whose ports they were to call, ran away with a great deal of his money – he marked down all the prices in his book of accounts and was grateful for a letter of credit from Rosetti on Mocha.

At last, on 29 June, having got up at five o'clock, they left at one and were very quickly in the desert. In fact Cleghorn was alone in the desert at one point since no one had thought to tell him that in Egypt the horses were trained to stop when the reins were slackened and gallop when they felt a check on the bit. As his horse bolted he lost carbine and pistols from his saddle, but managed to keep his seat and was retrieved by two Arabs of their party. He tried a dromedary after that but found it needed constant goading.

That night they camped and supped well and then slept under clear skies with the moon bright. They were off again at 2 a.m., Cleghorn this time on a camel with a mattress so arranged that he could shift his position when he felt stiff. They were in the saddle till ten, had a brief pause for food and rest, sheltered from the sun by a tent, and were away again by one o'clock. The basket of their water-melons broke on a camel's back, and thus they lost their fruit, knowing it could not be replaced at Suez. At eight that night they were allowed two and a half hour's sleep and then rode on. When the sun rose the next morning they were troubled with mirages – but they arrived at Suez at noon, having taken thirty-two hours on the seventy-mile journey. They took possession of an empty house. Literally empty: 'We are as ill-provided as in the Desert but much more dirty' – back to the flies and mosquitoes, with fleas, bugs, lizards and the fear of scorpions and rats thrown in! They managed to replace the water that had been used from their eight goatskins full from a tank of rain water. They were not too sure how good it was and were glad they had brought water from Cairo, even though it had been expensive.

'The tedious and dangerous navigation of the Red Sea': 6 July – 21 August 1795

With the help of Marquetti and the Governor of Suez, negotiations were opened with the proprietor of the only boat available on which they could take passage to Jedda. Contrary to what they had been told in Cairo, the ship was *not* ready to sail and, Cleghorn noted gloomily, 'unless I bribe the proprietor, she will not sail for a fortnight . . . but he knows our anxiety to get away and has availed himself of the necessity of our situation.' So a bargain of £300 for their party of seven was struck and Cleghorn paid over £200 to the Arab and promised the rest would be paid at Jedda. The captain of the ship then appeared and demanded *his* present but they put him off with promises to give it to him at Jedda. When they saw the ship itself their gloom deepened:

'The vessel is not seventy tons, has no deck and carries upward of a hundred pilgrims. We have hired the cabin if it deserves that name – there are two small cabins in none of which can two mattresses be laid with ease during the night and we have no place to walk during the day.' Worse still, 'the ship's timbers are slight and almost rotten and she is very imperfectly caulked.'

On 6 July they were up at four o'clock but only got on board at seven in the evening. They found the galley, which they had been promised for cooking, crammed with packages; only strong words from Marquetti prevailed on the crew to remove them, and then their own baggage filled it so that they could hardly turn round there. They borrowed, as the cook room, 'a small hole opposite to our cabin door, made by removing packages.' To accommodate their trunks they put them on the cabin floor with their mattresses on top. The pilgrims then piled on to the ship, which settled lower and lower in the water. When at last, on 7 July, the anchor was raised, there were so many people crowded on the deck that the mainsail could hardly be moved, and in addition the captain had taken a large boat in tow, also full of people. They sailed for only half an hour and then dropped anchor again and the captain went ashore. In the evening Cleghorn went up on deck, and, sitting or standing on their own luggage, enjoyed a little fresh air and exchanged civilities with other passengers, mutually incomprehensible but occasioned by goodwill. The next day the captain came back with thirty more passengers and somehow they pushed their way on board. When Cleghorn went up on deck that evening to escape the smell from the bilge water under the cabin he shared with de Meuron, he found 'upwards of 220 people in space not 50 feet long or 18 at its greatest breadth'. Suppers were being cooked on fires, every man on deck was standing, women were scolding, children crying, some were singing hymns and other's praying and striking their foreheads on the deck. 'The air was suffocating and I found myself soon obliged to retire to my hole below.'

The next morning the wind was favourable and with no regret whatever they saw Suez disappearing in the distance.

Cleghorn got out his charts of the Red Sea and became the centre of an admiring circle when they found he could name the towns and villages they would be passing. The Arabs were curious about many of their things: 'My snuff box has gone the rounds of the greater part of the company; the telescope, spectacles etc. have all been reviewed, but above all a silver watch of mine, having a cover of silver instead of glass which shuts with a spring and opens by a pressure behind, has excited much wonder. All have tried to open it but in vain . . . They were also much surprised to see me use a pencil; they had no conception that it was possible to write without ink.'

They came to anchor at four o'clock, 'tho' the wind was perfectly fair and not too strong . . . and we might have continued near three hours longer our course.' But, there was nothing they could do about it, and in practice they found the captain – Hadgi Hassan Tishiai – most civil. Each day they gave him part of their provisions and, in the evening, coffee in their cabin. And through their 'interpreter', Hassan, they found him most communicative, though after a few days he took to eating with their three servants.

The wind freshened, with the result that the sea began to break into their cabin. It also proved too much for the foresail, which split at the bottom. The crews fixed it somehow with a rope but the accident had taken up time and it was eight o'clock before they reached Tor. The next day had to be spent mending the sail but at any rate it gave them a chance to get good water. They were very alarmed by the Comte's suffering a sharp attack of gravel, especially as there was nothing to treat it with, except fomentations of dried herbs which the Comte had with him. Cleghorn privately believed that the Comte ate too freely and planned 'on his account to observe a more simple regimen in future'.

It was while they were at Tor that they had a splendid view of Mount Sinai and met the Lord of the Mountain, who came on board. He demanded money, which they positively refused, and wine – of which they gave him a bottle. The other passengers knew his reputation as 'a most determined robber' and begged Cleghorn to get rid of him.

They had a good day's sailing on 13 July, from six in the morning till four in the afternoon, when they reached Rass Mahomet – merely the point of land where the Mount Sinai range of mountains met the sea. They were out of sight of land for the first time for the next twenty-four hours, with only a light wind and a heavy swell, so they made little headway. In due course the wind freshened and they came within sight of the Arabian coast again and anchored opposite to Sharr some miles from the coast whose coral banks were very dangerous for shipping – especially 'for a vessel so unmanageable as ours and manned by such unskilful seamen'. At least Cleghorn saw now why the captain never sailed at night. Even during the day, on 19 July, they very nearly drove into a coral bank and, in coming suddenly to anchor, 'the shrouds of our vessel have been carried away by the cable and her mast nearly broken.' They were then plagued with a dead calm which at any rate gave the sailors the chance to fish. Cleghorn and his party ate a lot of fish and found it very good: 'This sea abounds with many kinds of fish which we never saw before.'

On 21 July they had an anxious evening from the time the sun set, just after six, till midnight – trying to find an anchorage, 'surrounded on every side with rocks and breakers,' and the captain with no sounding line or compass, and in this danger because: 'he had tried to push his vessel to an anchorage which the failure of the wind made it impossible for him to reach.'

Cleghorn's role on board widened to include giving medical advice and doses – mostly 'cream of tartar and tea' – and their party was constantly applied to for water. They were not in danger of running short, partly because the water was so tepid and full of worms that they did not drink it 'so often as our thirst may demand'.[27]

Once past the island of Hassani the crew came around demanding another Baksheesh. Cleghorn offered them less, for it was the second demand, but they refused to accept and the captain threatened to make things difficult for them with the Vizier at Jambo (Yan bu'al Bahr). The rest of the party persuaded Cleghorn to pay up, but then were further discouraged to hear that the captain meant to stay some days in Jambo. They decided therefore to ask a merchant, Hadgi Abdeen, with whom they had made friends on board, and who proposed to hire a boat from Jambo to Jedda, to take letters to the captain of the English ships which were reported to be at Jedda, and to the merchant, Gellani, to whom Cleghorn had been recommended.

Their progress was slow because their mast was 'in so crippled a state that we dare not carry a mainsail'. The land was barren: nothing green, just sandy plain and high craggy mountains; these, however, 'when gilded by the morning and setting sun are highly beautiful . . . all their various shapes present themselves to the eye and the rays of light give them a variety of colour and shade which hides from the view and makes us forget their native sterility.' And at night they were struck by the luminosity of the Red Sea: 'when the fishing lines are pulled up, they appear like a wire of fire.'

They reached Jambo, the port of Medina, at last – on 22 July – and with some apprehension, having heard that the Vizier was a drunkard and had a reputation for fleecing and imprisoning foreigners, and because they did not trust their captain. He was becoming greedier for their wine and liquor, and might make some sort of a pact with the Vizier in the hopes of dividing the spoil. Cleghorn dared not himself go ashore at Jambo, though from a distance the town looked delightful, because he had no letters of recommendation; so he had to rely on Hassan, his interpreter, and Hadgi Abdeen. After a long search they returned aboard to report that they had made a provisional agreement with the owner of an open boat who would take them there. They themselves had been seized in the bazaar by order of the Vizier, been brought before him, and had had demands made for the customary presents.

Hassan had explained why his master was not coming ashore and had no present, and they were allowed to return to their ship.

Cleghorn, fearing they might be plundered or detained, hired a boat to take letters to the senior English Captain at Jedda and in them asked him, if they did not arrive within eight days of that date, to try to find them, or at any rate Cleghorn's papers, which should be taken to Lord Hobart at Madras. Regretfully Cleghorn turned down the hiring of the open boat. He thought it would be too much for the Comte to be exposed to 'the insupportable heat of the day and the heavy dews of the night' for four or five days. Hassan had much trouble and great expense in procuring water but in the end they got all their jars filled. Many of the passengers were not so lucky and Cleghorn realised they would be asked for theirs, 'and hard is the heart which can resist gratifying their sober but pressing wants.' Otherwise there was nothing to be obtained in Jambo but charcoal and limes, 'which were the finest I ever saw.' But fish from the sea was a plentiful luxury – sometimes rock fish, 'some very large and of beautiful colour.'

They were three and a half days in Jambo and felt themselves lucky on the whole not to have tangled more seriously with the Vizier. They were feeling the heat increasingly and the stench from the bilge was becoming intolerable, 'although our cabin is well washed at least twice a day with vinegar,' and Cleghorn sponged himself down with vinegar and water frequently. They had the additional irritation of being unable to escape from the loud, shrill reciting of the Koran for five hours after sunset by a blind female passenger from Jambo, who seemed to know the whole thing by heart. Cleghorn's digestion was affected by lack of exercise, so he: 'lived abstemiously, seldom eating anything but rice . . . I find limes of much use and generally take lemonade tea for breakfast and the same after dinner.'

On 30 July they again could not find safe anchorage. For two hours they groped their way towards the shore between two reefs of rock, 'which we were only prevented from striking by the calmness of the evening.' But later that same night they dropped anchor again and the Comte de Meuron was so anxious that he got his strong box out of his chest to secure his papers, and called Cleghorn down to do the same, which he did – 'though I did not,

perhaps from ignorance, think the danger as great as he did.' In
the end they somehow edged their way out, and: 'so pleasant is
escape from danger that we all slept better last night than we have
ever yet done, and the little feverish complaints which have been
hanging about one for some days are entirely gone.'

Two days later and almost within sight of Jedda, they again
faced, even more acutely, the danger of shipwreck through nearly
driving on to a long and rough ridge of rocks. 'There was no time
to be lost: I made a packet of my most valuable papers which I
enclosed in a towel tightly tied up and committed them to the care
of Hassan who is an excellent swimmer, with orders to deliver it
to Lord Hobart at Madras in case any accident befell me . . . I
distributed my money between my friends and servants.'

They were in acute danger because the ship: 'could not have
kept long together for the rotten state of her timbers and slight
construction would have broken her in pieces on her first encounter against the rocks. This was the first time I apprehended real
danger . . . the companions of my voyage who had often braved
death in the field declared that they never had been exposed to
six hours of such inquietude,' especially as the Comte de Meuron
and Captain Bolle could not swim, and M. Choppin's limbs were
swollen.

A slight breeze from the east saved them in the end, and they
crept slowly towards Jedda. There they found to their bitter
disappointment that all the English ships for Madras had sailed
nine days ago, three days before the arrival of the Arab courier
Cleghorn had sent from Jambo. He confided to his journal: 'I
have to affect cheerfulness and support the spirits of others who
may have more to make in point of fortune but who have not
half so much to lose in point of character as I have, should our
object fail.'

It was on the morning of 22 August that Cleghorn went ashore
at Jedda and stepped into an entanglement of collusion, imposi-
tion and threats which left him a good deal poorer both in money
and goods. The collusion was between an English-speaking Bombay merchant, the Vizier of Jedda, and the merchant Gellani to

whom Cleghorn had been recommended. The Bombay merchant gave Cleghorn no alternative but to go to the Vizier's house, although his letters were to the Pasha. The Vizier directed the Bombay merchant to help Cleghorn get a ship but Cleghorn insisted that he be taken to the Nabob's Vakeel and then to Gellani. He seemed friendly and sent for the owner of the only vessel in port who would go to Madras. It seemed to Cleghorn that he had no choice but to pay the £800 demanded: he knew it was too high and in the contract he laid down as a condition that the ship should sail on 5 August and that their party should be the only passengers. While he was arranging this, the luggage of all the party was taken, their wines stolen, their papers tossed about, and 'the tenth part of everything that would divide seized as duty at the Custom house'.

Cleghorn sent his servants to retrieve the papers, which they did successfully, but then the Bombay merchant appeared with the news that an embargo had been placed on the newly hired ship because the Vizier had not been a party to the bargain. Gellani then turned up and said that without 300 crowns being given between the Vizier and the Pasha, the ship would not be permitted to sail. Cleghorn knew he was being victimised and resisted the demand, but they put on the pressure. He was denied his own interpreter, he discovered that he was a prisoner in Gellani's house and in the end he promised his bill for 200 crowns payable at Mocha. Once this had been extorted Cleghorn was allowed to return to the ship. The next day, when Cleghorn was ill, a new demand arrived to pay 76 dollars as presents to the officers of the customs house, to ensure the release of their goods. So, early on 5 August, Cleghorn with his own interpreter alone, bearded Gellani in his own house but was kept hanging about.

When at last Gellani saw him, Cleghorn insisted that he should keep his own interpreter and that the Bombay merchant should be sent out of the room. A stormy interview followed, with Gellani threatening to prevent them sailing to Madras at all. In the end Cleghorn agreed to pay the 200 crowns for the Vizier and Pasha which he had previously promised, plus 70 dollars for the Customs house men (although Gellani had pitched his first demand that morning at 300 dollars). In the course of their exchanges Cleghorn had offered Gellani things he had with him from Europe – dressing-box or pistols. Gellani's reply was always the same: 'Money; nothing but money.'[28] However, he did take Cleghorn's watch; during their high words he had thrown it back at Cleghorn, but as he left, Gellani sent his boy after him for it.

Cleghorn insisted on returning to the ship at the time appointed for sailing but found there no captain; only a crowd of passengers, and three of the captain's wives. The delay did, however, give him time for the buying of provisions: seven kids and many chickens, water purpy, onions, grapes, bananas and limes. Since all their wine had been stolen, they bought a barrel of local wine made by the few Greeks resident in Jedda. They were kept hanging about till 8 August – when just as they were leaving, the Bombay merchant brought, opened, the letters which Cleghorn had sent to the Senior Captain of the English ships. He realised that these 'might be one of the reasons for their obliging me to pay so high a freight'. They probably assumed that Cleghorn had power, 'which in this country is wealth.' At any rate in this whirl of events Cleghorn took some comfort at finding the name of Sturrock and Stewart, Dundee, on the mainsail of their new vessel: 'I little expected to find Angus canvas on an Arab ship.'

Their progress down the rest of the Red Sea, though still slow and subject to exasperatingly avoidable delays, was a little less of a physical ordeal. For one thing, they could take exercise on deck in the cool evening and though they had less room than they had paid for, the ship was less crowded. Cleghorn again found that: 'the medical chest with the directions of my friend, Dr. Grieve . . . had been of infinite service to us all.'

By this time Cleghorn was forced to accept that Hassan, their interpreter, was both a libertine and a cheat. His proposal to buy a slave girl at Hodeida and bring her on board was firmly vetoed by Cleghorn, and he was taxed with persistently cheating them when he was sent to buy their goods. He did not bother to deny it and showed no remorse when reproached by Cleghorn, who noted in his journal:

'The mildness of this fellow's looks and the gentleness of his manners have completely taken me in. This however has so often happened to me that it has ceased to surprise me and I shall continue the same course, giving way to sudden impressions, and preferring the occasional distress of disappointment to the constant vexation of suspicion. What I chiefly regret is that it is no longer possible for me to serve him. I meant, and probably could have provided for him for life. He knew my intention but thieves are always fools.'[29]

They called in at two more ports in the Red Sea: at Hodeida, though the captain had promised not to, and then at Mocha. Here at last Cleghorn found some help. He went straight to the English Factory and found there two agents of the East India Company, Soper and Ramsay from Bombay, who were there to buy coffee. The first, Soper ('well bred and intelligent',[30] noted Cleghorn with relief), was perfectly satisfied with the authorisation from Dundas which Cleghorn showed him and both paid his Jedda bills and advanced him money for casual expenses to Madras. This was a great weight off Cleghorn's mind. He was further comforted to learn from them that no ship of any kind had left Suez since the departure of the one Cleghorn's party had come on and that Cleghorn had been lucky to get a ship at Jedda, 'as none will leave that port for India for many months.' Soper also assuaged Cleghorn's hurt pride by telling him of other Europeans who had been treated in the same cavalier way at Jedda as he had been. Cleghorn also took advantage of landing at Mocha to send an explanation to the Governor of Bombay of why: 'I am under the necessity of drawing upon your presidency for the sum of German crowns 3714.37 which have been advanced to me by Messrs. Soper and Ramsay.' He gave Soper an extract of Dundas' letter of authorisation to show the Governor, and he asked him to send a letter to Lord Hobart at Madras in case Cleghorn's previous account of his business had not reached him.

Across the Indian Ocean to the coast of Malabar:
21 August – 6 September 1795

So, with a much easier mind, they set sail from Mocha on 21 August, 'having laid aside our whiskers here, which have been nourished since we left Venice.' As they finished their 'tedious and dangerous navigation of the Red Sea', Cleghorn noted in his journal: 'We are now entering into the great Indian Ocean and we trust that the omnipotent Being who formed and sustains universal nature, who has made us sensible of the miracle of our own existence, than which no modification of Being in the after life can be more surprising, will protect us, as long as our pursuit here can be subservient to his general plans.'

It was generally a much better-found ship than their first one, but the crew's seamanship was far from reassuring: 'Nothing can equal the general carelessness and neglect of duty which prevails,' while: 'there is no getting the pilot who is a Moorman of Malabar to keep awake during his watch.' Off Aden, it was Colonel de Meuron who noticed that the wind had shifted and who, with difficulty, got the pilot to understand his signs and alter the sails.[31] After ten days of this neglect of duty by the pilot, Cleghorn made a formal complaint against him and was backed up in this by the rest of the ship's company. On the whole the weather was favourable and they made good progress. Cleghorn observed with interest the slave boys and, as he watched the boys wrestling, 'one has become so great a favourite that I am resolved to purchase him.'

He had other things on his mind, when on 5 September they were informed by the captain that the ship only had water for four days, and it was made clear by a dispute between the captain and the pilot that they were not sure where they were or how near land. However, the coast of Malabar came into view that day – at least they had made it to India. Discussion followed: the captain said he would land for water where Cleghorn wanted, but when he opted for Anjenjo the captain said that the sea roads there were too dangerous. In the end Cleghorn decided on Tellicherry, which was definitely within the Presidency of Bombay, so that if he alone went ashore, he could use his own credentials without inviting further speculation, and seek reliable information from the chief of the fort on the state of relations between the Dutch and the British.

Cleghorn landed at Tellicherry on 6 September and learned from Mr Handley, the chief, that the British and Dutch were at war, Cochin being attacked by a British force under Lt. Col. Petrie, and Ceylon by another under Col. Stuart. The Dutch defence in both these places included companies of the Meuron Regiment. Cleghorn therefore sent Captain Bolle at once to Cochin, charged with orders from the Comte de Meuron to switch sides to the British. He himself wrote to Lt. Col. Petrie there, explaining the situation and the terms of the new Capitulation. He also set out orders for Captain Bolle which included the sending of the Meuron companies to Ceylon if possible, and in particular asked that Lt. Dardel, a young friend from Neuchâtel, should join Cleghorn in Ceylon. He also wrote privately to his friend, Lt. Alexander Walker, son of the minister of Collessie in Fife, whom he had last seen in St Andrews and who was in the Grenadiers before Cochin, concluding with the assurance: 'I am not here merely to eat mangoes.'[32] The writing of his dispatches kept Cleghorn up all night at Tellicherry. They were then entrusted to Mr Handley ('very civil' but not 'polite, elegant and liberal' like Mr Soper at Mocha) and Cleghorn spent the following morning buying vegetables and coconuts.

It took them until 12 September to crawl down the coast to Anjenjo, and there a boat coming alongside said it was too dangerous to carry any of them ashore, because of the surf. Cleghorn decided to attempt it nevertheless, put on light clothes and fixed in a box under the bench his most important papers, that they might be safe if the boat overturned, but in fact he got safely through the surf and on the advice he received there, decided that the whole of the party should make the rest of the journey to Madras by land.

8

Mission Accomplished
September – November 1795

The Transferring of the Régiment Meuron

What decided Cleghorn to abandon his Arab ship at this point, and make for Madras by land, was fear of their ship being taken in the seas round Ceylon, compounded by doubt over the nature of their reception if they should land at Colombo. These points were put to him very strongly by the British resident at Anjenjo, Mr Hutchison.[1] Moreover, letters had just arrived which brought the news that the British had taken Trincomalee in Ceylon and with it two companies of the Régiment Meuron, while Cleghorn had been wrongly informed about Cochin and there were no Swiss troops there at all. As a result, Captain Bolle's journey to Cochin would have been useless and might have let the cat out of the bag.[2] All this increased the need for speed. So the Comte disembarked; all the luggage was brought ashore and their journey by land organised. They were given letters of introduction to Lt. Col. Campbell, commandant of Palamcottah, and prepared what they would need to carry with them in their palanquins, the rest of the luggage being sent on separately to Madras.

Once ashore, Cleghorn wrote again at length to Lord Hobart enlarging on the nature of his mission, giving him what news from Europe he could and assuring him that, if they had not already arrived, he would soon be receiving letters of recommendation about Cleghorn himself from England: 'They are intended only to open the way to confidential communication for I am not come to India, an animal of prey. The liberal manner in which his Majesty had behaved to my family leaves me little to expect and nothing to wish but to render my exertions useful to his interests . . . '

On 14 September they were ready to set off by noon and made their way along the beach till seven in the evening, when they arrived at Valetora – where they were hospitably received by European officers in the service of the King of Travancore.

The next day their route was still by the sea though sometimes, because the way was so uneven, they went on foot through the woods. On the 16th they struck inland and 'by bribing highly the bearers, we are carried at a great pace' along good roads. Their way then lay over a high range of the Cardamam hills and on the evening of the 17th they arrived at Palamcottah and the English garrison there. 'We can never forget', wrote Cleghorn, 'the liberal and gentleman-like hospitality of the Colonel . . . everything was kind, hospitable and elegant.' The next morning one of the captains, whose friend Captain Wilson had spoken enthusiastically about Cleghorn as professor at St Andrews, was delighted to supply him with articles of dress he was in need of. The civil resident at Ramnad, Mr Powney, arrived and was an immediate ally and a valuable source of information. Cleghorn gave him all the intelligence from Europe that he could, and he gave Cleghorn letters of introduction to people in Madras. That evening, in the officer's mess, Cleghorn was comforted to hear from Major St Leǵer that he too had been given the Gellani treatment at Jeddah, and in addition, as St Leger spoke French well, he: 'most politely freed me often from the painful office of interpreter.' Cleghorn felt enormous pleasure at meeting so many young Scots officers, especially those who had been students in St Andrews. By contrast: 'in the evening we had dancing girls but I was by no means interested in that exhibition. It came far short of my expectations.'

On 20 September there was a review of the cavalry but it was spoilt for Cleghorn because nothing he said would dissuade the Comte from donning his General's uniform, reviewing the troops and publicly accepting the compliments due to a general officer. Cleghorn notes with exasperation: 'This conduct not only notifies his arrival in India, but leads the whole army to believe that his rank is greater and less circumscribed than it really is.' Cleghorn also wrote again to Col. Stuart, who was commander of the British forces in Ceylon, because he, above anyone else, should be aware of the plans for the Régiment Meuron and should try to get information about them to the Comte's brother, Col. Pierre-Frédéric de Meuron.

Cleghorn even suggested that Captain de Meuron de Rochat, now a prisoner of the British, should be sent to Col. de Meuron in Colombo to smuggle the information to him, and enclosed letters from the Comte to his relative explaining the situation.

Wanting to push on as quickly as possible, they made their way to the east coast and took a boat at Tuticorin. It was an open boat, 'but a part is covered with plaintain leaves for us and above the sand ballast we had to spread mats for our beds.' They did not reach Nagapatnam till 26 September and there Cleghorn found a letter waiting for him from Lord Hobart, the Governor of Madras, which reassured him and directed him to meet up with Major Agnew at Cuddalore, as he was sending Agnew on a new mission to Colombo and had given him a letter to the Dutch Governor of Ceylon, Van Angelbeck, informing him of the transfer.

Since these were the first directions which Cleghorn had received from his new chief in India, it would have seemed advisable to pay them some heed. But at the same time he heard other news which led him to fear that Major Agnew's somewhat leisurely progress to Colombo might be too late. This was that Col. Stuart had suddenly, and without advising Lord Hobart, ordered the embarkation of the 52nd Regiment for Ceylon and that it was generally accepted that Stuart was planning a thrust against Colombo before the monsoon broke – and of course before he knew of the switching of the Swiss regiment to the British. At the same time the Dutch were withdrawing from all their garrisons in Ceylon to strengthen that of Colombo, where they intended to make their main stand. Cleghorn, therefore, to avert 'effusion of blood', and if possible to effect the transfer of the Swiss Regiment before the siege of Colombo started, decided that he himself must act as the news bearer to Col. Stuart in the British camp and – more hazardously – to Col. de Meuron in the Dutch.

He asked the Comte to meet Major Agnew at Cuddalore and explain the situation to him, and Cleghorn himself found a small boat from Tranquebar loaded with Madeira, linen and cheese for the forces in Ceylon, but as these were all on the move to muster at Trincomalee, the owner had no market for his goods. Cleghorn prevailed on the owner to allow him to hire the boat and he sailed first to Point Pedro where he met Col. Stuart, to whom he explained the whole situation and: 'furnished him with a political arm against Colombo which if circumstances render it necessary, he will no doubt know how to use.' Cleghorn then persuaded the owner of the boat to sail to Colombo:

' . . . to carry an open note to Colonel de Meuron from me. In this note I only said that I had seen his friends well in Switzerland some months before. But the owner of the ship agreed to give him a Dutch cheese, into which I put a letter informing him of the arrival of his brother in India, of the general articles of the Capitulation, and that the transfer of the regiment would be instantly demanded on the part both of the British government and his brother, the Colonel and Proprietor of it.'

This expedition of Cleghorn's took three days only, and on 30 September 1795 he was in Madras.

In the meanwhile the Comte de Meuron had gone by land to Cuddalore and there he met Major Agnew and gave him a full account of their mission so far. Agnew was planning to go by land to Tuticorin and cross from there to Colombo and was put out not to meet Cleghorn, and alarmed at the damage to British prestige that Cleghorn's secretive methods of conveying information might do if they became generally known. He wrote to Cleghorn explaining how it was considered at Madras that now: 'open communication from us is the best – not subject to risk or suspicion of sinister intentions.' He went on to describe how 'public report has been so busy spreading' the news of the switch of allegiance by the Régiment Meuron that 'it is impossible it can be concealed from the Dutch Government' – though, in the event, he was proved wrong in this assertion.

The Comte's letters to his brother and to Cleghorn at this time each shed some light on motives and attitudes. In his letter to his brother, the Comte commended Cleghorn as a friend: 'of proven worth over a number of years and above all, in the journey we have just made together . . . He is a man of great spirit who enjoys the confidence of the minister . . . you could never have an advocate more astute, warm-hearted or sincere than he to help you deal with the English government . . . he is one with whom you can safely think aloud . . . '[3] The letter to Cleghorn expressed the Comte's regret that Major Agnew's party was not to include Cleghorn, so that he would not be in Colombo to witness the transfer of the Régiment, but the Comte went on to say that Lord Hobart had gained a high opinion of Cleghorn from his letters – his ones from Tellicherry being the first to inform him of their mission from Switzerland concerning the Régiment Meuron; no government dispatches on the subject had yet reached Madras.[4] Those letters were written on 30 September, the day that Cleghorn reached Madras from his three-day expedition to Ceylon.

It was not until 8 October that Major Agnew reached Colombo. He arrived at the Governor's palace just as Col. de Meuron and his officers were about to dine with Van Angelbeck. Agnew presented Lord Hobart's letter together with others for the Colonel from the Comte and from Cleghorn.[5] There was no doubt that news of the transfer of the Régiment came as a complete surpise to the Governor and probably to the Colonel as well. His first reaction to the news was to reaffirm his regiment's loyalty to the Governor and their duty to defend Colombo. Evidently Cleghorn's message in the Dutch cheese had not been found – if it had reached him at all. The Governor's Council was dismayed at the news and begged Van Angelbeck to resist the English demands: perhaps a French fleet would come to the rescue of the Dutch settlement, or perhaps France's ally in India, Tippū, would provide such a serious diversion that the English would not have the resources to take Colombo. At all events, the Régiment Meuron should not be allowed to go. But then over Saturday and Sunday there were no official meetings, but much private airing of views, and balancing of commitments.[6]

So on Tuesday morning, 13 October, Pierre-Frédéric and his officers went to the Governor and formally gave him notice that they proposed to accept the new Capitulation which the Comte had negotiated with Cleghorn acting for the British government. Van Angelbeck's fury led him to threaten to imprison the Colonel and all his officers. The Colonel, enraged by this, snapped back that the Governor would be hard put to it to find the forces to disarm and guard the Swiss soldiers, since the five hundred men under the Colonel's command were the only reliable troops in the Dutch defence. The Governor then completely shifted his ground and told Col. de Meuron that he could take his troops and go – the only condition that he laid down being that they took no part in any future fighting in Ceylon.[7] The Colonel was only too pleased to agree to this: for one thing, many of his own men had families in Colombo, against whom they would be reluctant to turn. Otherwise, the Dutch rejected the terms of peace offered in Lord Hobart's official communiqué.

Thus it was on 13 October that the Colonel and his officers were officially freed from their oath of fidelity to the Dutch company and informed that they were now in the service of His Majesty, the King of Great Britain. Major Agnew then returned to Madras, half his mission accomplished (Cleghorn's half) and convinced it would not take much more of a push by the British to end Dutch rule in Ceylon. Cleghorn was on tenterhooks and his quick mind saw only too clearly where Agnew – and Lord Hobart for that matter – had failed to make adequate provision for organising the means of transfer for the Swiss soldiers. For one thing, Agnew should not have argued with the Dutch governor over the cost of sending the Swiss regiment to India (in the end Agnew and Pierre-Frédéric de Meuron hired vessels and charged the expense as a regimental concern).

Another suggestion which Cleghorn did actually make to

Lord Hobart – in suitably respectful terms – was to have ships ready to bring the regiment over from Ceylon. This was not done, though there were two Bombay cruisers which could have been commandeered for this purpose. Thus it was not till November that the five companies of the Meuron Regiment from Colombo arrived at Tuticorin. As a result of the delay, they were caught in monsoon weather and one ship was swept away, feared lost, though in fact it turned up later. Cleghorn also thought that Major Agnew should have gone straight from Colombo to Point de Galle, where there were still two companies of the regiment, and explained the situation to them. Then they would not have had to learn their fate through rumour and report – as a result of which forty-four men and a quartermaster sergeant had deserted. All these men, in Cleghorn's view, should have been marched out of the garrison together and kept in temporary huts if necessary till transports came. He was also uneasy about the inadequate English naval presence. 'I often expressed my opinion and my alarms on this subject to Lord Hobart,' he noted in his volume of correspondence. He could not understand Commodore Rainer's complete failure to back up the operation in Ceylon and instead go off cruising in the Dutch East Indies, where 'he cannot take Batavia with the force he has with him', while one British ship only, the 'Heroine', was left somewhere in the seas of Ceylon, but no one knew exactly where.

Cleghorn was also rather more than disconcerted when Mr Duncan, the Governor of Bombay, publicly stated that not a man should be sent from the Coast of Malabar for the defence of the Carnatic or the taking of Ceylon, if he had the power to prevent it. Cleghorn's uneasiness was understandable and his criticisms valid but technically now it was none of his business because the mission on which he had been sent had been accomplished, and his orders from home had included nothing beyond that.

Besides, his stay in Madras was not all a matter of dancing with impatience on the sidelines. He had met up again with his eldest son, John, and had found him in good health and much improved, 'both in mind and body tho' he still has much to acquire,' and well regarded in his regiment, the Madras Engineers.[8] Also, Lord Hobart, while putting the Comte and his family into a large cool house in Fort St George, insisted that Cleghorn should join his own household. This had its advantages: 22 October saw him sitting in the Governor's garden writing to Madame Du Peyrou, giving a fairly light-hearted account of his adventures and of the possibility of his being sent on an embassy to the King of Kandy, who would no doubt welcome him as a liberator, '*et il ne manquerait pas de me donner au moins deux éléphants et une vingtaine de filles . . .* '[9] Also, staying with the Governor spared him household expenses; on the other hand, somehow or other Cleghorn had acquired thirty servants: 'I am a complete contrast to Midas . . . money always slips through my fingers.' In addition, for the time being, Madras society lionised him – as he wrote to Andrew Stuart: 'I have received much credit here both for the plan I suggested and for the measures I pursued.'

At the beginning of November the Swiss troops arrived at Tuticorin and Cleghorn was able to write to Dundas that the purpose for which he had been sent to the East had been achieved – not as completely as he had hoped, but with definite advantage to the British in India. Thus, through his expedition, 'we have withdrawn from Ceylon alone 600 Dutch troops by Capitulation and 200 by capture before the Capitulation was known.' The European force remaining in Colombo was thought not to exceed 400 and in Point de Galle not 200 men, and as a result Governor Van Angelbeck would probably be ready to surrender Colombo whenever a respectable British force appeared against it. This would be because: 'the loss of the Régiment de Meuron, by depriving them of the most efficient part of their European force and by leaving them almost destitute of officers of experience and ability, affords the strongest ground of hope that the only remaining garrison in Ceylon where the Dutch can make a stand will soon fall, a bloodless conquest, into our hands.'

Moreover, from Pierre-Frédéric de Meuron, now at Tuticorin, the army could learn the position and strength of the defences of Colombo – which, again, would help to save casualties. British forces in India would be strengthened by the addition to them of a battle-hardened, disciplined, acclimatised European regiment now in the Carnatic, with no expenditure necessary on the cost of their transport from Europe to India (that alone represented a considerable saving). For Cleghorn, even before the final conquest of the Dutch in Ceylon, it was a reassuring tally of advantages.

9

Dealing with the Dutch in Ceylon
November 1795 – March 1797

November 1795 – January 1796

The official orders which Cleghorn had received from Dundas had directed him to return after the transfer of the Meuron Regiment to the British army had been achieved, and there *was* a packet boat on which he could have embarked if he himself had been determined to carry home the official dispatches on the success of his mission. But Lord Hobart asked him to remain until the Articles of Capitulation with the Meuron Regiment should be finally settled, though as the outstanding questions concerned British liability for the arrears due to the Regiment from the Dutch East India Company, about which Cleghorn had no knowledge, it was not clear what role Hobart expected Cleghorn to play, except to hold the hand of the Comte – who hardly needed it, since he had a much shrewder idea of striking a financial bargain than Cleghorn. That Cleghorn was aware of this is shown in his letter to Dundas earlier on:

'I have observed that there are two passions which have much influence on the Comte de Meuron: one is a strong attachment to his own interests and the other, a deep-rooted resentment against the Dutch East India Company.'

There was certainly nothing in the Capitulation of Neuchâtel which bound Cleghorn to be a party in the final settlement after the transfer of the regiment. Cleghorn's own inclination was to stay at the centre of action, to meet Col. Pierre-Frédéric de Meuron, and to see that the knowledge of Colombo's defences that he could give the British would be used to good effect. And, of course, to be there when the Dutch surrendered.[1]

His natural curiosity to see more of Ceylon than the brief glimpse he had had of Point Pedro also prompted him to wait

the three months till the monsoon had blown itself out before
his return. His own inclinations did not move him to stay and
make a fortune in Madras though that was possible enough for,
at the same time as he was writing to Dundas to assure him that
he had received no recompense whatever from the government
of Madras (considering himself responsible to Dundas alone), the
Comte de Meuron was writing to his brother in Neuchâtel that he
was realising how easy it would be to pile up an immense fortune
in India, *'presque en dormant.'*[2]

Cleghorn's mind was for the moment wholly bent on thinking
out the best way to bring about the fall of Colombo with as
little loss of life as possible. His actual status now was that
of an observer on the sidelines but he was still a member of
Lord Hobart's household and therefore able to drop hints directly
to him. On 24 November 1795 Lord Hobart acted on these hints
and authorised Cleghorn, Captain Mackenzie and Major Agnew
to go to Trichinopoly to meet Col. de Meuron and as a result of
what he could tell them about the defences of Colombo, lay plans
for its siege.

In the event, Cleghorn was detained longer than he had
expected at Madras, becoming involved in the proposed terms
of a treaty with the King of Kandy. For the King was following:
'the traditional Kandyan policy of seeking foreign assistance to
oust the European power established in the maritime regions.'[3]
This also was not really Cleghorn's province, because Robert
Andrews, British Resident in Jaffna since September 1795, had
already been on one mission to Kandy and was planning another.
But Cleghorn hoped that, in the course of the tour of the island
that he was planning with Lord Hobart's blessing, he would be
able to visit Kandy, pay his respects to the King and bring back
more solid information than at present the British possessed. They
had no exact knowledge for instance of the terms of the treaty
of 1766 between the Kandyans and the Dutch, and in general,
as Cleghorn wrote to Dundas: 'At present we are as ignorant
of Ceylon as of Japan.' This was something he intended to
remedy.

He had hoped to be joined on his expedition by James Dardel, a young cousin of the de Meurons, a friend of Cleghorn and of Madame Du Peyrou in Neuchâtel. Dardel was on the Bombay establishment and Cleghorn hoped that, by accompanying him for the purpose of accurately mapping the island, the young man would have the opportunity to make his mark and win the notice of the British authorities. This particular scheme did not come off – Bombay, true to form, being unco-operative – but Cleghorn was always ready to use any influence[4] he had to help the young and to lend them money to tide them over – as he did to D'Ivernais when he arrived from Colombo, and George Gillespie stationed at Seringapatam – to whom he lent money because he had been ill and for whom he wrote letters of recommendation. He also lent his nephew, Cornet Peter McGill, a hundred pagodas because he had lost all his possessions in the floods at Arcot.

In the meantime it was the meeting between Col. Pierre-Frédéric de Meuron and Captain Mackenzie which was of prime importance. Colin Mackenzie, who was on the way to becoming one of the most distinguished Indian topographers and antiquarians of his generation, was already a friend of Cleghorn's and was now given charge, as Captain in the Madras Engineers, of planning the logistics of the siege of Colombo. By way of preparation, Cleghorn had already written to Pierre-Frédéric de Meuron asking him to bring with him, to their meeting-place in Trichinopoly, his plans of Colombo and marine charts of the coast of Ceylon, and he had translated into French all the questions which Mackenzie thought most necessary to provide him with the basic information.[5]

The meeting on 10 December was as fruitful as Cleghorn hoped it would be, both from the military and from the political points of view. Giving an account of it to Adderley, Lord Hobart's private secretary, Cleghorn wrote: 'I am persuaded the Colonel is a very sound headed man, capable and willing to give much information, and who always carefully distinguishes *what he knows* from *what he believes*. There appears to be no nonsense or vanity in his character.' The political points made by the Colonel were that the Jacobin pro-Patriot party was numerous in Colombo, and if they tried to seize power they might put Van Angelbeck to death and then it would be a tough fight to win Colombo. On the other hand, the Malay troops were devoted to the Dutch Governor and therefore would never fight for the Jacobins. The political confusion in Colombo was emphasised by D'Ivernais of the Meuron Regiment, one of the last of the Swiss to leave Colombo, who reported that the universal question there was: 'For whom are we fighting?' The Colonel also suggested the British should send young Prince Roeping, now a prisoner at Madras, back to Ceylon, where he might help win over his countrymen to the British, just as the Modeliars (the native chiefs of villages and districts) should also be wooed.

On the military side, Col. de Meuron pointed out that Negombo was the place where the British troops should land. From there, artillery and stores would have to be taken by canal to Colombo – so that many boats of very shallow draught would be needed and the assembling of them should be put in hand straight away. He advised sending rice with the British forces to Negombo because they were short of it there and its sale at moderate prices would create goodwill. He made clear that the fort at Colombo was not as strong as the British had believed but the garrison was more numerous. Col. de Meuron agreed to Cleghorn's suggestion that he should send some of his men who had been taken at Trincomalee, and were at Madras, to act as guides for Captain Mackenzie in Ceylon. In the event he sent him twelve men, with an intelligent English-speaking sergeant.

On the question of whether the British government should take over the funding of the Dutch colonial debt of Ceylon, Cleghorn and de Meuron were of one mind. As Cleghorn pointed out, both to Adderley and Dundas, the property of many individuals, native as well as Dutch, was involved and if the British refused to guarantee this Dutch paper money (reckoned at about £50,000), there might be much more resistance to their rule. He was also worried both about British naval weakness on the Coromandel coast and about Agnew's idea to send the Dutch inhabitants of Ceylon off to some of their other possessions – 'and a more foolish measure could not well enter the head of a sensible man.'

After the conference Agnew went back to Madras, while de Meuron, Mackenzie and Cleghorn made their way through the Southern provinces of the Carnatic – staying at Madura and Tanjore, where Cleghorn was introduced to the Rajah, 'who presented me with a handsome dress.' De Meuron then returned to his regiment while Mackenzie and Cleghorn went on to Ramnad and from there crossed to Rameswaram:

A 'beautiful island [and] one of the most sacred spots of the Gentoo Religion. Here we met a number of pilgrims and saw many instances of those voluntary and almost incredible mortifications with which the votaries of Brahmin inflict themselves. The chief priest, a child of about seven years of age, was waiting for us on the beach under a tent of muslin attended by Brahmins and priests who accompanied us till we arrived at the choultry adjoining to the Great Pagoda.'[6]

They stayed there a day and a half and Cleghorn gathered his thoughts on what he wanted to find out about Ceylon.

Cleghorn's interrupted tour of Ceylon: 7–24 January 1796

He first made a list of the subjects on which he wanted to gather information – such as revenue, commerce, harbours, natural history (including agriculture), population, and the character of inhabitants. Under each of these subjects he drew up lists of questions and then could enter the answers in parallel columns. In addition, in the districts he passed through, he noted down much information and the conclusions he drew from what he had observed.[7]

On 7 January 1796 he and Captain Mackenzie crossed to Ceylon from Tanni Cotta, but instead of landing at Talaimannar (where there were palanquins and bearers ready to carry them) they followed the advice they had been given and tried to make for the Fort of Mannar; so they had to walk ten miles past crocodile-infested pools. However, they were given a warm welcome by Captain Bowser when they arrived about nine at night – 'ample compensation for the little fatigues we had suffered.' From his observation, Cleghorn believed that the island of Mannar could be made much more productive if irrigation from its many small rivers was more effectively organised. He believed that immediate action should be taken by Madras to pay the Dutch civil servants who were settled on the island, the old ones especially being in desperate straits.

On 10 January Cleghorn and Mackenzie went their separate ways – Cleghorn northwards to make for Jaffna. It was a tedious journey: the sun setting at six meant hours in a dark, wet cabin, and then when daylight came the boat, though over a mile from the shore, had to be pushed along by the crew wading in water only knee-deep. At last on 14 January they turned a point of land and entered the bay of Jaffna. The town itself was considerable but Cleghorn stayed at the Fort with the garrison there under the command of Major Barbet. Here too he enjoyed generous hospitality and had a profitable four days, gathering information which ranged from the unofficial duties which had gone straight into the Governor's pocket to the excellent quality of the horses on the islands in the Bay of Jaffna. 'The mares are of a size, strength and bone sufficient to breed for the cavalry,' and Cleghorn was quick to seize on the military advantage this would bring to the British army in India which always had 'difficulty in supplying the cavalry establishments there'. He was intrigued too to hear about elephant sales and the way in which each was advertised and how 'eight were decoys necessary in taking wild ones' of which 'at least about sixty are yearly caught' by driving them into a Kraal and then linking them to the

1   William Hamilton 1669–1732. Great-grandfather of Hugh Cleghorn
2   Miss Sarah Cleghorn, c. 1727–1825
3   Rt. Hon. William Adam, 1751–1839
4   Adam Ferguson, 1723–1816

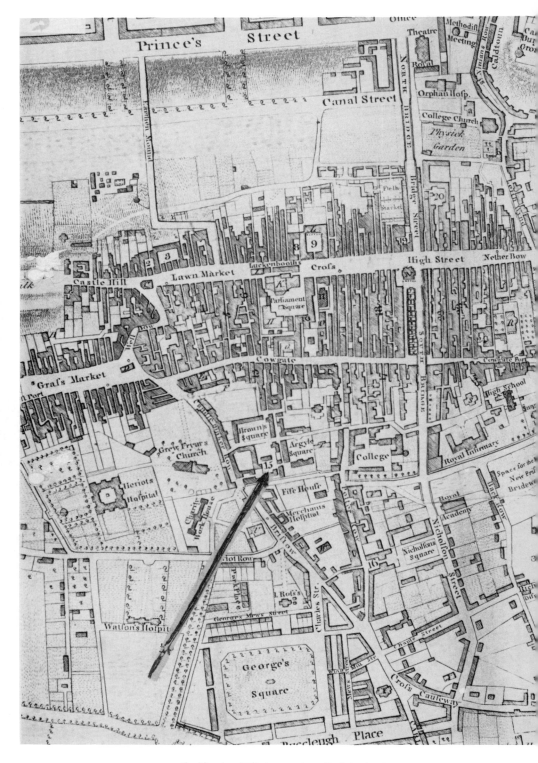

5 Number '15' shows where Society stood

6   Adam Smith, 1723–90
7   John Millar, 1735–1801
8   Edward Gibbon, 1737–94
9   Lt. Col. John McGill, d. 1818

10   South Street, St Andrews, c. 1797
11   St Leonards Chapel, c. 1797

12 Hôtel de Peyrou, Neuchâtel, Switzerland

15　La Petite Rochette, Neuchâtel, Switzerland

16   The Rhine Falls – c. 1840
17   Malta: the Lazaretto

18 Henry Dundas, 1st Viscount Melville, 1742–1811
19 Frederic North, 1766–1827

20 The Comte de Meuron being carried from Fort St George to Madras

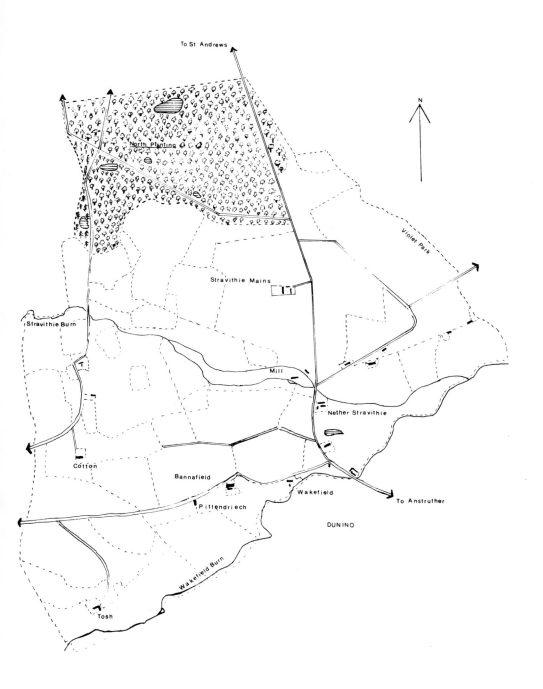

22 Stravithie. Based on a plan by Alexander Brown

23 Wakefield. Seat of Hugh Cleghorn Esq
24 'My place is in great beauty . . . '

25   Adam Ferguson in old age

ST. ANDREWS - 1820

26   Adam Ferguson's house in South Street, St Andrews

27   Hugh Francis Clarke Cleghorn. Grandson of Hugh Cleghorn

28   Rachel Jane Cleghorn, married Alexander Sprot

decoys.

Cleghorn and the Civil Resident at Jaffna, Mr Jarvis, had some useful sessions. Col. Stuart had ordered the suspension of the payment of all taxes for a limited period and both men agreed this was a mistake – as well as Robert Andrews' alterations on the method of collecting taxes. Cleghorn analysed for Jarvis the nature of the Dutch taxes, and the mode in which they should be collected, so he felt he had contributed something in return for all the information Jarvis had given him. Cleghorn's reaction to the social and political problems facing the new English authorities was marked by common sense and showed no contradiction of the principles which he had propounded to his students in St Andrews; for example, his hatred of the domestic slavery in Ceylon and his description of the means the Madras government might take to eradicate it, and his recognition of the valuable aspects of the Dutch administration. He believed that the Dutch should be well treated, so that as good farmers or efficient collectors of revenues they might: 'become attached to our government and forget their old connection with Holland.'

Jaffna was the meeting place Cleghorn had arranged with the Rev Dr Rottler, a Danish missionary at Tranquebar, who, both as a botanist and as one fluent in the Malabar language, would be a useful ally for Cleghorn. When they left the Jaffna garrison, on Monday 18 January 1796, it seemed like the parting of old friends – 'A more hospitable corps cannot exist than the 73rd.' Major Barbet gave him a gun and cartridges and arranged for an escort of sepoys to Mallative, which was halfway to Trincomalee; he was given introductions to the lieutenant who commanded there; Mr Jarvis had sent off a runner to ensure provisions, servants to carry the baggage and 'to attend me with tom-toms to keep off elephants and bears'.

So easily had Cleghorn slipped into the oriental approach to servants that he noted without a blink in his diary: 'I took the precaution to hire bearers and coolies at Mannar and Dr. Rottler's suite and mine, in which there is not one unnecessary retainer, amounts to near a hundred persons.' Their way lay through many paddy-fields and Cleghorn again comments on the abundance of water and the absence of tanks and reservoirs to retain it for the dry season.

At one of their stopping-places, a solitary mansion called Passen, belonging to a Dutchman who had been an army sergeant, they were joined – surprisingly enough – by an Anglican cleric. He was the Rev Mr Owen, formerly chaplain of the 'Suffolk', the flagship of Commodore Rainier. 'If I was surprised', Cleghorn remarked, 'to meet an English gentleman accoutred in this wilderness in the manner as he would have been in a county in England, I was not less so to hear his extraordinary adventures . . . ' He was bearing Lord Camelford company and had pushed ahead of him to arrange for transport from Jaffna. In November 1795 Camelford had, for the second time, been discharged from the Royal Navy for insubordination – this time in Malacca.[8]

Cleghorn writes:

'At Prince of Wales Island, Lord Camelford resolved to purchase a vessel to conduct him to Bombay and from there proceed to Britain by the Persian or Arab Gulf and the Desert. They found a ship which they manned to the number of twenty men of all nations; but she soon proved extremely leaky, and after suffering very great fatigue, they could no longer keep her afloat and in the midst of a dark night, she went to pieces between Baticaloa and Trincomalee . . . They have been for some time at Trincomalee and are passing through Ceylon to Madras, to carry their scheme into execution; his Lordship seems zealous to try what possible hardship may be encountered between India and Europe. I expect to fall in with him this day . . . I knew (him) some years ago at Neuchâtel while his Lordship lived with Monsieur le Ministre Meuron.[9] At present the Admiralty ought to be his station and I wish I could presume to advise him and should be so fortunate as to persuade him to repair there . . . [in the meantime] he was pursuing his journey and the wild beasts of the country on foot . . . '

Cleghorn was not in fact to meet this wild young man till his return journey from Ceylon, when they went on the same ship as far as Suez.

Making their way through the jungle had its own fascination: 'It is impossible', Cleghorn wrote, 'not to be delighted with the fragrant scenery which intercepts the view; trees of huge size surrounded with shrubs of every description perfuming the air and charming the eye. No shrubbery, however abounding in exotics or however nicely disposed, ever conveyed to me half the pleasure of these natural nurseries where nature sports untamed and unseen.'

Cleghorn in his journal noted 'peacocks in great numbers' and many other wild birds; plentiful traces of tigers, elephants and wild bear, and 'not the rivers only but every little tank was full of crocodiles'. There were, too, 'vast numbers of large monkeys of a silver grey colour with faces perfectly black . . . we were told, tho' they do infinite mischief to the trees and gardens of the people, they never willingly permit them to be killed. They in fact are held sacred by such Malabars as are pagans and the most of them still are so . . . '

He never failed to be astonished by the banyan tree: 'Twigs from its different branches catch the ground and there taking root, soon equal in size the parent stock, these again drop their tendrils in the earth till the tree covers an immense extent, forms natural windings or alleys between its various trunks and under its shade some thousands of people might find shelter from the sun and rain.' Dr Rottler, as botanist, was hard at work on 'many curious and undescribed plants', and as missionary he was preaching to the Malabar Christians when a group could be collected. He had with him a black Malabar catechist to help him, who, Cleghorn noted, 'attaches himself to me, and as he has much simplicity and bodily strength, I find his manual exertions more useful to me than his spiritual instructions.'

When they reached their halfway post at Mallative they were

well received by a Lieutenant Fair, the son of Mr Fair of Colinsburgh in Fife. They were lodged in a fine house which had been built by Mr Negal, a Dutchman who had rented Mallative from the Dutch East India Company. He had cleared the jungle, planted rice and brought in cattle, so that the province was now populous and productive. He was an excellent example to prove Cleghorn's point that the British administration would do well to win over the Dutch as allies in developing rice production in Ceylon and in collecting revenue according to the familiar ways. 'As there are vast extents of waste lands capable of great produce, the ancient Dutch settlers should be encouraged to occupy them . . . as they are all disposed to be farmers and gardeners, and as it is difficult to find English who will submit in India to this slow and patient method of acquiring independence . . . '

The worst hazard they faced on their way to Trincomalee was water: there was the salt-water lake near Alembeil which had to be crossed, 'more than a mile broad and very long, the bottom of black mould and very deep'; there was the swiftly flowing river where they needed a catamaran to help them cross (it was late arriving because the soldier who was sent to have one ready got drunk and failed to deliver the message). They all got a wetting but, very dangerously for some, 'the rope by which the catamaran was dragged to the opposite rocks, broke and as the raft was full of people and the current extremely rapid, the poor men were carried down the river to the bar,' from where in the end they were rescued.

Two days later (26 January) there was yet another river to be crossed, which: 'turned out to be more alarming than we thought. There were many deep holes and for more than an hour the poor men had to carry the palanquin with the pole on their heads, while they were sometimes in water up to their chin.' These perils past, Cleghorn presented a bottle of arrack to the bearers, 'which gave them such spirit that they set off at full speed but unhappily carried us out of our road . . . ' Nevertheless, they reached Kuchhaveli, their intended overnight stop, only a day and a half from Trincomalee. Here they were able to buy rice and fish and they could bathe and change their clothes, a positive pleasure after their strenuous exercise, and in the evening they sat: 'in the open air with our candle in a lantern while our numerous attendants under trees are preparing at many little fires their different suppers . . . '

The next day they reached Nilaveli and there Cleghorn found letters from Col. Stuart and a fresh palanquin with fast bearers which the colonel had sent to carry him to Trincomalee. There were letters waiting for him here, the one of most immediate concern being from Lord Hobart, ordering him not to go to Kandy after all, or at any rate not till the conquest of the Dutch in the coastlands had been completed. A letter from Adderley filled in the background to this order. Adderley himself had wanted Cleghorn to go: 'I know your activity and perseverance in accomplishing what you have undertaken, your abilities and your information. I therefore thought you well calculated to acquire that local knowledge which would go far towards convincing the ministry of the positive and relative importance of this possession . . . ' This was an issue – the strategic value of Ceylon to the British in the Carnatic – on which Adderley and Cleghorn were in full agreement and on which they realised there was division of opinion both in the British cabinet at home and in the Supreme Government in India. But Lord Hobart had been listening to Robert Andrews, who had convinced him that the failure of the Supreme Government in Calcutta to back the principle of alliance between the British and the Kandyans had made the Kandyans suspicious and resentful because: 'the reasonable expectations which we ourselves raised we have disappointed and their conclusion must be that we have acted with an illiberal cunning and duplicity.' Andrews' reception in 1795 had been hostile enough – 'he remained there a prisoner watched with the most wakeful suspicion' – Cleghorn's would certainly be worse. So he had to give up all thoughts of going to Kandy.

The British conquest of Dutch Ceylon completed:
30 January – 15 February 1796

There was no doubt that Cleghorn was disappointed, but Col. Stuart suggested he should accompany the army in its advance to Colombo and he jumped at the opportunity. He was only three days in Trincomalee and then embarked with the army on 30 January for Negombo, where they arrived on 5 February and joined forces with troops from Bombay under Col. Petrie and a detachment from Mannar with the Light Infantry Company of the 73rd Regiment, whose officers Cleghorn had found so congenial at Jaffna. The Dutch had abandoned the fort at Negombo, so once the business of landing troops and supplies was completed they set off for Colombo, twenty-four miles distant.

It was difficult country and their way lay through numerous defiles surrounded by thick jungle, and through many swamps and rivers. These last would have been a decided check if the Dutch had made a more thorough job of destroying the bridges over them: as it was they left the piers, with the result that planks could easily be placed on these and the guns dragged over. It was not till they reached the banks of the River Motual, only about eight miles from Colombo, that they met any opposition, coming under fire there from a Dutch battery on the opposite bank. The river was wide and too deep to be forded, so while scouts searched for somewhere to cross they had to wait in the rain, without tents and under pretty regular though not well directed fire, for two days. Then, as they were preparing to move upstream, it was realised that the Dutch had retired, having thrown most of their guns in the river. So the British crossed at once, left the Bombay Grenadiers to guard the passage of the Motual, and moved forward.

Cleghorn was with the officers of the Flank Companies of the 73rd, and saw some native troops gathering at the side of a lake – above which the British were stationed. Soon after, a European passed whom Cleghorn hailed and spoke to, learning from him that the Malays were planning an ambush a mile ahead (though Col. Stuart had already heard this). However, the night of 12 February passed quietly. Then in the early morning the first attack was delivered on the 73rd by a small group of Malays, wrought up to frenzy by using 'Bang', which Cleghorn described as 'a herb resembling hemp which they smoke, chew or drink, and which intoxicates them to madness'. The Malays did not capture the Royal Artillery gun they were aiming at, but a black servant of Major Barbet who was close by Cleghorn was killed, his body being carried off and decapitated. The main attack then followed, still falling on the advanced corps, consisting of the Royal Artillery and the flank companies of the 53rd, 73rd and 77th Regiments.

Cleghorn wrote: 'Musquet and grape shot was poured upon us but being directed too high, did little execution.' In fact only two officers were wounded and fifteen privates killed or wounded. British fire against the Malays did much more damage and Major Barbet, with the 73rd, counter-attacked and completely routed and dispersed them. This action lasted little more than half an hour and then the British were free to resume their march on Colombo. They halted that night in a village close to the Pettah, not a quarter of a mile distant from Colombo. One of the reasons for the fury of the Malay attack had been their belief that the British had massacred all prisoners taken at Trincomalee, consequently when they saw one of their own princes with the British troops – as Col. de Meuron had suggested at Trichinpoly and Cleghorn had recommended to Adderley – the fury of their temper was placated.

On 14 February Major Agnew was once again sent to Governor Van Angelbeck with a flag of truce and generous terms. Cleghorn wrote in his diary (not in his official account to Dundas): 'I had the good fortune to persuade Col. Stuart to hold out the most liberal terms.' He had obviously subjected the colonel to a formidable battery of unremitting argument, and the Dutch asked for twenty-four hours to consider them. Agnew was then sent again, the terms of Capitulation were agreed upon, and on 15 February 1796 the British army took possession of the city and fort of Colombo, finding to their surprise that the number of fighting men in garrison was nearly equal to their own. There was no doubt that the Dutch had lacked the will rather than the means to resist the British: there were the ideological differences between the party which supported the Stadholder and the pro-French patriot party; there was a split between the Council and the rank and file; there was the resentful attitude of the King of Kandy against the Dutch. But equally, and in military terms as importantly, the defection of the Régiment Meuron played its part in establishing the British in the coastlands of Ceylon.

The articles of the Capitulation followed the conventional lines: the yielding up of all Dutch forts, artillery, ships and their cargoes; the arrangements for those who had been taken prisoner of war. What Cleghorn had been most concerned to persuade Col. Stuart to include was in Article 4, in which the British gave their pledge to fund the promissory notes which the Dutch government had borrowed in the island and circulated as the current money of the market. It was to bear an interest of three per cent. As Cleghorn went on in his letter to Dundas: 'The government debt of Ceylon in actual circulation did not exceed £50,000 . . . the holders of this species of property now look for its realisation to the permanency of the English power and England holds the Island of Ceylon for the payment of a quit rent of £1,500 per annum.'

Cleghorn had a penchant for last lines with some punch to them and he felt that the purpose for which Dundas had sent him to the east had been well and truly achieved. *Now* was the time to go back home: the monsoon was over and there was a ship sailing direct from Ceylon to Suez. On 17 February he was writing from Colombo to Andrew Bell in Madras: 'I am at this moment almost decided to return to Britain by land.'[10] And on 22 February he embarked on board the East India Company's armed ship 'The Swift' for Suez. To his friends, old and new in the east, his departure seemed very abrupt. The Comte de Meuron wrote a long letter to him which was one long wail of complaints including the reproach that they would not now be making the journey back to Europe together.[11] Dr Rottler wrote on his return to Tranquebar to thank Cleghorn for the arrangements he had made to meet the expenses of Rottler's journey and to say: 'how my pleasure throughout the journey would have been perfect if I could have enjoyed it in your agreeable company or if I at least could have seen you once more before your departure.' But he had made arrangements to send the chest containing specimens of the five hundred different species of plants which he had collected for Cleghorn on his journey through Ceylon, and he was pleased to think that Cleghorn would mention Rottler's work to Sir Joseph Banks, 'whose acquaintance would be most encouraging and favourable to make the most desirable progress in the excellent study of Botanic.'[12]

There was another letter from Walter Wilson, who had been Cleghorn's man of business in Madras and who enclosed 'an account of the disposal of all your money that went through my hands' – the balance being 250 pagodas. He went on: 'I received your letter from Colombo and was very much concerned that we must meet no more . . . It was just at the time when I could have enjoyed your company . . . '[13] There was also a long letter from Colin Mackenzie grumbling about being inadequately paid for the work he had done in Ceylon, not only for the siege of Colombo, but for a survey he had carried out in the south of the island. He remarked bitterly: 'I have had my labour as my reward, further than some compliments – a coin very cheap.' His postscript contained news of Cleghorn's eldest son: 'I left John at Colombo with Mr. Castle where he is as well situated as could be done immediately, as for going a wandering with me and leading the life of a wild Arab or a wild Highlander, it would never do – the rogue does not write me but I have heard of him and will hear more soon from my friends there . . . '[14]

The Return Home:
22 February 1796 – 30 March 1797

Compared with the outward journey Cleghorn's return to Suez was carefree. In just over three weeks from leaving Ceylon, the ship in which he was sailing – 'The Swift' – arrived at Mocha, where he was greeted as an old friend by the Banian broker whom he had met on his outward journey, and who advanced him £100. During the passage up the Red Sea the strong contrary winds tried the patience of some of the passengers (one imagines Lord Camelford was probably among them), who formed wild schemes of landing at Jedda and crossing the desert to Cairo. To Cleghorn's relief, they did not put in to Jedda at all and by 15 April they were at Suez. Mr Rosetti, the Imperial Consul in Cairo, appealed to by Cleghorn, once more rallied round and sent Marquetti to organize his crossing of the desert. This time Cleghorn rode on an ass, 'and never met with an easier or better conveyance.'

In Cairo they heard how very uncertain passage across the Mediterranean was and decided it would be better to separate and each group go different ways and each take with them a copy of the dispatches about Ceylon. Baldwin in Alexandria arranged for passages on two ships, one going to Malta, the other to Zante. To Cleghorn's lot fell the Ragusan ship going to Malta and he found he would have two congenial Britons as travelling companions: 'Mr. Coxe and Mr. Wilkinson expert collector of gems, medals and busts.' Their journey to Alexandria took them through plague-stricken country. Cleghorn learned that Mustapha, the janissary who had been so attached to him on the way out, had that very month died of the plague. In Alexandria, Cleghorn, in spite of the danger of infection, went to Mr Baldwin's house because he wanted to renew his acquaintance with 'this most intelligent, zealous and cruelly used servant of the government'. To ward off the plague Baldwin recommended rubbing oil on the body and smelling camphor, and Cleghorn decided to sacrifice 'some days' cleanliness to this simple antidote'.

The passage from Alexandria to Malta took thirty-six days – when it was possible to do it in eight – and when they entered Malta, because they had come from Egypt, they were towed straight away to Marsanxott Harbour, where opposite the health office each ship which had to go into quarantine: 'has its separate little alley, divided from others by a large chain, of iron fixed in stone posts.' They then transferred their bedding and luggage across Lazaretto Creek to the isolation hospital . . . 'The building is magnificent and can hardly suffer from fire. We have one room 100 feet in length which is our kitchen and sleeping room of the Guardian and Servants. It has benches each side and from the number of iron rings in the wall, it must be the place where the poor Turkish and Barbary slaves are confined when performing quarantine. We have besides two other rooms of 15 feet square – one is our bedroom; the other is our dining room and sitting room. We have a long spacious terrace on which we can walk and a smaller one close to the sea.'

There for thirty-seven days they spent their quarantine. The fumigation rules were very strict and made visits from acquaintances on the island hardly worth their while. They persuaded the perfumer of the Lazaretto to allow them to bathe every morning, a privilege they especially appreciated as their rooms were beset with fleas. He arranged for a boat to take them each day at seven to the opposite side of the creek, where they bathed in the sea and walked in his garden. They could get plenty of fresh fruit and 'the bread is the best I ever tasted'. In fact they found that their days passed 'without the least ennui', Cleghorn writing public and private letters, Coxe and Wilkinson arranging their gems and medals. When they had finished their quarantine, they spent about a fortnight paying courtesy visits and obtaining passports for Naples, and Cleghorn, with his inexhaustible thirst for knowledge, collected enough material to write a politically and socially perceptive description of the constitution and history of Malta. They were in fact lucky not to have carried the plague with them from Egypt: 'I have just heard', Cleghorn wrote in his diary on 16 July, 'from the Count de Montferre that the plague was constantly in the Lazaretto during our confinement.'

On 30 July 1796 Cleghorn arrived at Naples but found that any prospect of a simple journey back through Europe was blocked by Napoleon Bonaparte's victories in North Italy: 'Eighteen million people will be forced to yield to a small army for want of confidence in each other,' Cleghorn remarked in disquiet. The British plenipotentiary in Naples was still Sir William Hamilton, whom Cleghorn had met on his earlier visit, and he strongly pressed Cleghorn to go to Corsica – both to carry letters from Naples to Sir Gilbert Elliot, the British governor there, and to give him the chance to entrust letters to Cleghorn for the British government at home. It was back in 1794, on the invitation of the Corsican nationalist Paoli, that Hood had attacked the French in Corsica and, with the vigorous backing up of Nelson (who lost his right eye at Calvi), had completed the conquest of the island. But then Hotham replaced Hood as admiral of the British fleet in the Mediterranean and, lacking Hood's dash and resolution, failed to build on British success in Corsica and secure command of the sea in the western Mediterranean. It was this failure more than anything which compounded the irresolution of the Italian states and enabled Bonaparte to keep his army in Italy supplied and drive back the Austrians.

It was at the beginning of September that Cleghorn arrived in Corsica having travelled up Italy through Rome and Siena, where he conceived the deepest suspicions of the motives of those politicians and churchmen gathering for the Congress of Florence – suspicions which he described to William Wyndham, Minister Plenipotentiary in Florence. His voyage to Corsica had run true to form: he had embarked from the mainland for Elba to the west but the crew of the boat he had hired sailed towards Civita Vecchia with the idea of handing him over to a French privateer, which turned out to be a Corsican ship with Letters of Marque in the English service. The Corsican gave short shrift to the Italian captain and escorted Cleghorn's ship to Elba, where its master was committed to jail.

In Corsica, Cleghorn learnt to his dismay that the British

government had ordered its evacuation. 'The real interest of Britain as connected with the general system of Europe, has thus been sacrificed, while her armies have been destroyed and her wealth dissipated in the fatal and deceptive enterprise of extending our empire over the unhealthy possessions in the West Indies.' So Cleghorn was still in Corsica when, on 5 October, a British fleet of nine ships of the line arrived to evacuate the British. 'The Corsicans were sad to see the British go – not a shot was fired by old enemies or deserted partisans nor were our troops impeded . . . I went on board the "Elizabeth" transport under the perfect conviction that our destination was England.'

But it was not to be so simple as that for Cleghorn. Sir John Jarvis ordered the fleet to Elba and, when it became clear that they would stay there for some time, Cleghorn made two attempts to get himself to the mainland, only to be driven back to Elba by storms. On 24 December he at last landed safely in Italy and made his way over the Apennines to Rimini on the Adriatic. Here he embarked on a Tortan (a large one-masted vessel) bound for Venice. During their second night on the way there they were struck by a hurricane, their mast was carried away and their helm unshipped, but they were rescued by another ship and taken back to Rimini. This time he went by land to Ravenna and then hired an open boat to Chioggia. From there he wrote to Sir Richard Worsley, British Consul in Venice, for passports, and arrived in that city on 28 January 1797. Here he learned that the French were in Treviso and Friuli so he decided to go to Trieste, in the meanwhile writing to Dundas about the setting up of the Cisalpine Republic of Ferrara, Bologna, Modena and Reggio and describing its constitution, sending his letter via Sir Morton Eden in Vienna. Cleghorn had a poor opinion of the British Consul in Trieste: 'Mr. Stanley, who I think rather a timid man, is preparing to fly.'

There was a desperate shortage of horses, which delayed Cleghorn, but he went by Laibach and then north west towards Salzburg. On that journey, because of the snow, he had been obliged to have six horses and twelve oxen yoked to the carriage to prevent it from falling down the precipices. The reports he wrote to Dundas give a good deal of information. He caught up, for instance, with the retreating Austrians: 'I could easily observe there was no gaiety in the manners or conversation of the officers . . . they seemed to me to be already vanquished in their own opinion.' From Munich Cleghorn wrote to Dundas: 'I much suspect the importance of Italy is not justly estimated at home.' The rest of the journey, via Augsburg, Nuremberg, Hanover and Cuxhaven, was comparatively straightforward. He finally arrived back in London at ten in the evening on Saturday 30 March 1797, after a journey of over twelve months.

Unsettled Accounts
March 1797 – February 1798

The morning after Cleghorn's return – Sunday 31 March 1797, that is – saw him walking 'in the Park', presumably St James', just a little over two years after he had left England for Neuchâtel. The only encounter he mentioned – that with Dundas – was the one he really wanted. He was greatly reassured to find Dundas genuinely pleased with the part he had played in the British acquisition of Ceylon at so little cost in lives and resources, and when Dundas asked him for information on the revenues of Ceylon, he went off to think out the best way of presenting it. He wrote asking for a brief interview, which Dundas gave him on 17 April. In fact it turned out to be lengthy and wide-ranging: it covered the relative importance of the different settlements which the British had taken from the Dutch – and as the Dutch in Ceylon had defied the Kew Letter from the Stadholder and offered resistance to the British, they were in a different category from the Cape of Good Hope settlement, for example, where the Dutch had surrendered. Thus the British were under no moral obligation to restore Ceylon at the end of the war.

Cleghorn was convinced that the British possession of Ceylon was essential to their safety in the Carnatic and therefore to their whole position in India. It was equally important to the Dutch, for their communication with their possessions in the East Indies, that they should keep the Cape. Cleghorn believed therefore that the best line for the British to take in any future negotiations would be to put their main emphasis on wanting to keep the Cape so as to make the Dutch really afraid of losing this vital link with their East Indian colonies; as a result, they would be more ready to surrender Ceylon to the British. Cleghorn had obviously not wasted the opportunities, which university politics had given him, of learning how to out-manoeuvre his opponents, and the academic surfaced again when he arranged to give a question-and-answer form to the report on Ceylon that Dundas had asked him to draw up. He could also tell Dundas that the botanical collection which Dr Rottler had made in Ceylon at Cleghorn's direction had arrived in London through the good offices of Andrew Bell in Madras.

On that same day Cleghorn also went to see Lord Cornwallis, at his invitation, to discuss with him the best way to send troops to India. This interview was in response to a paper Cleghorn had written while he was in quarantine in Malta and his mind was ranging over the Mediterranean: how Swiss troops could be brought south to Corsica (which at that point the British still held) and thence to Alexandria, or from Trieste to Acre and overland to the Red Sea. It sounds a logistic nightmare – but Cornwallis must have been interested enough to discuss it with Cleghorn and agree with him on the importance of Egypt to both British and French ambitions in India.

On 25 April Cleghorn had his report ready, together with another paper he had written in Malta on the value of Ceylon to the British in India,[1] and was asked to go out to Wimbledon to discuss it with Dundas. The report survives among the Cleghorn Papers. The first part consisted of a description of the Dutch system of justice, its territorial basis, the composition of the courts and structure of appeals. The second section was on the Dutch administration, beginning with a brief description of the native inhabitants of the island, which included: 'the Widas or Bedas, nomadic forest dwellers who lived in tops of trees and subsist upon game which they preserve by immersing it in honey.'

The Dutch possessions had been divided into six residencies (Colombo, Jaffna, Galle, Trincomalee, Baticaloa, Calpetty). Each of these residences was subdivided into 'carles', which were under the jurisdiction of a 'Modeliar' or native chief, and supervised by a 'Dessare', who was a civil servant of the Dutch East India Company. It was the Dessare who made the day-to-day decisions and who could communicate directly with the Government at Colombo. Cleghorn likened them to the barons of medieval Europe. In the Sinhalese territories the office of Dessare was hereditary, but the King of Kandy had insisted on their attendance at court, and if they left the capital their families were held in Kandy as hostages for their conduct.

The third section of the report dealt with land tenures. Cleghorn gave some idea of the complications of these by listing nine forms under which property was possessed and in most cases the burdens upon these different ways of land-holding. 'This multiplicity of tenure', Cleghorn went on, 'led to many disputes especially by a people naturally inclined to litigation and chicanery.' In these circumstances it was absolutely necessary to keep the 'Land Raad', the local land courts which the Dutch had established – they were clear, swift and economical. Decisions would have to be made about the number of judges and how they should be paid, but the courts themselves were one of the most useful parts of the Dutch administration, and through them a public register could be drawn up in which the tenure and transmission of property might be accurately entered.

The section on Revenue must have been revised some time later, because it described the innovations since the island had been possessed by the English and condemned them as: 'increasing the oppression of the people.' But the main part of this section was probably that presented to Dundas at this time and consisted of a straightforward description of the land tax and the personal tax, which was in special need of revision because it was paid only by some castes, professions and areas, as a means of redemption from service for the public for a certain number of days in the year. Cleghorn was for the more just extension of this tax rather than its abolition. He completed this survey with a description of the customs duties and salt tax.

He ended his report by asserting that there was no reason why within six or eight years Ceylon should not be a flourishing country. 'To obtain this purpose, less writing perhaps and more activity would be required.' He included in his list of suggestions for improvement that water tanks should be built at public expense; uncultivated land should be granted to individuals tax-free for a certain number of years in proportion to the expense they incurred in the construction of tanks; that all monopolies except those on cinnamon and salt should be abolished; that cotton manufacture should be encouraged; that the personal tax should be regulated; that the personnel for administering justice and collecting revenue should be kept completely distinct. It was a report with plenty of meat in it: Cleghorn had obviously not wasted his time in Ceylon. Discussing the paper he had brought along with the report – on the value of Ceylon to the British in India – Cleghorn was relieved to find that Dundas agreed whole-heartedly with him on Ceylon, but felt that the British should keep the Cape of Good Hope as well!

Cleghorn now wanted to return to Scotland to see his family again. Moreover, he was finding the expense of living in London more than he had reckoned on, so in June he began his painful campaign to prise out of Dundas the 'liberal compensation' for the successful Ceylon mission and the pension of £300 for Rachel which he had been promised. He had no one else to apply to; he had trusted completely in Dundas and he had burnt his boats with regard to the academic world. Copies of the three letters he sent in June survive, and they show Cleghorn's awareness of the pressure government ministers were under in the crisis year of 1797, but the longer the question of what he had been promised was in abeyance, the less likely it was to be satisfactorily settled. Garthshore, Dundas' private secretary, was sympathetic when he could be tracked down, and gave him 'insider' advice on submitting the account of his expenses incurred during his Ceylon expedition. These accounts are all set out in his volume of correspondence, and on balance the government owed him eighty-five pounds, fifteen shillings and eight pence. Garthshore suggested that it would be better not to give the expenses accounts in till the promised compensation had been settled. Also, once the accounts were in he could expect no interim allowances from government, 'whereas by allowing them to remain till all my other claims were adjusted, I was entitled to demand an ample allowance for my establishment in London from my arrival there till the day on which Government and myself should finally settle the business.' The only record of such an allowance being paid is a cheque for £200 sent by William Huskisson on 27 July.[2] There is also a note of Mr Coxe, Cleghorn's companion in quarantine in Malta, repaying money he had borrowed for his return journey.[3] Cleghorn tried another tack when he wrote to Dundas asking for a writership in India for his son, Peter, ending: 'You cannot blame me for looking to that quarter for some provision for my family.'[4]

There was no response to this plea either, but in July Dundas ordered Cleghorn to discuss with Lord Malmesbury the relative advantages of our newly acquired possessions in the East. Malmesbury was being sent to negotiate with the French at Lille to see if there was any possibility of a peace. This really depended on the outcome of a struggle for power between the moderates and the Jacobins in the French Directory, but at the same time Britain was faced with the crumbling of the First Coalition, the threat of invasion, mutiny in her fleets, plummeting public credit and a wave of industrial unrest. In these circumstances Pitt was ready to offer generous terms to the French, including possibly an exchange for Ceylon. This was where Dundas came in. He was convinced that the British should keep Ceylon, so he sent along Cleghorn, whom he thought of as the most convincing advocate for its retention. Cleghorn acted at once but missed Malmesbury by a few hours, so was ordered by Dundas to put his arguments on paper – to be sent to Malmesbury, together with a directive not to give back Ceylon.

Cleghorn was obviously at this time regarded in government circles as the specialist on Ceylon. He was asked, for example, to discuss with Col. Murray of the Bombay Establishment the value of Ceylon to the British, and it was on his recommendation that the business of the payment of the Meuron Regiment was given to the military agent, G Kempe, an old schoolfellow of Cleghorn's in Edinburgh.[5]

However, it was not only his own financial straits and the

position of Ceylon that was occupying him during the summer of 1797. He was giving his mind to ways and means of checking the whirlwind advance of Bonaparte which threatened to knock Austria, our last ally in Europe, out of the war. To this end, he worked out his: 'Plan for the Protection of Italy and forcing the French to abandon that country.' First he analysed the reasons for French success in Italy – in addition, that is, to Bonaparte's qualities of leadership, to which he paid full tribute. One reason lay in the fact that some Italian princes: 'dreaded the Emperor as a Master as much as the French for an enemy.' Because of this ambivalance their efforts to repel the French were 'feeble, disunited and ill-directed'. Also, the French armies brought with them the appeal of revolutionary fervour to the Italian people and so could 'turn the arms of the People against their Ancient Governments', so that the French were able: 'under the name of Allies to draw from the country those supplies of Men, Money and Provisions which they could not perhaps have exacted under the name of Contribution.' Thus, by the summer of 1797, only Parma, Tuscany, Rome and Naples remained free from French domination.

What Britain and Austria therefore ought to do quickly was to make a firm military alliance with Rome and Naples. Britain should send a naval squadron into the Adriatic ('which our late splendid success against the Dutch may enable us to spare') and Austria should send an army from Trieste to the Romagna – to land: 'at any place between Ravenna and Forto Fermana, having for its debarkation a sea line of upwards of 100 miles. From any part of this sea line they are within a short march of the Apennines, and may there take post in situations from which it would be impossible to dislodge them.' If Britain could send troops (perhaps from the army now at Lisbon), so much the better. The Pope and the King of Naples would then have: 'every inducement to act with vigour, if they can act with the prospect of success.'

There followed an analysis of the factors which would per-suade the King of Naples in particular to fall in with such a plan. 'But to facilitate the success of this Plan for the Defence of what remains and to regain what has been lost in Italy, the most perfect understanding should take place between the Cabinets of London and Vienna with those of Naples and Rome. For this purpose a Confidential Agent should be commissioned to treat with his Imperial Majesty and if he succeeds in his arrangements at Vienna, he should proceed without delay to inspire confidence and energy into the Councils of the Italian powers.'

Above all Cleghorn emphasised the need for *speed* in putting this plan into action. For one thing, the Pope, old and becoming feeble, might die and the French influence the election of his successor. 'The Landing of the Austrians in the Romagna will give a pretext to Rome and Naples to win and the united forces of these powers acting with that of Austria would place Bonaparte between . . . the army of Istria, which would prevent him from pushing to Vienna; that of the Tyrol which would hinder him from seeking shelter from that quarter into Germany and that of the Apennines which would resist his advancing into Italy. His only resource would be to retire into and consume Piedmont with an army which the produce of that country could not maintain.'

Cleghorn finished by pointing out what an enormous accession of strength the control of all Italy would give to France. Not only from the wealth of the peninsula, but from its strategic position in the Mediterranean, France would: 'become the permanent power at Constantinople and Egypt and by force or by treaty she will cut off all communication by land between this country and India.' This summary does not wholly do justice to the persuasive force with which his plan was set out: the basic strategy was, and appeared to Cleghorn, obvious enough; but his detailed knowledge of the situation in Naples and the clarity with which he analysed the possible developments in the Mediterranean, showed a bold and far-sighted mind at work.

He obviously tried out his plan first on Sir John Macpherson, who had been Governor at Madras, to test his reaction. The reply from Tunbridge Wells which he sent to Cleghorn (21 September 1797) showed his approval, though it was qualified with a number of quite interesting political reflections. For example, he wrote: 'Little as I am indebted to your friend Dundas, you know I always did him the justice, if the present business, like Ceylon, were in his department, you might give in your idea with advantage and you could obtain for it success in Italy. But never, never will Lord Gr[enville] or the Duke of P[ortland], this side of the scaffold, adopt any plan but a counter-revolutionary one in favour of monarchy in France.' What gives point to this is the lavish amount of government money which went through Wickham's hands from Berne to counter-revolutionaries, compared with the parsimony shown in the government's dealings with Cleghorn.

Macpherson also remarks: 'The undertaking is, besides, perilous – you would for that reason like it'[6] – an interesting comment on a middle-aged, one-time professor. At any rate Macpherson had not been so discouraging that Cleghorn put the thing in a drawer. In fact, on 16 October, he wrote to Dundas sending the plan and asking for an interview to discuss it with him, ending the letter: 'And altho' I think you have treated me with unmerited neglect, yet in the interview I ask, I shall consider it as a point of Honor, not to mention one word of my own affairs, nor under pretence of Public Business to steal a meeting which is to be subservient to my own.'

Dundas replied from Walmer Castle, where he was staying with the Prime Minister, expressing his approval of the plan and promising a meeting when he returned to London, which would be in a few days' time. He went on in his letter to say that he had taken exception to Cleghorn's use of the phrase: 'unmerited neglect . . . but that where he really wished well and saw real merit, he was not disposed to feel angry at any expressions which the impatience of the moment might suggest.'

Four days later Cleghorn was having his interview with Dundas. He began by straightaway dealing with Cleghorn's own affairs, saying that both the Directors of the East India Company and himself were determined that Cleghorn should not be put on the shelf; that he should be given £5,000 for past services, and that a liberal provision should be settled upon his wife. He then asked

Cleghorn to return to Ceylon as Secretary of State in the King's government which was to be set up there. Cleghorn's immediate reaction was to refuse the offer, saying that at this point he was determined to return to his family, 'with whatever recompense His Majesty might be pleased to bestow upon my past services.'

Dundas accepted that, for the time being, and went on to tell Cleghorn that he had read over his plan for Italy with Mr Pitt when they were at Walmer. Both had been so convinced of 'its practicability and prospect of success that they would have carried it into execution', had not the news come almost at the same time of the treaty the Austrians had signed with the French at Campo Formio, which obviously put paid to the idea. But the warm goodwill which Dundas showed Cleghorn at this time convinced him that it was his idea on Italy which had determined Dundas to have him as Secretary of State in Ceylon. The interview ended with Cleghorn telling Dundas that: 'I would rather accept emolument with labour than an equal income with having nothing to do.'

During the ensuing weeks Cleghorn was invited 'rather more frequently than usual' to dine with Dundas, and then at the beginning of December he was bidden by Dundas to dine with him and to come an hour before dinner, 'as he wished to have a long conversation with me.' The purpose of this turned out to be renewed pressure to take the Secretaryship of Ceylon: 'He requested it as a personal favour; he was so convinced of the importance of the conquest of Ceylon to which I had so much contributed that he was determined to leave the Ministry, if ever they decided to cede it.'

Cleghorn wavered under the force of such arguments, 'which might have staggered resolutions more decided than mine. I told him that as I had a numerous family dependent on my life, the offer of ten thousand pounds and excluding the Pension, might perhaps have induced me to accept an Embassy to Hell; he replied smiling: "I will make it as good and not send you on so long a journey." We parted however without anything decisive. He added as I was leaving him that besides three thousand a year salary, I should have every advantage which the Secretaries of His Majesty's Government enjoyed in any of the British Dependencies and should be in Ceylon what he was in England.'

Though Cleghorn does not say it in so many words, he would have been far happier with a government post at home or in the diplomatic service in Europe, for which he felt himself far better equipped. But Dundas was determined to have his way. He invited both Cleghorn and Frederic North, who had accepted the post of Governor in Ceylon, to Wimbledon for the night, and in the morning he renewed his argument to persuade Cleghorn to accept the Secretaryship in Ceylon, which he described as 'the best office then in the Gift of the Crown'. Since Cleghorn was still not convinced he should accept, Dundas said he would keep the offer open for a fortnight till Cleghorn could consult his family. So he wrote to Scotland and before the fortnight was up, he received letters from his brother-in-law, Col. McGill, recommending him to accept, and from his wife, 'reluctantly acceding to Mr. Dundas' proposition.'

So accept he did and a few days afterwards dined and passed the night at Wimbledon, where no one else had been invited and the financial position was thoroughly gone into. Rachel, Mrs Cleghorn, was to receive £300 a year and on her death their five daughters were each to receive £50 a year. Cleghorn himself was to have £5,000 as an assignment on the revenues of Ceylon and £1,000 more was pledged in consideration of the expense of the voyage and fitting out for the settlement, 'to be made up to me in some other way' (fatally vague phrase). Further, Dundas gave him 'a Cadetcy on the Madras Establishment for the son of the late Principal Gillespie of St. Andrews', and pressed him to put Peter, his second son, on the Civil Establishment of Ceylon. This offer Cleghorn declined, but he did obtain permission to spend a month in Scotland with his family.

It did not prove as easy to get away as he had hoped. The Comte de Meuron arrived in London and Cleghorn felt he should give the Comte more time and attention than he had at his disposal. Dundas wanted letters which Cleghorn had received from a certain Mr Darke, confidential agent of the Nabob of the Carnatic (with whom he had become acquainted in Madras), mentioning the sums which Darke had paid on the part of the Nabob to various individuals on the Council of Madras (notorious for its corruption). Cleghorn was trying to get his public accounts settled and his private affairs put in order; he was short of cash to meet his expenses. The beginning of 17 January 1798 saw him writing to William Dundas, of the Board of Control of the East India Company, asking if he might stay on in London till the Charter for Ceylon had been drawn up, so that he could take it out with him and in the meanwhile make himself better acquainted with the situation in Ceylon. He enclosed with this request, which was turned down, a paper on the Army and Revenues of Ceylon which he must have been asked to supply. All this kept him in London, as he wrote to William Adam, 'in the most tormenting state of anxiety.'[7]

Soon, though, his natural buoyancy began to reassert itself and cheerfulness to break in, as his letter to Dundas on 8 January showed. He wrote of his gratitude in accepting: 'the very respectable office you were so good as to assign me in the new arrangements for Ceylon.' He went on: 'I have now no wish but that of having my family assured of comfortable subsistence during my absence . . . I have at present five daughters; my jaunt to Scotland may produce another for during a long period of my life, a Child a year was the most certain part of my income. I shall be content with the Recompense you may be pleased to grant me . . . A few lines from you permitting me to pass a few days with my family and enabling me to assure them of the Pension would make me completely happy.'[8]

At last, in the middle of January, he was free enough to set out for Scotland. He had been three days only in St Andrews when he received a letter from Frederic North, 'which obliged me to return with all expedition to London.' He thus made a nine-hundred-mile journey in the depths of winter for only the briefest glimpse of his wife and family, but at least he could give Rachel good news of John, their eldest son in Ceylon. He was back in London on 26 January, and gave Dundas the names of his daughters, but heard to his dismay that Rachel's pension could not as yet be put upon the Scottish Exchequer, which was already fully committed. There was nothing he could do, however, with North demanding his presence, but trust to the promises of Dundas.

On the morning of 27 January Cleghorn breakfasted with Dundas and Pitt, the Prime Minister, at Wimbledon, and that night left London at midnight to join North early the next morning at Portsmouth. They were then held up by contrary winds. Cleghorn had time to write to William Adam to thank him for letters of introduction he had sent from the Duke of York to commend Cleghorn to the Commander-in-Chief in Ceylon.[9] Lord Keith also sent a letter introducing Cleghorn to Mr and Lady Anne Barnard at the Cape, which he was sure would be a help to him there.[10]

So, after all the rush of vainly endeavouring to settle his affairs, of a travelling-all-round-the-clock journey to Scotland, of a night ride down to Portsmouth, there was nothing to do but kick his heels in company with the new Governor, while they waited for the wind to change. For three weeks they were held up. Then, at last, on 17 February 1798, the winds shifted and they were able to board the 'Brunswick', and set sail for India.

11

The New Government of Ceylon
February – October 1798

A Slow Start

Cleghorn would have to work so closely with the new Governor of Ceylon that North's personality would be of considerable importance both in setting its seal on the character of that government and the role Cleghorn would have as number two in it. He would have met Frederic North first in Corsica in 1797, when North was acting as secretary to Sir Gilbert Elliot, the Viceroy, and he was the first to tell North in London of Dundas' intention to appoint him Governor of Ceylon. North was fourteen years younger than Cleghorn, having been born in 1766, the third son of the Lord North who had been George III's prime minister during the War of American Independence (until he insisted on resigning in the face of defeat).

As a boy, Frederic North had suffered from ill-health, so, although he was admitted to Eton, he had spent much of his youth in European cities with a kinder climate than England's, and felt himself at home in them. Writing from Ceylon to Sylvester Douglas, his brother-in-law, he authorised the purchase of a house in Conduit Street, 'which I shall make the seat of comfort on my return as I do not find the least inclination to purchase an estate in Yorkshire, and my Excursions will be to Naples or Vienna or other places of that sort.'[1] Part of his love of Europe must have come from his knowledge of their languages and literature. He was a brilliant linguist and spoke German, French, Spanish, Italian and Romanie, and read Russian easily. One of his early publications, first printed in Leipzig and reprinted in Athens, was *A Pindaric Ode in honour of ex-Queen Catherine of Russia*.[2] When he was at Oxford – at Christ Church – he became a noted classical scholar and a passionate philhellene and travelled much in Greece, entering the Greek Orthodox Church in 1793. And in the following year he was elected a Fellow of the Royal Society.

He at any rate saw the inside of the House of Commons, if nothing more of it, in 1792 – when he succeeded his brother in the pocket borough of Banbury and picked up a couple of sinecure posts as Chamberlain of the Exchequer and Comptroller of Customs. These did not prevent him travelling in Spain and then from 1795 to 1797 he was in Corsica. But however much he was detached from the political hurly-burly of the day, he was one of the governing class who expected high office, as was shown in his letter to Dundas of 7 October 1793: 'I have so much gout flying about me' (this at the age of twenty-seven), 'that unless I fix it by drinking the Bath waters, I shall neither have strength of body nor clearness of mind enough for His Majesty's service in case I should be wanted this winter.'[3]

Altogether, North was a highly intelligent, sophisticated and articulate aristocrat, but he had had little experience of decision-making under pressure of events and personalities. Even before he sailed he had provoked Dundas to irritation. In January 1798 Dundas was writing to him: 'Get on board your Ship when the wind will permit you, which I am sorry to think is not so favourable as it was in the morning . . . Be as active as you please but don't be what I believe is called "fidgetty".'[4] And in February Dundas was writing again with some exasperation: 'in the meantime, allow me to state to you that when you call upon me to make *haste* to push your appointment and get you the money you need, you seem to forget that I am neither the Attorney General, nor the Privy Seal, nor the Great Seal, nor the Court of Directors, nor the Court of Proprietors, all of whom it is more necessary to set a-galloping than me . . . It is impossible to control without being obliged to thwart and sometimes to disgust. It is sufficient on the whole to be able to keep the great wheels of the machine a-going and this can only be done by never allowing myself to be ruffled by the Rubs which the lesser wheels may occasionally meet with'[5] . . . though in justice to the Hon Frederic North, it must be said that he seems to have had a nice touch in 'ruffling' the Secretary of State for War!

North himself was unmarried; those of the new Establishment who went with him varied widely both in age and nationality. There was William Boyd, first Assistant Clerk, Cleghorn described him as: 'perfectly attached to Mr. North, gentle and obliging; has a knowledge of figures . . . he is honourable and do not think will ever betray a confidence.'[6] North, writing to his sister about Boyd, says: 'you know nothing but that his manners are not remarkable for Elegance but you do not know that he is Integrity, Activity and Intelligence personified.'[7] Then there was Henry Marshall, whom Cleghorn described as: 'aged about twenty-two; has received a classical education and has profited by it; but he is vain and assuming, has no very accurate conception of things and if business of importance was committed to his charge, he would neglect it for pleasure or betray it from ostentation.' There were also three boys under the age of fifteen, one of whom, Sylvester Douglas, was North's nephew, the other two being Robert Barry and George Lusignan, all of whom, as Dundas explained to the Court of Directors: 'Mr. North was desirous to carry out . . . with a view of employing in extra services on the Island, such as the interpretation of languages, the investigation of the natural productions of the Island . . . likewise intending them to assist the Servants on the regular Establishment in writing letters, copying papers . . . ' (For these boys North was given an allowance 'not exceeding eight hundred pounds sterling'.[8])

There were also Josef Joinville, a French emigré of 'the most amiable manners, destined to be the Naturalist to the settlement', and Anthony Bertalocci, North's Corsican private secretary: 'of respectable abilities, but he is ignorant of business, of our language and manners' (Cleghorn's comment). Cleghorn's own Secretary was Gavin Hamilton, of whom he wrote: 'I shall say only that he has been regularly bred to business and that I would not exchange his services for those of any other Servant of the government.' The last in Cleghorn's list was Joseph Bethune, 'destined to go to an uncle at Bengal; not provided for in Ceylon but whose services have been very useful; he understands accounts, writes a good hand and is very diligent. He is superior to every person (Mr. Boyd excepted) on Mr. North's list. I never saw him till the day of our departure from London; he was as strongly recommended to Mr. North as to me and he is the most efficient of all the younger Servants.'

As head of the Medical Services to be organised in Ceylon, Dr Ewart was appointed on the recommendation of the Duke of York. Perhaps this gave him the confidence to spend freely – before they set out he had run through £2,000 for the Ceylon Medical Establishment, for which Dundas had agreed he should be indemnified out of the revenues of Ceylon.⁹ He was evidently endued with a sense of his own importance. Cleghorn mentioned a visit from the Doctor but corrected it to: 'or rather a visitation which has delayed me from finishing sooner.'

The new Government had 'a very prosperous voyage' to Bombay, landing there on 4 June 1798. They found to their dismay that their Commissions and Final Instructions, which Dundas had promised would arrive before them, were not there. Governor Duncan offered house-room to North and Bertalocci, 'but to every other person he has behaved with the most ungenerous inhospitality and most studied neglect,' as Cleghorn noted privately. This meant that all the others had to find their own accommodation. Cleghorn hired a house in the country but was concerned about the younger ones, 'some of them almost children,' who were living most expensively and unsuitably in taverns in Bombay. They inevitably ran out of money and North had to give Drafts to a Bombay banker to obtain money to tide them over, Cleghorn joining North in pledging his security as well on the advances.

Quite apart from the money question, Cleghorn's sense of what was proper to the new Governor was offended by the set-up in the Bombay Governor's residence. North's apartments were: 'a Bedroom in a Palace; in it only, he must receive the visits of those who are connected with his Government; and he has not the power, or at least he does not presume to ask any one of them to dinner, or not to offer them, after some miles journey in this climate, the smallest refreshment.' One result of this odd set-up was that there survived more correspondence on the subjects exercising the minds of the Governor and Secretary of State than might have been expected. For instance, letters passed between them on what should be the form of the courts of Ceylon with speculation on whether a Governor 'can of his own authority erect courts of Justice and name Judges'. And whether an Edict: 'of the Governor can revive Dutch Law and give efficacy to its decisions; suppose it could – would the English inhabitants be liable to its Jurisdiction? Are the Governor and the Government Secretary Justices of the Peace?'[10] North and Cleghorn were both intellectuals who enjoyed speculation; they were in some sense testing each other's reactions, though there was also perhaps an element of one-upmanship in the setting down of their opinions.

North, of course, as much as the rest, chafed at the necessity of waiting for his Commission and Final Instructions from London. He was led to consider seriously a suggestion made to him by Governor Duncan that the Supreme Government in Calcutta should confer on him the administration of Ceylon. The more Cleghorn thought about this idea, which North passed on to him, the less he liked it. At the end of a letter to North on the question, he promised to stand by him whatever North decided but begged him not to trust Duncan, 'who may make a merit with his employers in submitting the authority of the King to the Servants of the Company.' Then in a postscript, feeling he had gone too far: 'Excuse, my dear friend, this letter, written in a hurry, in which I have been more intent in expressing my sentiments than in softening my expressions.' But the letter was taken seriously by North, who made alterations in his own to Lord Mornington at Calcutta and to Dundas in London.

Cleghorn, also restive, applied for permission to go to Madras, where he felt it would be possible to pick up reliable information on what had been happening in Ceylon. It sounded, from hear-say, alarming enough: breakdown of order, widespread rebellion against the new English administration, government now in the hands of commissioners who would inevitably at first have the new government in their power because they had the knowledge of what had been going on. 'We need to know what have been the actions of others before we are called upon to act there ourselves,' Cleghorn wrote for his own records. Dr Ewart, for his part, wanted to go straight to Ceylon to initiate the changes he had planned in the running of the hospitals. He held very strongly to the opinion that: 'his Superintendence extends generally over H. M. troops in India and over the King's and Company's troops employed in Ceylon.'

Cleghorn went on in his report to Dundas: 'He proposed that the Physician General should have sole control for the furnishing of Medical Hospitals with provisions, medicines, beds . . . ' etc. Cleghorn was critical of Ewart's scheme; he believed it would open the door to abuse: 'To unite the character of Physician General with that of Contractor for the Hospitals under his management is to destroy all kind of check and control, and to put his interest as directly as is possible to put it in competition with his duty.' He set out his other criticisms and ended by saying that North viewed the Doctor's plans with equal misgiving. However, North gave permission to both men to go, and he agreed – after consulting with Governor Duncan – to the necessary financial arrangements of the details, of which 'very uninteresting subject' Cleghorn made a note in his records. Characteristically, he preferred: 'an allowance whatever it may be, rather than be under the disagreeable necessity of keeping accounts of trifling disbursements and disputing concerning deductions where feelings may be hurt though the point of interest is to be despised.'

North also sent Gavin Hamilton with Dr Ewart to Ceylon on a reconnaissance to find out the position in Government House with regard to living quarters and offices; prices in the markets and government purchasing practices; the way the law courts were run and the best books on the subject, 'either in the Dutch, German, Portuguese or Latin languages.' This letter to Hamilton ended: 'As you will probably be sifted to know my sentiments on a great many points, I will desire you to declare that the only one

I know you entertain is that I am determined to make my house and government as agreeable as I can to persons of every nation and of every description in the Island.'

North's official letter to Cleghorn, giving him permission to go to Madras, allotted Joseph Bethune to him as secretary and directed him to find out about the claim of the Nabob of the Carnatic to: 'some interest in the Pearl Fishery of Mannar concerning which I believe our Government has made only a temporary arrangement. I should wish you to obtain a perfect knowledge of the Politics of his Durbar and of the persons supposed to have most influence in it . . . ' North included a hint about timing: 'I only wish that you may not be absent from Colombo after my arrival there and I do not believe that you would like to arrive there long before me.' It was with some uneasiness that Cleghorn left North in the clutches of Governor Duncan, who seemed to him to have: 'all the littleness of cunning but none of the greatness of design.'[11] Still, Cleghorn had to accept that: 'If the mediocrity of his talents is capable of producing any improper effect on Mr. N., it is impossible far me to counteract it.' He was apprehensive because he suspected 'the facility of Mr. North's character', though he noted that 'in all our Intercourse hitherto I have found him polite, communicative and candid', and he hoped there was no reason why this should not be so when they met again in Ceylon.

It was not till 1 August that Cleghorn and Bethune sailed for Madras on board the East Indiaman the'Earl Howe'. The pilot who saw them out of the Roads of Bombay told them that the 'Margaret', on which Dr Ewart and Hamilton had sailed for Ceylon, had 'struck on a reef of rocks near Old Woman's Island and was unable to proceed'. There were no casualties, he believed, but Cleghorn, fearing they would have lost their baggage, sent them, by the pilot, a credit on the house of Bruce Fawcett & Co. The 'Earl Howe' reached the Madras Roads safely and Cleghorn landed at the Fort on 16 August. He had seen no sign of any Royal Navy ship along the whole coast of Malabar, and found in fact there was none to protect the trade and shipping there. He was sure this was a dangerous gap – with Tippū Sahib still the active ally of France.

A week after Cleghorn's arrival in Madras, the new Governor arrived there: Edward, Lord Clive, son of the great Robert Clive. Cleghorn took careful note of the protocol for his installation: the salute from the guns of the ship and fort; the troops lining the way; the reading of the Commission, first to the assembled civilians and then to the troops. Lord Clive alone was dressed 'in full Windsor uniform'. A few days later Lord and Lady Clive also held a Levée. 'In truth, it was a splendid display,' Cleghorn wrote to North. 'But I really pitied Lady Clive who for three or four hours was so curtseyed and bellowed at that she was constantly ducking like a cork in agitated water.' A few days later Cleghorn had a private interview with the new Governor and they discussed the question of whether any troops could be withdrawn from Ceylon. Most important of all, in Cleghorn's view, Lord Clive had brought out with him a copy of the Instructions which the Directors were sending to North. Cleghorn was allowed to have it copied and to send the copy to North at Bombay.

These Directions contained no surprises. They grew out of the dual control system between the government and the East India Company, which had been regulated by Pitt's India Act of 1784 – almost as much the work of Dundas as of Pitt. The main innovation of this Act had been the setting up of a board of control consisting of six privy councillors nominated by the King and changing as ministers changed. This board had the right to see all the papers of the Company and to issue orders to its directors, and in emergencies to transmit direct orders to India. The East Indian elected directors, on the other hand, kept the right of appointment to offices in India, subject to the King's veto. The Governor General in Calcutta was supreme over the other presidencies of Madras and Bombay, especially in the control of foreign policy. The act also contained measures: 'to check oppression and punish Company servants who enriched themselves outrageously.' In 1793 Dundas had been made president of the board of control – an office he retained till 1801. It was therefore natural that when he had to decide on the form of the first British government of Ceylon, he should cobble it up from arrangements already familiar in his mind. Before Cleghorn left London he had noted in his own records: 'On the whole it appears that the measure of erecting Ceylon into a Royal Government, however long it may have floated in the mind of the Minister, was in the end, hastily adopted . . . the Plan which involves a double government, is neither likely to last long nor to act with vigour while it lasts.'

The essential point of this 'double government' is spelt out in the first paragraph of the Directions: 'The Governor . . . in Ceylon, notwithstanding his appointment by His Majesty, should correspond with the Court of Directors of the India Company and with His Majesty's ministers through the medium of the Court of Directors and he may obey such orders as he may from time to time receive from them or from the Government General of India.'[12] Moreover, the Governor was to keep the Court of Directors (or its Secret Committee, whose members are named) informed on all that was happening in Ceylon. 'You are likewise to keep a diary of your proceedings and transactions, a copy whereof is to be regularly transmitted to us from time to time and another copy to the Governor General in Council.' It was also laid down that if he needed more men for the administration of Ceylon, they 'are to be procured from the Company's civil servants on the Madras Establishment on application to the Governor in Council', though this was modified in the last paragraph of the Directions.

The Governor was to be Commander-in-Chief and have military as well as civil authority and for the time being was to administer the courts according to Dutch law. 'All public acts and judicial proceedings are . . . previous to their being published, to be signed by the Chief Secretary to the Government.' On the financial side, the Governor could sweep away regulations 'which are ruinous and vexatious', but was to make a thorough report to the Directors on 'the different resources from which the revenue was derived'. The Governor was to honour the pledge given in the Capitulation of 1796 to take up the promissory notes of the Dutch government, but also to: 'report to us the exact amount of the paper money now in circulation.' The Governor is next directed to: 'conciliate the affections of the King of Candia and of the nation in general upon the island of Ceylon.' Religious toleration was to be observed. Then follow detailed demands for information and the heads under which it was to be submitted, and a grant of authority was given to require such information from Madras.

Thus, in essence, the East India Company shared the administration of the coast lands of Ceylon with the Crown and was to enjoy a monopoly of its trade. Cleghorn, incidentally, turned out to be right about the impermanence of this arrangement: it lasted until 1 January 1802, when these possessions became the British Crown Colony of Ceylon.

After these Directions had been dispatched to North, Cleghorn did his best to acquire just that information which the Directors were demanding. He interviewed General Sydenham, the Auditor General of the Madras Presidency, who was persuaded to give Cleghorn a full statement of the military expenditure in Ceylon and promised to discuss with him 'such parts of the Establishment as may be dispensed with and such as can bear considerable retrenchment' – all useful stuff as far as it went. Cleghorn also got on to good terms with Captain Blair, who had been recommended by North's brother, Lord Guildford, and Lord Hobart. He was 'a very worthy sensible fellow', who hoped to become North's ADC. Cleghorn was non-committal on that, of course, but teased North in his letter about it, saying: 'I should doubt of his making you a good ADC as he has long lived in a family of water drinkers.'

Another important contact Cleghorn made was with William Petrie, 'a clever man and has at present most influence with Lord Clive.' But there was a faction of young men in the government of Madras who aimed to cut out Petrie in order to 'blindfold the Master that they may plunder the larder'. Robert

Andrews, from Ceylon, was on the edge of this group. He proved elusive when Cleghorn first endeavoured to make contact, but: 'I got him into a corner at Lady Clive's hurricane where I contrived to calm the storm which I believe was brooding in his mind for he had an idea that he was going to Ceylon to undergo a kind of inquest, to deliver up his accounts and retire.'

The report he gave on the state of the revenues of Ceylon was not very enlightening. The Dutch: 'have carefully kept back all intelligence and the only information we have as yet received has been through the medium of Black writers and the Sinhalese formerly in their service.' He also reported that the Dutch were very averse to the British and simply refused to co-operate at all; old Angelbeck was a threat because of the devotion of the Malay Corps to him, and young Angelbeck was described by Andrews as 'a very dangerous character'. Andrews also suggested that Cleghorn should get hold of a copy of the report which de Meuron, Agnew and himself had drawn up on Ceylon after the rebellion had been put down. Cleghorn extracted a pledge from Andrews that on his return to Ceylon only the shortest possible leases would be granted. 'I observed that the produce of the Pearl fishery had been carried to the Credit of the Madras Presidency; that the produce of the Cinnamon had gone home as profit for the Company – and that it was not doing justice to you on the eve of your Government to deprive you of the only remaining Branch of revenue: the lease of the Tythe. He most positively assured me that it should be done as I desired.' With a little perseverance on Cleghorn's part he was given the Committee's Report, which brought him up to date on the measures that had been taken to fix customs duties, regulate the salt tax and check smuggling of cinnamon, etc.

Cleghorn was also in touch by letter with General de Meuron and Major Agnew in Colombo, Col. Barbet in Jaffna and the Hon. Lt. Turnour in Mannar, and of the reports he sent to Dundas he was scrupulous to keep copies, so that they could be shown to North. In conversation with General Sydenham and others in Madras, he realised how jealous the officials there were 'of the erection of Ceylon into a separate government as tending to deprive them in a certain degree of Patronage or Emolument', but he did manage to get a sight of the paper he wanted on the rules of the Audit Office of Madras, on the expense of subduing and maintaining the Island of Ceylon from July 1795 to 31 January 1798, together with an estimate of expenditure for six months from 1 July to 31 December 1798. On the whole Cleghorn found these quite cheering: 'for the apparent expenses of Ceylon are much greater than its real expenditure.'

He also managed to arrange an interview, at Arcot, with the Nabob of the Carnatic (8 September) and decked himself out in what he afterwards referred to as his 'Tippū finery'. The Nabob sent a letter to North by Cleghorn, 'but it is so covered with gold that it cannot be sent by post.' On discussing with the Nabob his rights in the rent of the pearl fishery, Cleghorn found that he claimed one sixth, while the Company allowed it to be one eighth, but as the revenue he received from the pearl fishery went to discharge his immense debts to the Company at Madras, it was something of an academic question. It was difficult, Cleghorn found, to pin down whose influence the Nabob was under, the only constant factor being that it was always some not very trustworthy character.

Cleghorn, whose political antennae seem to have been pretty sensitive, gained some useful ideas in Madras on the best orientation for the new government of Ceylon. Madras, it was clear, would remain obstructive and resentful. It would be preferable to employ the civil servants of Bengal, who were 'more expert in business and more liberal in conduct', and who would help to strengthen the ties with the Supreme Government. Too many Madras officials were involved up to their necks in the present abuses, whereas those from Bengal would come to the new administration with no axe to grind. Cleghorn foresaw it would be necessary to get round the Directions on this point, and for this purpose – and others as useful – someone from the new Ceylon government should go to Bengal and establish direct links. And who better than the new Secretary of State to that government?

After about six weeks in Madras, on 20 September, Cleghorn left there and by way of Tranquebar crossed to Ceylon, landing at Jaffna, to renew his friendship with Col. Barbet and to find out how he set about collecting the revenue in his district. He also wrote a report to Dundas on his doings in Madras, and in the private letter accompanying his report he ended by sending his compliments to Dundas' wife, Lady Jane, 'and I hope next season to be able to present her with two Jaffna horses, which are the gentlest and most tractable animals in the world – Your commission I shall not forget.' (This refers to Dundas' desire to present his wife with a really splendid pearl necklace as a symbol of his conquest in Ceylon.)

In the meantime, North in Bombay had also been collecting advice on government from Barnard in the Cape[13], for instance, for it had also been taken from the Dutch, and from Sir Thomas Strange on more legal points.[14] At last, on 22 September, North received his Commission from the King and set out for Ceylon in the 'Intrepid'. He reached Colombo on 12 October. On his arrival he had the Commission read on the parade ground and later at Government House, and took the oath of fidelity to the East India Company. This happened before Cleghorn reached Colombo, which he did about the middle of October. He merely notes that on his arrival at Colombo he found the new Governor had got there: 'a few days before me and had taken quiet possession of his government.'

'Reduced to a Cypher'[1]

October 1798 – May 1799

Growing tensions

Cleghorn may have been disappointed that the first British Governor of Ceylon had entered on his term of office with so little panache and without the presence of his Secretary of State, but he must have been reassured to learn, from the official Instructions to the Governor that North had brought with him, that Dundas had won the approval of the 'Chairs' (ie the Court of Directors of the East India Company) for the grant of £5,000 for Cleghorn and, from the revenues of Ceylon for the time being, a pension of £300 a year for Mrs Cleghorn and her daughters. It is worth quoting from Dundas' description of what Cleghorn had done on his first journey to Ceylon:

'It only further remains for me to bring under your view a circumstance relative to Mr. Cleghorn. The great and meritorious services performed by him, and to which indeed is principally to be attributed the rapid and easy conquest of the Island of Ceylon, are well known to the late and present Chairmen of the East India Company; they were unknown, at the time, to every Department of Government but my own; but there is no reason why the Chairs may not now communicate to a Secret Court of Directors the whole course of that Transaction and the whole train of the Correspondence respecting it and when that is explained to the Court of Directors, they will heartily concur with me in thinking that when I directed Mr. North to pay him £5,000 out of the Revenues of Ceylon, it was the instance of all others I ever witnessed in which the most meritorious Service had been performed to the Public at the cheapest rate. I was induced, from the useful information I received from Mr. Cleghorn relative to

Ceylon, and the great talents he had displayed, earnestly to request his again leaving his Family and going out as Secretary to the Government; at his time of Life and with a large Family, it could not be a pleasant service to him but he acquiesced and is gone there.'[2]

Cleghorn made arrangements through his friend in Bombay, Alexander Walker,[3] to present the bill for the £5,000 to the House of Bruce, Fawcett & Co. there, settle his account with them and remit the balance to Messrs William and John Wilsone in London, who would see that it was sent on to Mrs Cleghorn or Col. Macgill in St Andrews, 'as they are looking out for a small landed property for me.'

The main concern, however, was to establish the new British government of Ceylon. In 1796, when the British took Ceylon over, its administration had been put, as an interim measure, under the control of the Madras Presidency. The immediate object of Madras had been to recoup from the island the cost of its conquest. To do this they had sent out Robert Andrews as Resident and Superintendent of Revenue. He had in 1795 been made British Resident in Jaffna and Ambassador to the Court of Kandy – to which he had been on a mission, which had failed. The changes he had then proceeded to make in the method of collecting taxes in Jaffna had roused Cleghorn's distrust when he had visited there in January 1796: 'Mr. Andrews . . . has made the alterations without knowing sufficiently all the circumstances which might have rendered the Dutch mode of collection in this district preferable to ours.'[4]

Later that same year Col. James Stuart, Andrews' superior in Ceylon, felt the same distrust when he heard of Andrews' confident plans for more social and economic reforms for all the regions under British control, but he did not forbid their introduction, so Andrews went ahead. He began antagonising the headmen by withdrawing their 'accomodessans' (grants of land in return for services) and completed it by bringing in from Fort St George South Indian officials of the Madras Presidency, who from ignorance of Sinhalese custom and tradition, trampled heavily over: 'some of the most sensitive aspects of the lives of the people, such as caste.'[5] He tried to make a uniform system out of the welter of land taxes, which turned out to mean an increase in the taxation level. He introduced new levies, such as one on personal ornaments and another on coconut palms and other trees. The result of all this was rebellion, which broke out in December 1796.

The Sinhalese had already risen twice against the Dutch in the last forty years (protesting in 1757, for example, against service obligations which had kept them for eight months of the year in the forests peeling cinnamon). In both these previous risings they had forced the Dutch to retract their measures. This time Lord Hobart, Governor of Madras, crossed to Colombo to judge the situation for himself and on his return, condemned the South Indian civil servants (given the title of 'amildars' by Andrews, popularly called the 'Dubashes' or interpreters) for their rapacity and extortion. And in June of 1797 he set up a committee: 'to investigate the state of the revenue and other important matters on the Island of Ceylon.'[6] He named Brigadier General de Meuron as Chairman, the other two members being Major Agnew and Robert Andrews himself. The committee was: 'granted extraordinary powers to investigate the causes of the rebellion, recommend measures of reform and redress grievances.' It was given executive powers as well and from June of 1797 to November 1798 it was in fact the government of Ceylon. It took until March of 1798 to put down the rising, partly because of the help given by the King of Kandy to the rebels, who held strong positions on the borderland between the low country and the hills. They were also given help by Dutch officials reluctant to accept the permanence of British rule, and French agents may have added fuel to the fire.

Administrative measures to restore the status quo to the situation before Andrews' reforms also helped to quiet unrest. The South Indians, for example, were ordered to return to Madras and the headmen were to be restored to their former position. By October of 1798, when North arrived, he found that the remedial measures suggested by de Meuron were still in process of being implemented and his own conservative instincts led him very readily to adopt them. His first act was to restore the Sinhalese headmen – the modiliars – to office. Cleghorn, writing privately to Alexander Walker in December 1798, felt that an opportunity to inaugurate a better system of government had been lost. He joined wholeheartedly in the condemnation of the rule of the dubashes and was glad to see them go, 'but the Modiliar is a native of high rank and to the authority of his office adds that of his caste. He can be guilty of injustice and oppression in a thousand ways and the natives dare not complain; he is the only judge in the first instance, the leading one in the second, and what Justice can be expected where the Judge is the Oppressor? I am persuaded if the Poverty and Indolence of the natives of this country were traced to their true cause, these would be found to originate from the insecurity of their little property which lies at the mercy of the Modiliar.'[7]

But it was not Cleghorn but de Meuron to whom North listened and of whom he wrote so warmly: 'We have ever since my arrival lived in the most intimate and cordial union and I have found the greatest comfort in his society and the greatest assistance from his co-operation.'[8] It was not till later that North acknowledged by his change of policy that there had been much justice in Cleghorn's assessment. By a proclamation of 1801, (after Cleghorn had returned to Scotland) the modiliars were deprived of their 'accomodessans' and later on they were excluded from registering land-holdings.[9] North was thus accepting that in restoring the old order, he had benefited the headmen more than the people or the government.

North and Cleghorn were of one mind on the malign influence of the British civil servants of the Madras establishment on the government of Ceylon. While Cleghorn was still in Madras he had warned North of this and North within a year of his own arrival in Ceylon was writing bitterly to the Secret Committee of the East India Company of: 'that determined and systematic spirit of opposition and of hatred which has guided them (ie the

Madras people) in all their actions and which has made them turn every mark of confidence which I have shown them and every authority with which I have invested them into engines to discredit my government and thwart my person.'[10] North and Cleghorn remained at one over the problem of Robert Andrews. Ceylon must certainly be rid of him but he must not be drummed out in disgrace. There survives the draft of a letter which Cleghorn drew up for North which aimed at making the position clear to Andrews. They came to differ, however, on another Madras civil servant, Cecil Smith.

On 8 January 1799 Madras sent Smith over to Ceylon with the sort of formal recommendation which is given to those whom their employers hope to be rid of. He had been in the Accountant General's office in Madras and was sent to regulate Ceylon's audit and account offices. Cleghorn saw him very much as an intriguer and a man on the make. Writing of him to William Petrie, he said: 'Smith's object is to get McDowall removed from the office of Under Secretary and to procure that situation for himself . . . I should hardly think that either of these offices (ie audit and account) is compatible with that of Under Secretary: that the same person should pass in one office the Expenditure of which he is the efficient disposer in another. I know nothing of Mr. Smith's character but I understand he is involved in debt which the fair revenue of office can scarcely ever discharge and I have had sufficient experience to be convinced that the Secretary or Under Secretary here may acquire by improper, though undiscoverable means, any fortune he may choose to possess.'[11]

North, by contrast, saw Smith as one resolute to make a fresh start. Writing to Cleghorn from Madras, he said of Smith: 'He appears to me to have taken a manly and honourable resolution to retrieve his past indiscretions by a regular and zealous attention to his duty. If the countenance which I have shown him has contributed, as I hope it has, both to encourage him in that Resolution and to hasten the effects of it on the Public Opinion, it will be a most heartfelt satisfaction to me during life.' In the event, Smith who had gone with North to Madras, stayed there. Cleghorn, with his basic fairness of mind, acknowledged in a letter to North the gladiatorial element in public opinion. 'A man has lived with little observation if he has not had frequent experience of Characters being both unjustly extolled and unjustly run down.'

Col. Champagné, one of the senior military officers in Ceylon, was, however, very much of one mind with Cleghorn, to whom he wrote: 'I hope Mr. North is safe at Madras and that Smith will remain there, I desire never to see him again as long as I exist. Is it not wonderful that a man of his vile character should ever be employed? I trust he never will be here.' In connection with appointments Cleghorn also became critical of the way North rewarded favoured officers by creating posts with insufficient or nominal duties, which of course led to: 'profusion of public money with which their untried services are bought.' Maitland, North's successor as Governor, bore out this criticism by his wholesale abolition of many of the posts North had created.[12]

On another issue, Cleghorn faced squarely a fact that North evaded – that is, the refusal of Dutch officials to reconcile themselves to British rule. It was all very well to restore Dutch civil and criminal law, but since, because of the lack of Dutch co-operation, 'it would have to be administered by those who do not understand it,' this meant giving an undoubted and unmerited advantage to the Dutch. They also were benefiting unfairly, Cleghorn believed, by the way the question of the salt duties had been dealt with: 'We have very wisely renewed the Salt duties; we very unwisely have given the superintendence of the Salt works to Dutchmen . . . we have thrown every temptation in the way of those men to become smugglers themselves. We cannot expect that they will be more chaste under our government than they would have been under their own. And it is well known that Governor De Graaf preferred for his own brother the Salt Superintendence at Calpetty to a seat in Council. Yet we have given this office to a Dutch prisoner of war, who must necessarily regard the interest of our Revenue with the apathy of a stranger or the animosity of an enemy.'[13]

Cleghorn's own solution would have been to divide the salt districts into different allotments and to let them to different persons. 'Had a maximum of price been established Government would at once have got a larger revenue and the Kandyans would have been infinitely less exposed to extortion.'[14] One begins to see why comfort-loving North sought for expedients to escape from the advice of a councillor ready on any question to fire off such well-directed volleys of criticism.

This expedient presented itself in the shape of the 1799 Pearl Fishery. When he was still in Bombay Cleghorn had written to Col. Barbet and the Hon. Lt. Turnour for reports on their districts, which included the oyster beds which were annually dragged for pearls.[15] Turnour, commanding at Mannar, sent Cleghorn: 'many important papers concerning the Pearl Fishery and I have not a doubt that the Banks may be fished this season with every appearance of success.'[16] In thus writing to Dundas, Cleghorn was going directly against a report he had sent him earlier, 'that the Pearl Fishery would for several years be altogether unproductive,' because of the way it had been over-fished in 1797 and 1798. Turnour, however, had convinced him that there were some banks 'which have escaped the general rapacity and which may be dragged next February with every appearance of profit'.

Cleghorn believed that the reason why Robert Andrews and other Madras officials engaged in the 1797 and 1798 Pearl Fisheries were so anxious that there should not be one in 1799 was that: 'they still have very considerable quantities of pearls to dispose of. It is obviously therefore their interest to prevent, if possible, the fishing of the Banks next season as the additional quantity of pearls which may thus be thrown on to the market must naturally diminish the value of those which they mean to dispose of.' Cleghorn was in fact being too clever here – to his own future downfall – but he had raised the question, so he was sent in November 1798 to Arripo, just south of Mannar – 'a desert district', in his phrase – to carry out an inspection. He was prevented from beginning by the weather. 'The season', he wrote to Alexander Walker, 'is too far advanced and the weather too

uncertain to enable me to attain anything like accurate information on the subject.'[17] What he did get was a somewhat startling
insight into the prevalence of bribery in everything connected
with the Pearl Fishery. 'Since I have come here the sums of
money which have been offered me in this miserable district, to
continue occupants in their offices, exceeds belief.'

On 1 December he wrote to North in Colombo that he had just
been offered 2,000 Pagodas by a go-between for the aumildar,
placed in the Arripo district by Mr Andrews. Cleghorn described
how he had demanded to see the aumildar, so it was arranged
that he should come after dark and bring the money. In return
for it, Cleghorn was to give him a chit for the governor, which
would enable him to obtain the office, and was to keep the
affair secret – so, Cleghorn continued: 'Whatever letter I may
judge it expedient to give him to you . . . you will know how
to appreciate it and if he presents it in person before my arrival at
Colombo, you will determine whether he ought to be secured.' He
finished his letter to North on a confident note: 'Philip's Specific,
it would seem, is of universal application but it shall work no
wonders on me. Moderately speaking, there is at least 5,000
Pagodas now ready for my acceptance and brought by those who
have not the appearance of being altogether possessed of ten.'

Big business also was reluctant to lose the advantageous
position it had enjoyed in the two previous years. A letter
from Mootiah Chitty suggested that, if Cleghorn and Turnour
would give the positions of manager, dubash and cashkeeper
to his friends: 'Yourself and Mr. Turnour can undoubtedly get
an advantage of about 20,000 Pagodas besides your commission.'[18] Mootiah Chitty and his brother, Wydelinga Chitty had
been sureties for Wydelinga's son, Cundapah Chitty, to whom
the whole fishery for the season had been let by the Madras
government in both 1797 and 1798. The size of the bribe they
were prepared to offer Cleghorn and Turnour showed how
great their own rake-off had been in the previous two years.
The bribe was refused but instead of being warned off by the
evidence of endemic corruption and in spite of having to rely on

Turnour's opinion on the presence of sufficient pearls, Cleghorn went ahead: he and Turnour and John MacDowall, Collector of Colombo, were appointed commissioners for superintending the 1799 Pearl Fishery. MacDowall was included because he, unlike the others, was a servant of the East India Company.

Cleghorn was back in Colombo in January 1799 to find North increasingly popular with the European community. There were probably not more than about a hundred and twenty English civilians in Colombo but North also wanted to win over the Dutch and their wives – great sticklers for etiquette, apparently – so he entertained them all to dinners and balls, moving from a house in the Fort of Colombo which he found 'hot and confined' to: 'a more eligible situation surrounded with pleasant prospects and fanned by perpetual breezes. It formed the theatre of all gay and festive entertainments.' But among government officials it was a different matter: the administration 'is at present divided into factions and hardly anything heard but the voice of discontent', Cleghorn wrote to Walker. Dr Ewart, for instance: 'is at open war with the Company Surgeons and has put the surgeon of the 19th Foot in arrest. I was absent and do not know the cause of the quarrel but I am sorry the harmony of our little society is likely to be broken by parties and courts martial.'[19]

North, civilised intellectual though he was, yet lacked experience of administration: praising his personal secretary William Boyd, for 'the degree of economy, regularity and order which he has introduced into all departments'. North goes on: 'Now these are points in which I do not shine.'[20] He also seems to have lacked the personal authority to impose his will on his subordinates. Writing to his sister, Lady Douglas, he reflected unhappily: 'It is a sad thing to drive restive Horses that long for nothing so much as to break one's neck and that is just my case. Everything is kicking and flinging . . . Dr. Ewart is engaged in a paper war with all the Powers of India and is moreover not on speaking terms with me.'[21]

North certainly made no effort to channel Cleghorn's energies into worthwhile work. On 25 January Cleghorn was writing to his friend William Petrie, in Madras: 'We have got into no system and the labour of yesterday does not smooth that of today – would you believe that I am dying of idleness in a new Government?' There was something of Cleghorn's verbal extravagance in this because his dispatches to Dundas show a detailed understanding of many of the problems of Ceylon as well as his fears prompted by the French presence in Egypt and the implications of this for the British in India. He had decided to send copies of these dispatches by William Petrie to Lord Mornington, the new Governor General in India.

Mornington, in fact, needed no warning on the dangers from the French in India. He had arrived in Calcutta in May 1798 and had soon determined not to allow French influence to gather head through the activities of Tippū Sahib in Mysore. While negotiating with Tippū through the winter of 1798–9 he prepared for war. Moving to Madras in February 1799, after galvanising everyone to tremendous exertions, he ordered General Harris and the Carnatic army 'not to delay the march of the army one hour', but to enter Mysore and advance on Seringapatam.

The flare-up of war in India showed Cleghorn how inadequate were the defences of Ceylon: 'At Colombo, there is, of every description, but 2,000 men; the works are in disrepair and the firing of a salute endangers the Embrasures . . . We have not among us talents for Defence: De Meuron has not yet left us . . . but he never was in real service, was advanced in life before he was a soldier, has received his only military education in a Dutch garrison and his Science, of consequence, cannot be expected to exceed that of a Captain of a City Guard . . . We have other difficulties to encounter of a nature sufficiently urgent to challenge attention: upwards of 500 Malays straggle in the neighbourhood of Colombo and if these are not hired to fight for us, they will fight against us . . . '

In addition, those Europeans formerly in the service of the Dutch, would seize any opportunity to renew hostilities and, 'above all, that absurd and dangerous measure of de Meuron, the re-establishment of the power of the Modiliars will arm and

give Chiefs to the natives who are ever looking for a charge.'
Behind these possible dangers was the actual one of famine:
vigorous measures were needed to procure supplies, and they
should be taken soon, 'for a change of monsoon will in a
few weeks deprive us for six months of all communications
by sea . . . ' The anger which comes through this analysis of
Ceylon's weakness had been sparked off by North's decision
to go himself to Madras to meet Lord Mornington. Cleghorn
had been hoping to be sent; instead he would be in the 'desert
district of Arripo'. But quite apart from his own disappointment,
he was genuinely convinced that the Governor should remain
in Ceylon: 'During the absence of the Chief, no subordinate
officer may possess energy or power sufficient to take necessary
measures . . . I have hinted at a distance,' Cleghorn went on in
his letter to Petrie, 'of these considerations to Mr. North but I
would not push them lest we should have thought that my only
object was to be sent to Madras myself . . . ' There was a final
shot from Cleghorn's battery of arguments:

'But there is yet another [reason] of a private nature which I am
surprised he has allowed to escape him. By his Commission he is
expressly forbidden to leave his Government except on account of
his health. The Commanding Officer, who is ex-officio Governor
during his absence is not required by the letter of his Instructions
to resign the government, if the Governor is absent from any
other cause – and India has furnished examples of what bold men
may do when invested with what was thought only a temporary
government . . . '

Despite this North had made his decision and needed to wait
only for the loading and departure of the cinnamon ships in the
middle of March. The letters Cleghorn had from him before that
were mostly addressed to all three Commissioners and concerned
the organising of the pearl fishery. There was also one, from the
irrepressible Mootiah Chitty – setting out his claim to 74,250
pagodas which were owing to him from his nephew, Cundapah
Chitty. Mootiah accused his nephew 'of employing more than
twice the number of boats allowed by his contract and cheating

him of his share' – in what was, of course, a flagrant fraud. Mootiah ended his petition to North by explaining: 'This affair must be investigated at the Pearl Fishery as it is now the best opportunity, for the people that were present there last year, will be now again there by which means then this affair will be proved.'

Cleghorn investigated and reported confidentially to North: 'I never wrote to you with so much reluctance . . . In this investigation Lord Hobart and Mr. Adderley will be implicated. And I am assured the late Renter [Cundapah Chitty], when pushed, will accuse himself of having given considerable sums in Secret Service money to them. Write me privately what you wish done. These gentlemen are not here to vindicate themselves – and consider the odium of committing such names and characters upon Black evidence. After reading your answer to this, I shall return it to you to be destroyed if you require it.' Here was another warning to Cleghorn on the ease with which reputations could be tarnished by involvement in the pearl fishery. But on this occasion the accusations were not taken up. North replied: 'I am therefore of opinion that the Business had better not be entered into: it can do no good.'

The 1799 Pearl Fishery

In 1799 a different system of organising the fishery from the previous years was to be tried. It was not let, 'but carried on for the Company's account under the Administration of three Commissioners appointed by the Governor of Ceylon.' On 24 January 1799 North drew up their formal 'Instructions'. Macdowall, Collector of the Revenue, was to have the right of naming the servants to be employed in the management of the fishery; Turnour was to command the troops which were to be stationed there. The Commissioners were to: 'take especial care to hinder any combination to the detriment of the public interest, by facilitating the bidding of every person who wishes it for each separate boat . . . '

The exact boundaries of the banks to be fished were to be marked out; the supply of provisions, especially rice, was to be organised; financial and administrative details were settled and finally: 'as an indemnification for your trouble and expense you will receive (to be divided equally among you), one per cent of any sum produced under one Lac of Pagodas, two per cent on any sum from one to two Lacs . . . up to ten per cent on any above three Lacs.' The only modification of these instructions that the commissioners asked for was permission to accept local bills of exchange from the Sinhalese who would come to Arripo, as: 'it is hardly to be expected that such persons can have time to apply for Paper at the Carnatic and British Banks.' Because of the enormous expense of the Mysore War, the Supreme Government had prohibited all exporting of coin from the mainland and had further ordered the commissioners of the pearl fisheries to send immediately to Madras any sums they might receive as the price of boats.

These boats were the property of individuals who, naturally given to gambling, were ready to bring their boats to 'the Lottery of the Pearl Fishery', in Cleghorn's phrase. The full complement for the crew of a boat was ten divers and five stones (the crew took turns; when one dived the other had to be ready to haul up the stone which had taken the diver down). The boats, each with its numbered passport, went out from the shore in the morning, guided by the pilot and accompanied by the shark charmer; they fished for a certain number of hours and then, all together, returned to the shore and landed the oysters. They were then, boat owners, crews, pilot, shark charmer and all, paid for a 'complete' day by a certain number of oysters from each boat, the rest of the oysters going to the proprietors of the fishery – in 1799, that is, the three commissioners on behalf of the government of Ceylon and the East India Company. Sometimes contrary or shifting winds and currents, sometimes a lack of divers or stones meant an 'incomplete' day. Then the boats fished on the account of the proprietors of the fishery, who purchased their oysters. Boats came from the Carnatic and

Malabar coasts as well as Bengal and, of course, Ceylon itself. So, although on paper the organisation was clear, in practice, for Europeans who did not know the language of the fishermen and divers or find it easy to distinguish one from another, control was difficult and they had to rely on their dubashes for enforcement of the regulations.

At the beginning of February Cleghorn left Colombo. On the 5th he drew up their advertisement for the 1799 Fishery, giving notice that 350 boats and no more would be disposed of by auction for the usual period of thirty days. The commissioners also decided that the divers should be impartially distributed so as to equalize their value as much as possible before the sale (with a view to keeping up the selling price). At the same time they wrote to North asking him for discretionary power 'to bid for such number of boats as they may judge necessary to keep up the price'. They also wanted a surgeon for Arripo and they emphasised the need to be sent more rice. This was usual at the time of the fishery, and North and Company officials in Bengal and the Carnatic did their best to respond. No actual date had been fixed for the first sale but the boats were dilatory in coming. The commissioners had hoped to begin early in February but by the 15th neither boats nor divers had arrived – so the 22nd was fixed on. But Cleghorn had obviously overrated the gambler's instinct among the pearl fishers or else they had better information than the commissioners: another postponement proved to be necessary. They wrote to Lushington, Collector at Ramnad on the Carnatic coast, asking him to stir up the divers there as the weather was now favourable. On 27 February came the first sale of boats.

This was preceded by the public reading of a proclamation which stated: 'as deposed to by Damoodera Rilla, Permal Naig and Wydelinga Chitty and elucidated in the Deposition of Daniel Roderigo (the pilot) that a boat would bring in from eight to ten thousand oysters in one day's fishing.' This encouraged the purchase of twelve boats at a high price, averaging 1902½ Porto Novo Pagodas per boat. By 4 March eighty-five boats had been sold for varying prices but the commissioners had felt obliged to step in and purchase some for the government, 'to prevent the price being commanded by few monopolist partners.' The fishery did not begin till about 3 March and then it soon became clear that there were nothing like enough oysters on the banks to have justified one – but the commissioners battled on, hoping to save something for the government and the Company.

On 5 March they ordered that the whole number of oysters brought in by the different boats was to be delivered at the banksaal set aside for the oysters of the boats which the commissioners had just bought on behalf of the government. In addition they declared that a full day's compensation was to be given to all boat-holders who delivered their oysters there. They next tried shifting the fishing grounds slightly, ordering the boats to row to Ammani, led by the pilot; and though they sold fifty-nine more boats the yield remained small.

On 16 March they were reporting to the Governor an arrangement they had come to with Wydelinga Chitty, the father of the previous year's renter. This, they admitted, 'is not desirable but it will yield something.' It was the best of the offers made by those who were in a position to take advantage of the misfortunes of the commissioners: Wydelinga Chitty would buy eighty-two boats at 1,250 P. N. Pagodas per boat, 'with a remission when the number of oysters shall fall short of four thousand.' During the fishery of 1797 a boat with ten divers and five stones brought eight thousand oysters up a day on average, and in 1798 six thousand oysters. Therefore the commissioners were trying to take account of the relative poverty of the banks in 1799 by calculating four thousand oysters as the daily produce of a boat, so that whenever that number should not be completed by a day's fishing, a proportioned remission should be made in the purchase money and the commissioners forgo some of the full amount for which it had been agreed to sell the boat to the purchaser. Those who had bought boats at a high price at the beginning of the fishery then put in a claim for a similar remission, and this was granted to them.

The adoption of this system may have been aimed at reassuring the speculators; but one more calculated to open the whole working of the fishery to administrative chaos and wholesale cheating, it would be difficult to devise. It was at this point that North arrived at Arripo on his way to Madras, and gave his official approval to the remission scheme, whatever his private doubts may have been. The commissioners inevitably found that: 'the great proportion of the boat holders did not give in a fair ration of the number of oysters delivered by their boats at their respective banksaals.' To counteract this the commissioners: 'fixed the remission universally at one half Fishery from the commencement of the fishing to 15 March and as one fifth from that date to the conclusion.' They reached this rate, which was 'neither hard nor inequitable', by taking: 'the profit of the government boats which are undoubtedly the worst as they were left on the hands of the Government for want of purchasers as the Criterion of the Profit of all the rest.'

But there was no escaping the stark fact of failure: the fishery ended on 13 April, having hopelessly dragged out more than its thirty days. Enlarging on this, the Commissioners explained: 'The wind has been quite contrary for some days past and consequently no fishing has taken place and even during many of the latter days that the boats did get to the Banks the quantity of oysters taken was so small [not above two hundred] as to leave no encouragement to the divers and boatmen to make the necessary exertions.' On top of this, the commissioners ran into trouble over their fixing of the remission, part of the way through the fishery, at a rate below that which had been promised the boat holders in the original proclamation. Indeed, North was so uneasy about this that in Madras he asked Lord Mornington to disavow it officially. This was done in a directive from the Council of the Supreme Government at Fort St George on 16 May, ordering that: 'the accounts of the late Fishery should be adjusted upon the terms of the original engagement with the purchase of the boats and setting out as a general principle: "As we are satisfied that the Permanence of the British Interests in India is inseparably connected with the Preservation of Public faith, we are desirous that this characteristic principle should be preserved throughout all the departments of Government.'"

The annulling of the commissioners' decision about the remissions was clear enough; what was left in the air was where the money was to come from to pay the original boat-holders, since the commissioners had, as directed, already sent their takings to the Supreme Government and Colombo.

When North left Ceylon at the end of March, he had named Col. Josias Champagné, now senior military officer (on the return of de Meuron to his regiment in India) as deputy Governor, and it was he who passed the problem of Col. Torrens on to the commissioners. Torrens, with singleminded devotion to his own interests, was pursuing his claims against one of the principal merchants involved in the fishery at Arripo, and Cleghorn was reluctant to use the law on his behalf since those who came to the fishery were under Government protection, unless they did anything in the fishery itself to forfeit that protection. The Commissioners took some steps in answer to Champagné's request but then regretted them and asked Champagné privately to 'knock the business on the head'. Writing to North, Cleghorn commented: 'Col. Torrens is here and gives us more plague than all the divers' . . . an accurate assessment, judging by all the letters in Cleghorn's records on the subject.

Inevitably the search for reasons to explain the failure of the fishery turned attention on to Turnour, who had recommended it, and Cleghorn was writing privately to North even before it ended, that Turnour: 'is completely under the management of his Dubash who may make him a bankrupt tomorrow. Our banksaal was robbed and upwards of 3,000 Pagodas' worth of pearls carried off. It was done I believe by the Dubash and Turnour dared not take the least step to an enquiry. I declare I am not sorry for the loss – we have abandoned our speculations of the profit or propriety of which I had always great doubts.' North's reply to this point showed little sign of his later moral outrage: 'I am sorry for the business of the banksaal and particularly for the weakness of one of the Co-partners. I am afraid that beaupère and belle-mère are a little in the Dubash style.'

There was only one other reference in Cleghorn's papers to the venture. It came in a letter of Turnour's in December 1790. This was mainly about Cleghorn and MacDowall living in the castle at Arripo and sharing with Turnour the 'little bungalow' as a common dining apartment. At the end, he said how ready he was to take 'a chance in this concern'. As there is no mention in the later indictment of Cleghorn of this concern, and as North obviously knew about it and did not include it in his charges, it must have been above board. Cleghorn for his part had good reason to recall earlier reflections on his own impulsiveness in judging character: 'Giving way to sudden impressions and preferring the distress of disappointment to the constant vexation of suspicion'[22] – though in this case the distress was indefinitely prolonged.

There remained the financial and administrative loose ends of the fishery to deal with. The commissioners had sent twelve bills of exchange payable at Madras (the purchase price for the boats) to the Supreme Government as directed. They now had to write to Lord Mornington explaining that the fishery 'has been so unproductive as not to balance the one third of the purchase price paid in advance by the speculators, and we have not the means of paying them the difference in cash' (this had been sent to Colombo). They were therefore giving the council notice that they proposed: 'to suspend the payment of the Bills on Madras – and we shall induce the speculators in lieu thereof to grant others for the exact sums due to government.' To North they sent: 'a list of the Boats sold by public outcry and private contract during the Fishery – the total number of boats to 344 including 26 fished on account of government. The total price received amounts to Porto Novo Pagodas 86398. To the above sum is to be added 33½ lbs, of pearls, the produce of the Boats fished on account of Government which as we could not find purchasers . . . we shall carry to Colombo to be disposed of as Government may direct. The pearls from the boats fished in

Ammani amounting to 53 [lbs] are likewise unsold and shall be carried with the former to Colombo.'

Officially the 1799 Pearl Fishery was wound up on 23 April and Cleghorn was back in Colombo by 1 May, having in health 'held out better than either of my colleagues', McDowall being afflicted with boils and Turnour with 'fear of smallpox' – but he spoke too soon for he developed some sort of feverish complaint caught from 'the putrid exhalations of the oysters at Arripo'. However, he threw it off and had to set about explaining the failure of the enterprise he had backed so wholeheartedly. He wrote on 2 May to North: 'I confess I was deceived and I regret that I may have been the means of deceiving you . . . When Turnour asserted that there was full fishing for 350 boats, I naturally concluded that each boat would have daily averaged what would be considered a full day's fishing and did not conceive it to mean, as it has since been explained, that the extent of the Bank could allow 350 boats to anchor upon it . . . Turnour's plans which looked so well on paper, were all fallacious in practice.'

Cleghorn went on ruefully to hope that North had not been as explicit in his claims for a productive fishery as Cleghorn had been in writing to Dundas. Similarly apologetic letters reflecting Cleghorn's disappointment had to be sent off to Dundas himself[23] and William Petrie in Madras. But in financial terms as North pointed out in a letter to Lord Mornington (30 April 1799), what his Government had suffered, through the failure of the fishery, 'was in fact only a Diminution of Profit and a failure in the Resources of Government, not an actual charge on its revenue.' But failure was there, and it was Cleghorn's, and there was no escaping it.[24]

13

An Engineered Disgrace
April 1799 – February 1800

In the weeks which followed the failure of the pearl fishery, the letters which passed between North and Cleghorn were friendly enough in tone in April. Cleghorn, responding to a suggestion by North to shift John MacDowall from the post of Sub-secretary, wrote: 'For my own part I certainly do not wish to part with MacDowall whom I consider as a man both of talents for Business and the strictest integrity. But if Business could be carried on better or more smoothly I do not care though the Devil was my Deputy – and I dare say you think he would be a proper assistant to such a principal.'[1] If Cleghorn could mock his own explosive personality and expect the Governor to enjoy the mild joke, relations were not yet too strained. On 11 May North wrote to tell Cleghorn of the British victory over Tippū Sahib at Seringapatam and then wrote again when he heard that John, Cleghorn's eldest son, who had been in the battle, was safe and had 'behaved very well in every respect during the whole campaign'.

On 13 June North asked Cleghorn to send him information on 'the sum total produced by the Pearl Fishery', and continued: 'I have got a very good form for your accounts drawn up which I will send you tomorrow and which will facilitate your labour exceedingly.' Three days later North was writing to the Lieutenant Governor officially directing him to obtain from the commissioners of the late pearl fishery a statement of what it had yielded and saying that 'in an early stage of their Commission', he had sent them forms from Colombo for their accounts, 'to be kept and forwarded to the Government.' He set out the heads under which information was to be provided and the whole tone of his directive was sharp and critical. When he received this from

Champagné, Cleghorn, responding to the tone, wrote to North to explain:

'I have been pressing MacDowall to have the accounts ready that they might be presented for your inspection whenever you called for them but his Dubash, Narrain, was taken very ill and asked three weeks permission to go to Rameswaram. He had not yet returned tho' he is now on his way here. I took upon myself some time ago to write to Narrain and to desire him to lose no time in coming to Colombo to get the accounts ready and from what I have heard MacDowall say, I suspect they cannot be made out before he arrives. This circumstance cannot now create much delay . . . ' and he goes on to report progress on a review of justice and revenue which North had asked him to draw up. Cleghorn next reported the measures he had taken to deal with one Petitpas, suspected of being a spy, and when North wrote telling him that he would not yet be able to return to Ceylon because of painful toes – 'applying a burning ploughshare to them would not give them more pain' – Cleghorn responded at once sympathetically and ended his letter light-heartedly enough:

'I am now a country gentleman and sleep at my Bungalow. Champagné one of the best men that exists, Blair's horse is as fat as himself and these are all the articles which the Colombo Gazette at present furnishes.' Apart from his work, Cleghorn was at this point enjoying himself in seeing to the selection, boring and stringing of two sets of pearls: one for Dundas, who had given him a commission for a necklace of the choicest pearls for Lady Jane Dundas, his wife, and the other presumably for Cleghorn's own wife, Rachel.

However, the three commissioners had met to draw up their official reply to the governor's letter, defending themselves from his censure and maintaining that they had not in fact received any forms at all on the way in which their accounts should be presented, while they *had* sent him a list of the boats and their purchasers and the amount paid by each purchaser. They ended: 'We are unwilling to contrast the former letters we have had the honour and pleasure to receive from Your Excellency to that to which we are reluctantly obliged to refer . . . We are persuaded that a mind so candid as yours will be happy to have an opportunity of doing away a with censure on our conduct . . . '

How wrong they were!

Cleghorn might irritate North, who at this time was writing from Madras to his sister: 'Cleghorn never does anything in his official capacity but passes his time in railing at me or in getting false accounts for Dundas of the tenure of property under the Sinhalese.'[2] But it was John MacDowall whom North was really gunning for on his return to Ceylon. He exploded in his report to the Secret Committee of the East India Company:

'But the violence of Mr. MacDowall, the Head of that Party [i.e. the British civil servants from Madras] has so far exceeded the bounds of Prudence, that it has broken out into acts of positive and direct Disobedience to my orders and those of the Lieutenant Governor during my absence and into the most contumelious and indecent Reflections on our Government in his official correspondence with an agent whom I allowed him to nominate . . . the sneering and contemptuous style of this letter bears too strong internal evidence of its being an Ebullition of habitual Rancour and opposition to me to attribute it to the momentary Impulse of Passion or Imprudence.'[3]

The letter had obviously touched a raw nerve in North but there were some grounds for taking action against MacDowall: that he had more than once refused to accept officially nominated Sinhalese headmen; that he had not yet arranged for the remissions promised to the boatholders at the pearl fishery; that his accounts were 'totally silent with regard to the amount of the Proceeds of Rice (2752 bags) purchased by Government or issued from public stores here and conveyed to the Commissioners at Arripo'. On these grounds, North suspended MacDowall from his posts and asked Major General Hay MacDowall, new senior military officer, who was in the vicinity of Mannar, to make a detour via Arripo and go into the whole question of receipt, storage and disposal of the rice which Government had sent there.

That Cleghorn was not under any cloud but that of the failure of the pearl fishery at this point was shown by North's plans to send him on a mission to Kandy. Before he went to Madras, North had met the Adigar (Prime Minister) to the King of Kandy and, as there was now a new King, it was obviously a good opportunity to make another approach. Cleghorn, replying to North, was happy at the prospect and full of plans on those he should take with him.

The next letter Cleghorn wrote to North on 12 August was in fact the last of his to the Governor that has survived:[4] the situation had changed and Cleghorn was obviously endeavouring to respond to a battery of accusation North had fired against him. The first was on the subject of the rice sent to the pearl fishery. 'There is no denying', Cleghorn wrote in reply, 'the justice of your remarks with respect to the responsibility of the Commissioners to indemnify Government for the full loss it has sustained . . . When the Government rice arrived, it was marked in our minutes and ordered to be sold at the price fixed by you. And I believed this to be as really done as if the business was transacted before my own eyes' – no defence in law, but a truthful statement of Cleghorn's inattention when it came to financial minutiae. The responsibility for the rice had been claimed by MacDowall and the others had accepted it. The next accusation concerned MacDowall's taking himself off to Mannar to meet North. Cleghorn's disclaimer showed again how little idea he had of the blaze of North's anger:

'I never imagined I had the smallest power to grant leave of absence to any person, except perhaps a clerk in my own office. When Mr. MacDowall notified to me his intention of meeting you at Mannar I observed that there were none here who could grant him permission. I think he replied that a Collector required none to visit any part of his own district. This appeared to be reasonable. And in truth I thought no more of it, till it was recalled by your letter.' As for Cleghorn himself: 'I know I cannot leave my office without your orders, or leave asked and obtained.' He went on to accept North's decision to delay his embassy – 'that will surely not hurt our interests at Kandy.'

Somewhere in the middle of July North was back in Ceylon, and: 'Government has passed on a sudden from the extreme of remissness to that of severity,' as Cleghorn commented in a letter to Captain Walker, and continued: 'Mr. North in passing from Trincomalee by land to this place, beat the Tom-Tom at many villages soliciting complaints. Among the many he received some impeached the conduct of the native agents of the late Pearl Fishery.'[5] As a result North fired off a volley of orders: the Fort Adjutant at Jaffna was to arrest Narrain Swamy Naich ('Cash keeper at the late Pearl Fishery') and to: 'Seize all papers, obas and other writings . . . together with all such trunks, chests and cases as cannot be opened.' Jaggaloo Naich, father-in-law to Narrain Swamy was to be arrested and all his papers and trunks seized; Nagapilinga Pillah, at Ramnad on the Carnatic coast, was arrested and sent to Ceylon. All these, with other Sinhalese witnesses were brought as prisoners to the Fort at Colombo and Narrain was kept 'in irons to force him to a confession'.

In the meantime, General Hay MacDowall had been carrying out his investigations at Arripo into the government rice and had come to the conclusion that there had been no fraud. It was true, he said, that John MacDowall had taken responsibility on himself for this aspect of the fishery: 'The rice which was sent to Kandatzie was invariably consigned to the Collector nor did the other Commissioners after perusing the Bills of Lading conceive they ought to interfere further than in regulating the price and directing the sale; indeed it would appear that a discussion had taken place on this subject but when Mr. MacDowall showed the Bills of Lading addressed to him individually, Mr. Cleghorn and Mr. Turnour were silent.'

General Hay MacDowall described how he had 'with scrupulous exactness' measured the quantity of rice in purrahs and counted the number in bags, and: 'I am happy in having it in my power to affirm that since the Rice was deposited here, no collusion, artifice or stratagem has been made use of to defraud the Government or impose upon the Lieutenant Governor during Your Excellency's absence.' True, MacDowall had been careless in not measuring all the rice received from the vessels at Kandatzie and in not reporting the balance and state of the rice to Government at the end of the fishery. 'These however, Sir, are but venial trespasses. Mr. MacDowall is completely acquitted.'[6] As a result, North reinstated him in his offices – only to dismiss him a month or so later, 'for an offence not connected with the Fishery and in itself of no criminality,'[7] as Cleghorn reported to William Petrie in October.

In the meantime, on 3 September, North had appointed a commission 'for the purpose of Investigating the Administration of the late Pearl Fishery at Arripo'. The three investigators were General Hay MacDowall, Col. Josias Champagné and Justice James Dunkin. (North's private opinion of his Chief Justice was expressed in a letter to Sylvester Douglas, his brother-in-law: 'My good old Dunkin twaddles dreadfully and will not live a year longer being now 110 years of age.'[8]) The commission worked in secret for three months and finally presented their report to North on 11 December 1799. They were three agonising months for Cleghorn, partly because he was so isolated. His own personal secretary, Gavin Hamilton, had left him because he had been offered promotion by the Governor. This desertion was particularly painful to Cleghorn because it had been Hamilton: 'whom I relieved from distress . . . paid his passage and advanced £500 at a time inconvenient for myself.' But it also caused Cleghorn some fear because: 'I may without breach of charity, infer that he has communicated to the Governor the careless expressions of my conversation, as well as the laboured details of my public correspondence.' It made it no easier that he had no one but himself to blame for the cutting edge of his own vigorous style. Cleghorn was writing with this freedom to Captain Alexander Walker in Bombay. He goes on: 'I have here no friend and no acquaintance of any standing.' He hesitated to ask Walker outright to stand by him but came very near it: 'It is impossible for me to express how much may depend upon the testimony of a friend who has known me for so many years, and who has had so many opportunities to witnessing my conduct.'[9] Walker wrote sympathetically but did not – or could not – come.

On 5 October Cleghorn was writing to Dundas, sending him: 'a memorial concerning the Administration of Justice and Revenue in the Island of Ceylon under the Dutch Government.'[10] He had also obtained: 'the necessary papers concerning the arrears claimed by the Regiment de Meuron – both the original and translations shall be forwarded to you by the first opportunity.' (The question of these arrears seems to have permanently soured the attitude of the de Meurons and their descendants towards Cleghorn, as may be seen in Guy de Meuron's history of the Regiment.[11]) He went over again his disappointment that the pearl fishery: 'instead of realising four or five Lacs of Pagodas, has hardly yielded one.' He is careful not to complain to Dundas about the Governor except to say: 'It has been unfortunate that the absence of His Excellency for near five months from the seat of government prevented him from sending us such orders or Instructions as he might have deemed necessary.' He went on to describe the setting up of the commission and their taking of evidence in secret, and continued:

'I have little experience of the character of the natives of this country tho' I'm told their testimony seldom spares such as can give them no favour or protection,' and rather desperately he wrote: 'And as a man of veracity, I affirm for myself that I never during the Fishery, nor on an other occasion, ever received a single pagoda.' He wrote in the same vein to William Petrie in Madras, adding: 'If the truth only comes out I have nothing to fear but I confess I am afraid of native depositions when by criminating the Commissioners [of the pearl fishery] they gratify the Governor and when, of course, by not doing so they proscribe themselves.' On 9 December Cleghorn was writing to Walker: 'I hope however a few days more will bring their proceedings [i.e. the report of the committee of investigation] to our knowledge and we will then have an opportunity of making our defence.' And coming back to this, he ends his letter: 'I meant at all events to have gone home with my very moderate fortune in the Cinnamon Ships but I now will not turn towards home, till my Conduct has been cleared.'[12]

The report[13] was in fact published on 11 December 1799, and its findings must have been a more appalling blow to Cleghorn than anything he had envisaged.

The three investigators expressed their regrets at not having been able to question the Cash Keeper, Narrain's brother-in-law and brother, and 'Gopaul Naig and others whose examination might have thrown much light on many dark and nefarious transactions which took place in the various branches of the Fishery', and a servant who belonged to Mr Andrews was also missing. They also lamented: 'that Narrain on the sixth day that he appeared before us, positively refuse to answer the questions which were put to him.' Rather in the way of a sixteenth-century treason trial, they assumed the guilt of those on whose conduct they were sitting in judgement: 'We have not thought it necessary to call before us Messrs. Cleghorn, MacDowall and Turnour as no Interrogatories could have been put by us to them from which we could expect satisfactory replies'!

They first criticised Cleghorn and Turnour for advocating the holding of a fishery at all in 1799 and then pointed out that they had never rendered an account for the oysters which were fished during the trial. Secondly, they asserted that the Malabar Writing, which was prepared by the commissioners and publicly proclaimed just before the first sale of boats by public auction, induced many to purchase boats at a high price. The commissioners were in this case guilty of gross deception for financial gain. Thirdly, the Government was cheated out of the best pearls fished by government boats at Ammani by the commissioners' total lack of supervision of the Ammani banksaals where the Government oysters were stored. From these not only Narrain and his family took their pick, but the coollies washing the pearls were, in return for bribes, allowed to carry some away. Fourthly, the commissioners had not offered the pearls from the Government Banksaals for sale at the fishery, as they claimed they had, but had them carried to Colombo: '33½ lbs of Pearls produced by the Boats fished on account of Government . . . with 53 pounds more, the produce of the Ammani fishing.' But it should have been more and when the pearls were examined at Colombo not only had all the choicest Ammani pearls gone, but the total value was less than that stated by the commissioners, who were thus guilty of another fraud.

The fifth accusation concerned Cleghorn alone: on the evidence of Narrain (before he dried up), Cleghorn had 'clandestinely secreted and carried off a quantity of selected pearls'. At Colombo Cleghorn had employed a pearl driller: 'to bore pearls at his bungalow near Colombo for fifteen days to the number of 2,600.' A pearl stringer gave evidence that he had been at Cleghorn's bungalow for two days to string these pearls. On this question of stealing, Cleghorn was also accused by Jaggaloo Naig (Narrain's father-in-law) of putting into Jaggaloo's hands: 'another collection of pearls which we desired him to keep as they were afterwards to be valued. Jaggaloo Naig then pointed out a chest which stood in the room where we sat examining him and which he said contained the pearls he was speaking of, when removed from his house after his arrest . . . ' So the three investigators opened the chest and found two sealed bags of pearls. 'The bag said to belong to Mr. Cleghorn (and which we believe to be the case from having found a small bit of paper enclosed with a portion of the pearls containing what follows we think in his handwriting: "No. 3: Bad") contained 2 pounds and nearly one third of pearls apparently of good quality and which were valued by the Pearl Merchants at Porte Novo Pagodas 847.'

The investigators then go in some detail into accusations against Narrian, his family and associates but come back to the commissioners with the sixth main accusation – that Cleghorn and MacDowall had ordered Narrian to fabricate a second set of accounts after the fishery was over, which cheated the Government out of 26 lbs of pearls.

The general conclusion of this committee of investigation was that: 'great and manifold abuses paraded in almost every department [of the fishery] and it is evident that owing to the remissness and inattention of the superintendents the Honourable Company's interests have been sacrificed deliberately and systematically and that Government has been defrauded to a very considerable amount, particularly in the Ammani Fishing and in the collection of the Sea Customs. It appears from the evidence of almost every person whom we have examined that the gentlemen to whom Your Excellency confided the management of the Pearl Fishery delegated their authority to Narrain Swamy Naig, a common Dubash, who seems from its commencement to its conclusion to have been constantly occupied in acts of extortion and embezzlement and in which he has been actively assisted by numerous accomplices, his relations and friends.' These were the essential points of a lengthy report and the day after he received it North was writing to Dunkin to ask him about the Governor's powers to proceed against the commissioners whether by criminal prosecution or by civil action for damages, and if such a case could be heard in the Supreme Court of Fort William in Bengal or should be sent to London.[14] We do not have Dunkin's answer but it must have discouraged North from immediate action, except for officially suspending Cleghorn from office.

Cleghorn, for his part, when he heard that he was charged with stealing pearls, in a revulsion of feeling, took every pearl in his possession and deposited them in the Treasury. He seems to have tried to explain to North about the commission he had been given, 'by a person of rank', for a choice set, which explained his possession of the pearls which he had asked Narrain to purchase. That he had not yet settled with Narrain was not a charge upon his honesty, since he acknowledged the debt. The trouble was that he had been told of the charges against him but not the evidence on which they were based: this made specific defence difficult. But it was entirely in character that, where his honesty was impugned, any calculation of financial advantage would go by the board: he would rid his house of everything which called to mind the humiliating charges brought against him.

A month later North was writing to the Court of Directors[15] on the report on the pearl fisheries. His own comments with their unctuous moral tone, their heavy sarcasm and their scarcely suppressed glee at the report's condemnation of Cleghorn and MacDowall, make distasteful reading. He worked in a peculiarly humiliating reference to Cleghorn by a skilful negative: 'These are circumstances [i.e. those proving the commissioners' negligence and dishonesty] not depending on future proof, not resting like the story of the pipkin-full of pearls emptied by Mr. Cleghorn into his handkerchief on the unsupported assertion of a rogue, but solemn facts . . . ' The story of the pipkin (or bowlful of pearls) did not in fact appear in the report so it was brought in quite gratuitiously by North. He got back into his stride with:

'Common fame, a fallacious Guide indeed and one whose authority they may fairly dispute but no contemptible Informer, had certainly carried to every ear but theirs, long before the close of the Fishery, an account of the Fraud, Oppression and Rapine of their Servants; and the positive Evidence of all men there will inform you what was the general opinion of the Oriental Seclusion in which they sheltered themselves against the noisy voice of Remonstrance or Complaint.' There followed more sarcasm at the expense of the commissioners and then: 'I have contented myself with requiring from them an obligation to answer any suit which the Company may bring against them within three years.' Then he was back again on to his high moral horse:

'There is one point however in which I am Judge in the First Instance and in which I should have considered a Delay of Judgement as a Betrayal of my Duty. I mean my official animadversion on their official misconduct. I have exercised the discretionary Powers which I possess to this effect so far as His Majesty's Commission and Instructions has entrusted me with them in the case of Mr. Cleghorn. [He is referring here to his suspension of Cleghorn from office.] If they have been improperly exercised, I myself lie fairly open to the retributive Justice of Government. But whatever be my Fate, my Conscience will never allow me to regret that I have not contributed to the degredation of our national character and the Dilapidation of our

National Resources, by overlooking gross and Scandalous Negligence and by encouraging in the Guardians of the public Interests that dangerous System of blind and idle Confidence in Agents of known Intrigue and Improbity which has proved the Scourge of our Subjects and will prove the Ruin of our Employers.'

The last point in North's report informed the Court of Directors that in place of Cleghorn and MacDowall he had appointed: 'the first assistant secretary, Mr. William Boyd . . . to whose merit I feel it impossible to do justice . . . To his assiduity, I attribute almost all the Regularity which exists in any of the Departments of this infant Government; to his penetration I owe the Discovery of almost every Fraud, to his Integrity, the prevention or Correction of almost every abuse . . . '

North informed Cleghorn, MacDowall and Turnour of the charges which had been brought against them, so that: 'a specific denial or satisfactory explanation on their part may in the first instance accompany these allegations to those to whom it is my duty to submit them.' He went on to say that he enclosed Cleghorn's reply to him in which he rebutted these charges. Unfortunately this is not among the records which survive; in fact there is nothing among the Cleghorn Papers either which throws any light on what Cleghorn said in his own defence. Certainly he was given no opportunity to confront Narrain or any of his accusers. North simply stated: 'It is impossible that they can be heard in a Regular Defence of themselves till I know in what manner the Court of Directors will proceed on the Information I now send them.' It is not clear why North thought this but the course of action he decided upon, that is, passing the whole issue to London, ensured for the three accused the maximum of uncertainty, delay and local humiliation. MacDowall took himself off to Madras, Turnour to Mannar and Cleghorn was left in Colombo – isolated and disgraced. He must have decided that with the whole business referred to London, which meant indefinite postponement, he stood no chance of clearing his name in Ceylon so he returned with the cinnamon ships to England, leaving Colombo at the beginning of February 1800.

North, writing to Lord Mornington on 3 February, was jubilant: 'Heaven be praised, the "William Pitt" and the "Preston" have weighed anchor from this place . . . Cleghorn is gone on the "Preston" . . . '[16] And of course these ships took with them North's critical dispatches. That it was a wretched time for Cleghorn was attested by North himself when he was writing to Dundas about Cleghorn's suspension: 'I have suffered so much from the idea of the sufferings which in the course of my duty I have been obliged to bring on him that I should rejoice extremely at hearing that he is not harshly or discreditably treated.' But at the same time he was expressing his delight in his letters to his brother-in-law about the 'departure of my beloved Hugs', who: 'I daresay has persuaded Dundas of his entire purity, great knowledge of Business and unremitting attention to his duty.'[17]

By the end of the summer Cleghorn was in St Andrews. On his arrival in England he had written to Dundas, who had put off seeing him because of the nature of the charges which had been brought against him, the evidence for which North had sent to the India House, and Dundas had not yet had the opportunity to study. But Dundas left North in no doubt of his disapproval of the way North had acted towards Cleghorn. In a letter written on 15 July, Dundas fairly weighed in to North.[18] First, he implied that if North wanted to get rid of Cleghorn, he had chosen a pretty shabby way of going about it: 'It is several months since I communicated to Mr. Douglas my intention of recalling Mr. Cleghorn on account of the misunderstanding which appeared to have taken place between you and him: for although Mr. Cleghorn was appointed to the situation of Secretary in part of his reward for very important services performed by him relative to Ceylon at a very critical moment, it is impossible to leave a person Secretary to a Government, who was not on the best habits with the Governor . . . If matters had remained on that footing, the mode of proceeding would have been short and simple.'

Dundas went on to tick North off pretty sharply for the form of moral blackmail he attempted towards authority at home by threatening to resign if all his actions were not approved by government: 'If I discovered any defect such as in my judgement rendered you unfit to remain in your Government, it would be my duty to advise His Majesty to recall you, 'without being desired by you to do so.' Dundas also took North to task for his expressions of anxiety for Dundas' own reputation: 'I really do not exactly understand the extent of your feeling upon it when you sometimes mention an anxiety on my account. I really feel no anxiety of any kind on that score. When Mr. Cleghorn says he was commissioned by a Person of Rank to buy a set of Pearls, he means me and speaks true. I did tell Lady Jane that I would make her such a present from the produce of one of my own conquests and meaning them for that purpose . . . If in the execution of that Commission, Mr. Cleghorn purloined pearls in place of purchasing them . . . I am not in any degree apprehensive that he will be supposed to have received my sanction for the abuse nor do I find the smallest apprehension that my impartiality will be one grain the less on examining that part of the charge than it will be on the investigation of every other.'

It is a pity that we do not have North's letter which touched off this furious response from Dundas but the last three salvoes he fired were surely well on target. First, he criticised the appointment of two soldiers as investigators: their training in no way fitted them for judging evidence. It would have been better to have asked Lord Clive in Madras for 'one or two of the most approved of the servants of experience in business to have been employed on the Committee'. Secondly, Dundas criticised the appointment of William Boyd (on whom North could never lavish enough praise) as secretary to the Committee, 'for such an appointment was liable to the imputation of a person, bearing an active part in an enquiry which might lead ultimately to his own benefit.' In fact North *had* made Boyd Deputy Secretary in the place of Cleghorn and MacDowall. (And he went further: he told Douglas that he was 'ready to give £2,000' to secure a post for Boyd in the administration at home.) Thirdly, 'I cannot help regretting', Dundas wrote, 'that the persons accused were not confronted on the spot and in the presence of the Committee with witnesses adduced against them, particularly Narrain. I am sure if that had taken place and had been skilfully conducted it would have led to a discovery of the truth more speedily and efficiently than there is a prospect of in any other way.'

There, certainly, Cleghorn would have been in full agreement although nothing of his in which he set out his own defence survives. Dundas went on to observe on Cleghorn: 'As he is now come home under a direct charge of criminality, his case as a matter of Justice must undergo an accurate investigation and that can with propriety be done only by referring the whole papers to such Counsel for the Crown or Company as are generally resorted to on such occasions. This will be more tedious than I could wish but there is no help for it.'

This considerable broadside did not have the effect on North of provoking him to resign. The Douglases feared it might: 'Your sister and I often talk . . . with apprehension that it may have induced you to take some still more hasty steps when you received it.' But North had no thought of resignation. He was writing to his sister in July of 1800 about his enjoyment of sea-bathing in Ceylon: 'I hope to bathe stoutly through my remaining three years until I have my 30,000 yellow boys [i.e. guineas] snug in my pocket.' And in another letter: 'I shall be really comfortable if . . . they do not send me another owl of a Secretary in the Hugs style.'[19]

In his official reply to Dundas, North rebutted every criticism and ended: 'All I require is a fair and dispassionate examination of my measures and the right of vindicating them and explaining my reasons for adopting them. [It did not seem to occur to him that he had denied this to Cleghorn.] . . . In relations as complicated and multifarious as those in which I have been engaged in an unknown country, after a crooked and suspicious administration, many errors may have been, or may appear to have been committed. I am at present conscious of very few; if more are discovered and pointed out, I will kiss the rod.'[20]

This impenetrable self-righteousness can be seen again in his total absence of self-reproach when he broke his promises to the Adigar of Kandy and the Pretender to its throne, and sent a British military expedition to disgrace and death in 1803. But North escaped 'all official censure for his crooked dealings . . . doubtless he has strong influence at home'.[21]

In the event it was not till 1802 that the case against Cleghorn and the other commissioners of the pearl fishery of 1799 was examined by Henry Smith of the East India Company. In June 1801 William Adam, Cleghorn's friend, had written to Robert Orme, Solicitor to the East India Company in Madras, to engage him to act on Cleghorn's behalf and Cleghorn had also written and sent him 'sundry papers'.[22] Henry Smith's report was submitted on 3 September 1802. It represents a level-headed, legal assessment of the case brought in December 1799 against the commissioners and dealt in detail with each of the charges. He accepted that there were frauds, abuses and corruption committed at the fishery. That the commissioners were 'parties to the greater part of these offences' rests on the testimony of those who admit themselves to be guilty, and: 'as the Commissioners were not present when the witnesses were examined and had no opportunity of confronting them, what they [the witnesses] have said must be received with reserve.'[23]

On the first part of the first charge against Cleghorn and Turnour (that they 'did not fairly and truly report to Government the state in which the Pearl Banks were found on the Examination previous to the Fishery') Smith gives the evidence. This is 'the translation of the Report made in the Malabar Language by the Pilot and Arapowers' which Lt. Turnour sent *together with the original* to the Governor. 'If he meant any wilful misrepresentation he was open to immediate detection and therefore I think this charge can affect the Superintendents no further than it shows their anxious wish that a Fishery at all events should take place.'

The second part of the first charge was that Cleghorn and Turnour had not accounted to Government for the pearls collected from the oysters taken on the examination of the Banks. Smith went on: 'both admit to the fact and state that they looked upon them as their perquisite out of which they defrayed certain expences of arrack, drams etc, to the Divers, which were not charged to the Company and that after deducting those expenses the value of the pearls they kept amounted only to 130 P.N. Pagodas.'

The second charge was that: 'the numbers of oysters taken on account of Government were not accounted for.' In their accounts the superintendents had given only the number of pearls produced for Government, not the number of oysters. The evidence was clear that Narrain had sold oysters from the Company's banksaal; what was not clear was that the superintendents had connived at this.

The third charge – that 'the most valuable pearls allocated from the Company's oysters were taken away and never brought to their account' – led to the same conclusion: that the best pearls taken at the fishery had certainly disappeared before they could be sold for the Government, 'but there is no evidence which fixes the Commissioners with any privity to their being purloined.'

The fourth charge concerned Cleghorn alone and is now given in full: 'Narrain (who admits that he was party to all the mal-practices which went forward at the Fishery) states that Mr. Cleghorn came into the Banksaal one morning and emptied an earthenware pot of picked pearls into his Handkerchief, telling Narrain to keep it secret. Narrain's Father-in-Law called Jaggaloo Naig, and other persons prove that afterwards they bored and strung sundry pearls for Mr. Cleghorn at his Bungalow, just out of the suburbs of Colombo, and a bag of pearls which Jaggaloo said were Mr. Cleghorn's property and delivered to him to be valued were found in Jaggaloo's house. The bag on inspection appeared to contain a note of the quality "bad" in Mr. Cleghorn's handwriting. This is the summary of all the Evidence on this Charge. The charge (but not the evidence) was communicated to Mr. Cleghorn; he denies having carried off any pearls from the Banksaal but states that he employed Narrain to purchase a set of pearls for him and that he [Narrain] brought two bags of pearls to his house which were bored and strung by Jaggaloo and others at his Bungalow and that two sets having been selected, he returned the remaining pearls to Jaggaloo – he did not pay Narrain for either set of pearls. After Narrain had been taken into custody to appear before the Commissioners of Enquiry, Mr. Cleghorn deposited the two sets of pearls in the Treasury; for whoever they might belong to, this was at his own request and upon his own suggestion as he did not consider the Pearls as his Property till paid for; if the transaction as explained by Mr. Cleghorn was "bona fide", it would have appeared more natural in him to have kept the Pearls and have offered to deposit their value. This is the only circumstance which creates any doubt in my mind as to this part of the Case. Nevertheless I cannot bring myself to think that Narrain's statement that Mr. Cleghorn carried the pearls off secretly from the Banksaal in the manner he described has any foundation.'

The fifth charge was that 86½ pounds of pearls were credited to the Company' account when there ought to have been 188 pounds. Moreover there was positive proof that: 'some of the Company's most valuable pearls were purloined. Whether the Superintendents were or were not blameable is a separate question.'

The sixth charge was that: 'Bribery, Corruption and Extortion were practised with respect to boats sold by private contract and upon shopkeepers, boat owners and others.' Here Smith pointed out that all the evidence for this was traced to Narrain, who admitted the charges. Yet it was on Narrain's evidence *alone* that the three superintendents were implicated. Furthermore, 'it is also proved that in some cases on complaints being made the Superintendents made Narrain pay back part of the sums he had received.'

The seventh charge was that some of the shell pearls were sold for 800 Pagodas but the Company had credit only for 550 Pagodas. Again, with this trifling fraud, 'there is no proof to bring it home to the privity of the Superintendents.'

The eighth charge was that: 'a much greater sum was received for Sea Customs than was carried to the Company's credit.' This charge was proved 'by the real accounts which were found in Narrain's house'. This time, Smith believed, there were grounds for suspicion of collusion by the superintendents in the fraud. The testimony of Narrain and Jaggaloo: 'leaves ground of suspicion that one thousand five hundred Pagodas out of the money received for Sea Customs was appropriated to the use of the Superintendents.'

The ninth and tenth charges Smith dismissed as trifling. (The ninth dealt with the levying of fines and the forfeiting of goods which were not brought to the credit of the Covernment; and the tenth with charging for expenses when 'in two instances, more was charged than was actually paid'.)

'The eleventh charge is most important viz: the fabrication of a complete set of false accounts in order to deceive the Government.' Smith went on: 'Of the existence of two sets of Accounts which differ from each other there cannot be the least doubt,' and he referred to evidence which he enclosed with his comments. 'Narrain stated that he was ordered to make out the fabricated accounts of the oysters by Mr. Cleghorn and Mr. MacDowall and that in the presence of Mr. Cleghorn and Mr. Turnour, Mr. MacDowall ordered him to make out the false accounts of the Sea Customs.' Again the accusation of the personal involvement of the superintendents in the fraud rested on Narrain's statement alone, and since the fabrication of the second set of accounts definitely took place after the fishery was over, when the superintendents had returned to Colombo and Mannar, this told against their personal involvement. On the other hand, the fishery had ended by 22 April and though they sent an account of the number of Boats sold and the number of oysters taken by each, they failed to note the number of oysters taken for the Company. And they were very tardy in rendering their accounts, had to be pressed twice for them (7 and 17 July 1799) and then could not say how many oysters the Company's pearls had been taken from. 'There is no other evidence', Smith concluded, 'which brings the fabrication of the false accounts against the Superintendents as their personal Act.'

It is the twelfth and last charge which really indicts the three superintendents of culpable irresponsibility: 'that the whole power of the Superintendents was delegated to Narrain and exercised in a most corrupt and scandalous manner, and that the Superintendents did not personally interfere either to watch the washing or sorting of the Pearls, or even, when washed or sorted, to take the charge of them, almost every part of the evidence proves, and that the Company was greatly plundered was equally evident; the Commissioners of enquiry estimate the Company's positive loss at upwards of 32,000 Porte Novo Pagodas.' Thus, in Smith's view, failure to superintend was what Cleghorn, MacDowall and Turnour had to answer, with the question of what happened to the Sea Customs needing further investigation. He concluded: 'I apprehend the evidence will not be thought sufficiently credible to ground upon it any positive charge of corruption against the Superintendents.'

The grounds for bringing a suit against them might be 'for an account of the produce of the Boats which fished for the Company'. The best form would be a bill in equity: 'it would have this convenience . . . that the testimony of the witnesses could be obtained under a commission to be executed in the Island of Ceylon . . . and the Supreme Court of Judicature of Madras where Mr. MacDowall (I believe) is resident, would be the proper tribunal to resort to.'

Smith's examination of and comment on the charges has meant some repetition but it amounts to a refutation of the *criminal* charges against Cleghorn, which were the ones which would have been most intolerable to him and which are the most incredible. Such reports by counsel for the East India Company did not automatically whitewash the accused as can be seen in the case of Robert Andrews, the previous superintendent of the pearl fisheries. His case also had to wait for legal opinion till 1802, and the counsel wrote: 'I am of the opinion that the information which was received respecting the conduct of Mr. Andrews . . . was

quite sufficient to create suspicion.' The Madras Government
should: 'proceed in the investigation, Mr. Andrews being called
on to attend . . . If there is a probable ground of charge, then
institute a proceeding at law *on a criminal charge* before the
Madras Judiciary where the witnesses and all the sources of proof
are at hand.'

In Cleghorn's case there is no record of any bill in equity
or suit for damages being brought in the Madras Courts, let
alone a criminal charge. North had seen in the failure of the
pearl fishery, and the subsequent accusations against the British
officials responsible, the opportunity to get rid of MacDowall
and Cleghorn at one sweep, seizing eagerly on any charge – the
more humiliating the better. As Cleghorn had written to Petrie
in October of 1799, all the native servants of the fishery and
a number of witnesses were being 'examined in secret by the
Governor and then sent to be examined in the same manner by
a Secret Committee appointed to investigate the whole detail of
the Fishery'. North had obviously seized on the story invented by
Narrain of the 'pipkin of pearls' stolen by Cleghorn, although the
investigating committee did not think it anywhere near credible
enough to include in their report. Cleghorn and the other two
commissioners had obviously been the dupes of Narrain, whom
they had allowed to get away with far too much.

Cleghorn could also be criticised for taking Turnour's expertise
too much for granted when he had recommended a full-scale
fishery. On the other hand, Turneur had taken part in the 1797
and 1798 fisheries and knew the locality. In North's Instructions,
responsibility had been firmly put upon MacDowall to appoint the
native agents for the fishery: he chose ill, but that cannot be laid at
Cleghorn's door. MacDowall, as Collector of Colombo, had the
financial expertise which Cleghorn lacked. Over thirty years later,
when he was considering with Andrew Bell what it was essential
for his grandsons to learn, he wrote:

'They must be educated to be men of business and the world;
a thorough knowledge of arithmetic and a progress in mathematics are not to be neglected . . . my own disgraceful ignorance,

particularly of the first, has been of infinite disadvantage to me in the different situations of my varied life.'[24] This ignorance certainly helps to explain why Cleghorn was so ready to leave the presenting of accounts to MacDowall. Why MacDowall left so much of this side in the hands of Narrain is a separate question.

Cleghorn had gone about selecting pearls for the necklace for Dundas and having them prepared so openly that he obviously regarded the whole operation as perfectly above board. His returning every single pearl in his bungalow to the Treasury was part of his impulsiveness: he had not yet paid for the pearls; he would not now pay Narrain, who had both duped him and then accused him of common theft. The knowledge that the Sinhalese made a practice of implicating Europeans in their own malpractices had given him warning – as in the case of Hobart and Adderly – but did not make it any easier when, having had the knife plunged in his back by Narrain, he found North twisting it in the wound with so much unction. And this character-assassination was made more bitter by the knowledge that in the course of the fishery Cleghorn had 'refused more money to grant favours than I shall ever possess', because he had been determined to uphold standards of honesty and integrity in the new British administration. But this same administration under North was only too ready to use the failure of and corruption in the fishery as a means to get rid of Cleghorn, although North must have known that he was not in fact guilty of the criminal charges brought against him. In any case the affair effectively brought to an end this stage of his career: no other opportunity of a place in the public service offered itself.

Dundas, in whom Cleghorn had trusted completely, had used him, rather meagrely rewarded him and did not unduly exert himself to see that his promises on family pensions were carried out. Of course the hounds were soon to gather on Dundas' own trail. He resigned in March of 1801 with Pitt. Addington, Pitt's successor, set up a committee of naval inquiry which in 1805 brought allegations of such seriousness against Dundas that they formed sufficient grounds for impeachment. Dundas resigned and never returned to office. Both he and Cleghorn had been guilty of negligence but not of the graver charges brought against them. But the circumstances in which they fell ensured that neither had any opportunity of ever holding office again.

14

St Andrews Again – Civil and Military
1800–1806

The circumstances in which Cleghorn left Ceylon must have left hurtful scars but he never referred to them in his surviving correspondence. There was no railing against anyone; no attempt at self-justification. His natural buoyancy began to reassert itself and his spirits rose at the prospect of reunion with his wife and children. He had achieved brilliant success and suffered undeserved humiliation in the East but in addition to satisfying his own desire for travel and adventure,[1] he believed he had achieved not only his main objective – the transfer of Ceylon to Britain – but also a secure income for his wife and daughters, independent of his own life. As he wrote to Rachel, his Ceylon venture 'was the only step which could have secured a permanent provision for you and the children'.[2]

He must have gone straight back to St Andrews because on 20 June 1800 Peter was writing to him there from London: 'I can assure you you were not far wrong in supposing I was very angry with you at your long and provoking silence and had it been one post later, I could not have received your last which has now put an end to all my troubles.'[3] John, his eldest son, writing from India, referred lightly to 'the unfortunate affair in Ceylon', hoping 'everything is settled to your satisfaction', and mainly concerned with the illness which led to the death of Peter MacGill – to whom Rachel, Cleghorn's eldest daughter was engaged.[4] (Peter bequeathed everything to Rachel. In the end, this amounted to about £800, but she remained single for life.)

Writing from India in November 1795, Cleghorn had asked Rachel to suggest to her brother, Col. John MacGill that they might together put up the necessary capital to buy a small estate[5] but that idea came to nothing. In 1797 Col. MacGill bought property on the north side of South Street:[6] Numbers 127 and 129. (Number 127 is now the general post office and in the middle of the nineteenth century was the home of Dr John Adamson, the pioneer of early photography.[7]) The Colonel had Jane, Cleghorn's second daughter, and his niece, to run his household and keep him company, until her marriage.[8] Cleghorn, himself, had not given up his ambition to put into action his ideas on improved farming methods. Moreover, property would, if carefully chosen, bring with it a vote, which he wanted. It was a privilege which acknowledged status and was not lightly regarded in rural Scotland. To become a voter it was necessary: to hold superiorities of the value of £400 Scots old valued rent; to hold this qualification for a year, since only those qualified could make a court; to elect the preses or chairman of this court, and generally to order the business of electing a county member. With this also in mind Cleghorn and Patrick Anderson, his Edinburgh lawyer, were on the look-out for property coming on the market. In 1801 Anderson was reporting that Stravithie was not for sale at present.[9] In December of that year Cleghorn bought Horseleys, 'that acre of land lying among the remanent acres of the Priory of St. Andrews', from the kirk Session of Kemback[10] and arranged a lease for grazing in the Abbey parks,[11] and in the next year was being advised by George Sandilands of Nuthill to go to the Angus markets for wethers.[12]

In May 1795 Cleghorn had remitted £800 for his wife and family from Venice to Col. MacGill by way of Switzerland,[13] and perhaps on his advice Rachel lent that same sum in 1795 to Dr Murison, Principal of St Mary's College in St Andrews, and as security had been given sasine of the 'lands of Gowkston' or Dewarsmiln on heritable bond by him,[14] on which he paid £40 interest a year to her. Dr Murison had acquired Dewarsmiln back in 1796 and was living at the neighbouring Denbrae, which was actually the property of David Martin. It was in May 1803 that Cleghorn decided to take advantage of his position with regard to Dewarsmiln. Anderson had £1,000 ready to be transmitted from Cleghorn to Murison 'when all the writings are signed'. Then Murison died suddenly, but 'left a Trust disposition of all his Property and the persons there named have power to grant all necessary deeds to complete the transaction with you', as Anderson wrote, adding: 'but I hope there will be no necessity to resort to their assistance.'[15] That Cleghorn acquired additional rights was shown in 1809 when he resigned them to David Wemyss WS and David Tod, and was paid £1,500 in part of the price for Dewarsmiln by Wemyss.[16]

Cleghorn's position over Denbrae is clearer, though complicated by his following the very general practice of the day in borrowing on land. In 1803 Cleghorn bought Denbrae from David Martin of Edenside, who had already at Martinmas of 1802 signed a heritable bond for £1,100 from him.[17] After Murison's death, Cleghorn began to pay interest on a bond from him to Murison's heirs, Mrs Lindesay and Col. Maitland.[18] Denbrae itself he sold to David Wemyss in 1810.[19] Cleghorn's motive in concerning himself with these properties is not clear; they did not bring with them any voting rights, nor did Cleghorn ever appear to have lived at Denbrae and certainly Cleghorn did not farm Dewarsmiln himself because the tenant, James Pringle, was in possession there during the period when Cleghorn was involved.

His principal purchase on his return from the East was in St Andrews itself: on 17 December 1800 Cleghorn bought the south range of St Leonards College buildings, which at the time was known as St Leonards Lodge.[20] This was indeed to announce his return to St Andrews with a flourish. Cleghorn had imagined only too vividly the sort of St Andrews tittle-tattle and innuendo Rachel had been subjected to while he had been away. He had written on his journey out east in 1795: 'If you do not like St. Andrews, the Colonel and you may go to any town in Scotland where my fortune can make you live.'[21] And from Ramnad after the transfer of the Régiment Meuron had been achieved: 'I hope you will not allow your mind to be in the least hurt with anything the Envy or Malevolence of the good Christians of St. Andrews can say.'[22] Now, on his return to his family, he could show both his former colleagues and the gossips of St. Andrews that his claims to have been on government service had been well founded, with rewards sufficient to ensure freedom from their sort of treadmill.

In 1773 Boswell described St Leonards as providing 'very comfortable and genteel accommodation' when Dr Johnson and he stayed there as guests of Professor Robert Watson.[23] It was only in the previous year that Professor Watson had bought St Leonards from the Principal and Masters of the United College,[24] who, since the union of St Leonards with St Salvators in 1747, had moved to North Street and had simply cobbled up a series of temporary and unsatisfactory leases of the St Leonards' sets of rooms, as application had been made for them. In 1770, for instance, they had to throw out one of their tenants, Bell, with his wife and daughter, because: 'they kept a bad house and were of bad fame.'[25] Bell had been in the south range (afterwards St Leonards Lodge) which had consisted of twenty sets of students' rooms, ten up and ten down, access to the upper ones being by outside staircases. Professor Watson, Principal after 1778, would have had to make considerable alterations to turn the building into a family house for his five daughters. Cleghorn, as a fellow professor with Watson, would certainly have visited and dined there in the 1770s.

Watson's sudden death, in December 1781, led to St Leonards Lodge being sold by his daughters to Sir William Erskine of Torry, who bequeathed it to his son on his death.[26] In 1800, therefore, Cleghorn was purchasing one of the more handsome and distinguished residences in St Andrews, as was shown in the Stent Roll of 1803, in which 'Mr. Cleghorn's house', assessed at £1/2/0, was the most highly rated in all South Street.[27] In addition to the whole range of the old college buildings, there were very pleasant gardens to the south again, enclosed on the west and south by Prior Hepburn's Wall, which he had built when he extended the old Priory Wall to include his new college after 1512. The garden's other attractions included its glass-houses. In September 1803 Anderson wrote appreciatively of a can of fruit sent to his wife in Edinburgh, 'filled with Grapes and Peaches in very High order, from the St. Leonards hothouses.'[28]

Once he was established in St Leonards, Cleghorn's hospitable instincts were allowed free rein. Patrick Anderson, who wanted to visit him on business asked about dates: 'I hear your mansion has been much crowded of late . . . your servants will need a recess.'[29] Cleghorn hoped to lure his friends, the Clarke family, from London to visit St Andrews. But Mrs Clarke, who was the letter-writer of the family – and a very endearing one too – could not commit her husband. Since Cleghorn was coming to London, she wrote: 'If you can bring half a dozen bottles of whisky, I will be satisfied. I say that to say something as you must have *a positive answer*. Never was such a *positive* man: how can I say that I *will* visit the land of whisky and fish in summer? I can only say I *hope* to do so . . . '[30] In the event, the visit was paid in the summer of 1806.[31] In another letter she teased Cleghorn:

'Tho' you may have made a little too free with the bottle after dinner, you were not quite so far gone as to send your letter without its proper cover; it appeared to be written with a very steady hand . . . .' She went on: 'As I said before, I think you are a set of very dissipated people in St. Andrews with your Pick Nick Suppers and I agree with Dr. Playfair and should not be at all surprised to hear of a masquerade next winter. I shall be very happy to be of the Fete Champêtre party in Dura Den . . . '[32] It seems fair enough to assume that Cleghorn's was the moving spirit behind these 'dissipations'. It was in 1802 that Cleghorn became Captain of the Company of St Andrews Golfers for the year, so he was well established in golfing circles – as the golf ball commemorating his year of office in the Royal and Ancient club-house showed.

He also set about picking up the threads of old friendships. George Sandilands of Nuthill replied to a letter from Cleghorn: 'It gives me I do assure you sincere pleasure to learn from such a good authority as your own that you are likely to become a stationary man amongst us and that we shall once more renew our old habits for, as to renewal of our friendships, this last never having sustained the slightest interruption on the part of either of us, we shall find it on our first meeting exactly as it stood at our parting.'[33] There were letters too from General Ross at Mugdrum[34] and Patrick Murray at Meigle, about visiting.[35]

His involvement with the young who came his way was also reflected in his letters. There is a tiny folded note, sealed with a large blob of red wax, enclosed in one of Mrs Clarke's letters: it was to Cleghorn from her youngest child, Mary Anne, whom he called his 'bonny lassie'. She called him her 'Man o' Man' and sent many spirited messages to him including bloodcurdling threats of what she would do to anyone who harmed him.[36] Sadly, the child died the following year.[37] Of the same family, Richard Clarke wrote from India, hoping that Cleghorn would find time to send him a letter.[38] Captain Alexander Vilant, son of a professor of the United College, wrote to Cleghorn from Trincomalee, worried that it would be some time before he could repay what Cleghorn had lent him. He added bitterly: 'I have written a very strong letter to my father . . . in hopes that he may be inclined to assist me a little in paying you: I don't expect he will . . . '[39] And Cleghorn took on what his wife had been doing for the previous years: writing to and supplying the needs of his sons. He sent John a theodolite: encyclopaedias and 'good English books'[40] chosen at his discretion. But 'half the Encyclopedias and some of the books were perfectly destroyed' on the journey, so 'the collection of plans and designs for public buildings of all descriptions' which John next wanted were to be 'packed in a white linen case and then in a wooden box'.[41]

Cleghorn went over to Glasgow in November 1801 to see Professor James Mylne at the University because Peter had been his student.[42] Mylne had considerable respect for Peter's abilities and obviously enjoyed exchanging ideas and books with Peter's father, who also did his duty by his son by paying his outstanding bills at the booksellers.[43] As far as his younger daughters were concerned, Cleghorn's main duty was to pay their school bills to Mrs Wilson, though they were nearly past that stage.

But what gave a bitter edge to these years of enjoyment was
the battle he had to wage with the Treasury for the pensions
for himself and his daughters which he had been promised by
Dundas.[44] On both his forays to the East, he had seen himself first
and foremost as a government official, not as a fortune hunter. As
he wrote to Rachel in November 1795 from Fort St George, when
he was being lionized by the English in Madras after the success
of his mission:

'I have refused very great situations here . . . but . . . I
reflected upon and determined in my own mind what the
Government at home had the right to expect of me. I am here by
Commission from the King and I am responsible to his Ministers
for my conduct. In this situation I neither feel it consistent with my
duty or my honour to accept of any employment which can make
me responsible to others. My fortune, by my present exertions,
must be improved. And you and my daughters must be provided
for. I am as rich as I wish to be, and I shall receive the most solid
of all recompences, that which a liberal mind derives from the
successful discharge of its duty.'[45] But in 1800 payment of the
pension, which his wife had been given while he was in India,
stopped.[46] Cleghorn was determined that he would fight to the
last ditch in Whitehall for his daughters' pensions. The provision
of these had been after all one of the main reasons for his Eastern
gamble. It proved a wearing campaign.

In February 1802 Cleghorn travelled down to London and took
lodgings at Number 4 Old Cavendish Street. His lawyer was
James Chalmers, to whom Cleghorn had handed over all the
papers that Andrew Stuart had held since Cleghorn's first journey
to India.[47] His main ally, however, was William Adam – whom
all knew and respected – and his main reliance had perforce to be
on Dundas: 'Whatever is done in the Secretary of State's Office
must be done thro' the medium of Dundas'[48] – and Dundas was
out of office, leaving the frugal Addington at the head of the
new ministry. Dundas, if not overtly sympathetic to Cleghorn's
claims, at any rate stood by his promise. In February 1802 he
wrote in answer to Adam's letter raising the matter:

'The Directors appear to me to act very strangely in stopping Mr. Cleghorn's pension. In a pecuniary point of view it will for some time be an advantage to the East India Company to be relieved of the expense of Ceylon; but independent of that circumstance, do they seriously maintain that the whole of their Indian Empire is not much more secure by the requisition of Ceylon than it was previous to that event? Upon that ground alone, they ought without cavil to have continued the Pension . . . '[49] On 23 June, Dundas sent a letter about the pension which Cleghorn agreed with Adam was very satisfactory, 'had I not been so long deceived by letters and promises.'[50] Cleghorn was right to be distrustful and was longing to leave London, 'scene of anxiety, idleness and expense.'[51] However, he waited till the end of the parliamentary session and could at least comfort himself with the knowledge that when William Adam saw Addington on his behalf, 'he admitted your claim and enlarged on your services and talent.'[52] But no official decision was made on how and from which fund the pensions were to be paid. As Dundas wrote to Cleghorn: 'Mr. Addington concurred with me in thinking that the provision for your family ought to remain as a debt to be paid by the East India company. They admit the justice of your claim but contend it should be paid out of the Revenues of Ceylon.'[53]

Cleghorn did not appreciate being the shuttlecock in this sporting contest between authorities. It must too have been painful to be rapped over the knuckles by Dundas for applying to the Treasury with the names of his daughters when he believed the warrant for the pensions had been authorised. Nevertheless, by the time Cleghorn returned to Scotland in July of 1802, some ground had been won, though he realised another approach to the Treasury would have to be undertaken.

Cleghorn's other anxiety in 1802 was the question of the pearl fishery of 1799: whether he would have to answer a charge or be faced with a bill in equity over the business, which he had given into the charge of Robert Orme, to act as lawyer on his behalf in Madras.[54] When Cleghorn asked William Adam whether it would be a good idea for him himself to go to Madras to clear his name,

Adam's answer was decisive: 'According to my recollection of your Bond, you are not required to return to India and should never think of it.'[55] This turned out to be wise advice because it was found by the East India Company counsel that Cleghorn had no case to answer.

In March 1803 Cleghorn took himself down to London again, for the next round with the Treasury. The help of his old allies was invoked and Dundas, now Lord Melville, saw Addington about: 'the claims you have on the justice of government. Mr. Addington admitted them and seemed hurt at the delay'[56] – a remark which must have left Cleghorn ruefully measuring degrees of pain! However, he saw Addington in Downing Street,[57] and Sargent at the Treasury,[58] and Castlereagh at the India Office.[59] He again supplied the names of his five daughters (Rachel, Jane, Anne, Hugh and Janet) and arranged trustees for Janet, the only one still under age.[60] In spite of this, Cleghorn's 1803 effort did not see the end of the campaign. In 1804 Dundas, now back at the Admiralty, was writing to Adam: 'I have received yours on the subject of Mr. Cleghorn. The delay is unpardonable and must be put to rights immediately.'[61] But 'immediately', in terms of Treasury action, meant Huskisson writing to Cleghorn in August 1804, asking (for the third time) the names of Cleghorn's daughters and whether any of them were under age. Cleghorn, thanking Adam for his exertions wrote optimistically: 'I have some hopes that their Pension is to be made payable immediately.' But the end of the year came and Adam was comforting Cleghorn with the reflection that the delay 'is mere stupidity in those who have to execute'.[62]

Cleghorn and his advocates were successful in the end over his daughters' pensions of £50 each a year for life, but the Treasury won a Parthian victory over Cleghorn's own pension. He had been promised £300 a year by Dundas, but the Scottish Exchequer would only bear £150 of this – and the Treasury simply shuffled out of paying the rest. Cleghorn wrote to Chalmers: 'The not obtaining that Pension of £150 a year, with arrears due upon it, is a very serious disappointment to me . . . '[63] It was a disappointment the effects of which he was to feel for the rest of his life.

A military imbroglio

The spring of 1804 saw Cleghorn fully embroiled in the affairs of the Royal St Andrews Volunteers. This transient body had been formed locally in response to the danger of French invasion in which the country stood from the renewal of war in 1803 until August 1805 (when Napoleon switched his armies from their camp at Boulogne to the Danube, to fight the armies of the Third Coalition). But the war which Addington planned against the French in 1803 was to be 'defensive and therefore cheaper'.[64] It would not, in Addington's view, be necessary to enlarge the army again after the drastic economies he had enforced after the signing of the Peace of Amiens. Instead, the government set itself in the first place to increase the militia. But, as the danger of invasion became more acute: 'the government appealed for volunteer companies to defend their country. The patriotic response was great . . . ' And among those coming forward were the St Andrews Volunteers, probably at the end of 1803. But the government had not thought out clear guide-lines on how the men were to be trained, equipped or paid, and these inadequacies were all clearly reflected in James Cheape's letters to Cleghorn concerning the St Andrews Volunteers.[65]

Lord Moira was at this time Commander-in-Chief in Scotland and was sending directions to the Lords Lieutenant in the counties where volunteers had been formed, to try to set on foot some system of training. The St Andrews corps was under the command of the Earl of Kellie, with James Cheape of Strathtyrum as Colonel, Cleghorn as Lieutenant Colonel and Cathcart Dempster as Major. Cheape's first letter, of 10 April 1804, to Cleghorn about the corps was concerned with the appointment of junior officers: 'Ensign Buchanan to be Lieutenant since Hay resigned; Mr. David Wright to be Ensign . . . ' and so on. He was writing to Cleghorn from George Street, Edinburgh, telling him how the previous week he had made the journey from Edinburgh to Cupar 'expressly for the purpose of attending a meeting of the Lieutenancy'. This had been chiefly marked by a clash over supplies, fought out between the Treasury and the Volunteers. Cheape went on:

'I am sorry to say that altho' no more than 345 against 1672, whatever we might be able to do in the field, they beat us hollow in the Cabinet; all that we were able to do was to save the Volunteers three shillings each in the price of their greatcoats.'

The contrast in numbers is quite interesting: over four times as many volunteers as militiamen. This was the pattern all over the country and the government had no idea how to cope, except to reduce expense allowances and to introduce new acts which further entangled the position. Certainly poor Col. Cheape became caught in the network. The previous Secretary at War, Charles Yorke, had in 1803 issued a directive which Cheape quoted to Cleghorn: 'It is intended to advance the Volunteers, in preparation to the time they may agree to assemble, a Sum not exceeding one Guinea for the function of assisting in providing Necessaries amongst which it is particularly desirable that great coats should be provided where they are wanted.' Lord Moira had made it clear that unless the various corps went on permanent duty for at least four weeks, they would not be entitled to the guinea. Col. Cheape therefore wanted to arrange a spell of permanent duty. 'It seems to me', he wrote to Cleghorn, 'that about 26 May will be the time our men can be most easily spared from their Agricultural occupations.' The best place to go for their basic training would be Dundee, in Cheape's view: 'As Dundee is so near and . . . our Officers and Men may have leave of absence when their occasions really require it. I hope . . . that they will have no objections.'

The articles of equipment that Cheape was concentrating on at this point were not weapons but greatcoats, 'good substantial shoes', hats and gaiters. 'I suspected', he wrote, 'that some of the hats and even gaiters had been worn privately which certainly tends to disfigure the appearance of the battalion,' – something in which no officer of a citizen army could take much pride, from Justice Shallow to the Home Guard of the 1940s.

Col. Cheape's problems originated from the time when in February 1804 he thought the Volunteers might really have to take the field to meet the French. At this point he had applied to Lord Kellie for permission to order greatcoats for the men, and, on receiving it, duly went ahead. But then it turned out, at a meeting on 7 April, that this could not be considered an 'act of the county' – which, he wrote ruefully to Cleghorn, 'occasioned me not to persist in my objection to 12/- out of the 15/- being deducted from the marching Guinea.' Nobody was at all clear on, or ready to take the responsibility of ordering the greatcoats out of the quartermaster's store. Cheape confided his anxiety on the question to Cleghorn:

'In fact, my zeal for the Interest of the Volunteers has brought the county under this imputation against it . . . and would it not be rather a hard return to this my attention to their comfort, if it should . . . be turned to my prejudice, which would probably happen if this imputation was attempted to be fixed upon the County through my officiousness . . . '

Cleghorn had handed on Cheape's letter of 10 April (about going on permanent duty) to Dempster. He must have replied to Cleghorn (though we do not have his letter), criticising the whole concept of permanent duty for a month, and enlarging on the hardship this would inflict on the men, paid only a shilling a day and not even ending up with the greatcoats which ought to have been *given* to the men. Cleghorn received this letter on 16 April, and – 'as it was written in consequence of his having perused yours of the 10th; *as* it was directly applicable to its contents; *as* it explained why your wish of calling the men to go on permanent duty was not complied with, and *as* it suggested no wish of the writer to have his sentiments concealed from you' – Cleghorn had felt at liberty to send the letter on to Cheape, only asking that he would send it back because in one paragraph Dempster 'had imputed motives to Lord Kellie and others which probably had no influence on their conduct'. A few days earlier, as full of enthusiasm as ever, Cleghorn had told Cheape that he intended calling a general drill and there would do all in his power to induce the men to go on permanent service.

On 26 April Cheape wrote to Cleghorn, answering Dempster's letter of criticism in detail and beginning with an explanation of his actions in connexion with the greatcoats. He went on: 'As to the men having only a shilling a day, they are, in this, exactly on the same footing with every other Volunteer corps in Great Britain and Ireland and I never before heard of this being stated as an objection to going on permanent duty . . . but besides the shilling a day, I believe there are other advantages, particularly that during absence from home on duty, the families of Volunteers are entitled to the same support from Government as those of the Militia.' He defended his decision to go on permanent duty and ended his letter: 'As you say you are sure he [Major Dempster] would have no objection to his letter being communicated to me, neither will he, I trust, to my having made the observations I have done when it is to you.'

Cleghorn, however, was very wide of the mark in assuming that Cathcart Dempster would accept Cheape's answer to his criticisms in a letter addressed to another. He wrote an angry letter to Cheape in which he blamed Cleghorn: 'I cannot but suppose that my confidential letter sent to you by Mr. C. was accompanied by some observations not warranted by my expressions and not in unison with the truth of my feelings.' The rest of the letter was taken up with defending what he had written. He sent identical letters to Cheape and Cleghorn. Cleghorn's reply to Dempster was straightforward enough: 'When I sent your letter to me to Col. Cheape, I accompanied it with no remarks unfavourable to you nor with observations of any kind but what tended to corroborate its contents – and to show that it is so, I shall write directly to Mr. Cheape for the letter I addressed to him and request him to send it directly to you. My reason for sending your letter to Mr. Cheape was owing to my being obliged to go to the country and being in a hurry I thought I could not explain the subject so well as you had done . . . ' and he ended by asking for an apology.

In his letter to Cheape, a copy of which he sent to Dempster, Cleghorn set out his course of conduct, explained his motives and asked Cheape to send his letters to Dempster to prove that he had neither impugned his patriotism nor 'insinuated any differences of opinion from him on the subject of the Great Coats'. He ended his formal letter to Cheape: 'It is impossible for me, after what has passed to have any intercourse of confidence or friendship with Mr. D. And as his services may now be more useful than mine, the only subject of deliberation now is my resignation or the laying of his conduct before the Lieutenancy.'

Before this letter had been sent off Cleghorn had received a frigid acknowledgement from Dempster: 'Mr. D. having only now come in from golf at 4 o'clock, had no opportunity of returning the letter sooner as he only got it after dinner.' So Cleghorn added a postcript in his letter to Cheape: 'It is perhaps of no great consequence to state that I had so little the Idea of having offended Mr. D. that I met him on Sunday and requested him to sup with me to read your letters. He was engaged but called on me yesterday morning when he passed with me a considerable time; walked with me in apparent friendship in the garden and never dropped a hint that I had done him the smallest injury. How he could in the evening put himself into such a temper I cannot explain . . . I shall only add that there was no previous misunderstanding between D. and me. I uniformly treated him with respect and hospitality and with that degree of kindness with which any right-thinking man treats him whom he regards as a degree in life below what he ought to be.'

The harassed Col. Cheape did what he could to patch up the quarrel but it rumbled on and in a note of 20 July he wrote to Cleghorn to: 'refer you to a copy of a Minute of the Lieutenancy assembled here [i.e. St Andrews] this day and to say that until you hear from me you have leave of absence from appearing with the Regiment.' The Minute referred to concerned: 'a meeting of the Lieutenancy of the County of Fife and district of St. Andrews . . . the Earl of Kellie, Vice Lord Lieutenant in the chair . . . his Lordship laid before them a letter from Col. Cheape, Commandant of the Royal St Andrews Volunteers, covering one from Lt. Col. Cleghorn of that Company and likewise a letter from Major Dempster of the same regiment; and these letters having been read in the meeting, they are of the opinion that these letters . . . should be transmitted by the vice Lord Lieutenant to his Majesty's Secretary of State and that his Lordship do request the directions of the Secretary in what manner the Lieutenancy are to proceed in this matter . . . '

A court of enquiry was set up: it drew up a report which was sent to Lord Hawkesbury. On 25 September Lord Kellie was writing to Cleghorn from Cambo that both Hawkesbury and the court of enquiry viewed the matter 'in a civil light' – in other words, it was up to Cleghorn to bring a civil action against Dempster if he wanted to pursue the matter further. On 27 September Cheape was writing to Cleghorn: 'You will please now to consider your leave of absence at an end and resume exercise of your Duty in the Regiment.' This he took up for the next few years, becoming commandant of the regiment till 1808. In 1806 he had to write a sharp protest to the local officer, David Laird, who had tried to press two St Andrews men into service in the navy, for an apologetic letter from Laird survives, addressed to Col. Cleghorn and assuring him that he would give the young men in question certificates 'which will prevent them ever being disturbed again'.[66] Cleghorn also involved his friend George Kempe in ensuring the promotion of Lt. McArthur, the adjutant to the St Andrews Regiment from 1804–6.

In 1805 Cathcart Dempster was a party in another row which at first involved Cleghorn, and which dragged on for many years. It was over the golf links. In 1797 the Town Council had sold them to two merchants, Gourlay ard Gunn.[67] From them, the Links passed into the hands of Charles Dempster and his son Cathcart, who aimed at exploiting them commercially as a rabbit warren. In 1803, therefore, when Cleghorn was still Captain of the Company of Golfers, a fund was started for the purpose of taking legal action against the Dempsters and the case duly came before the Court of Session on 17 May 1805 as 'Cleghorn and others against Dempster'. Here it was ruled, in 'the almost unanimous Judgement of the Court of Session', in favour of the golfers, preserving to them: 'the privilege of playing Golf on the Links of St Andrews . . . which would be completely destroyed if this judgement were reversed and the object of the suit of their opponent obtained, by their being converted into a rabbit warren.'[68]

The golfers' anxiety flared up again in June 1813 when they heard that Cathcart Dempster was in London, where their suit against him was 'shortly to be brought under the Judgement of the House of Peers'. In these circumstances, on the advice of Hugh Cleghorn, they wrote to his old friend, William Adam, to ask him to act for them in this matter, 'wherein their existence as a Society is at stake'.[69] However, 'the case never came on there for in the meantime an epidemic had carried off the rabbits.'[70] And in 1814 Cleghorn was asking Charles Grace to: 'let me know without loss of time what Resolution the golfers have come to as to paying their debt to Mr. Chalmers.'[71] He was Adam's instructing solicitor in London and had acted too for Cleghorn, particularly since 1810, by taking over the paying of his daughters' pensions after the death of Patrick Anderson in Edinburgh (who up till then had made the necessary arrangements).

In spite of all these flurries of activity, Cleghorn needed more satisfying outlets for his considerable energies than walking in the gardens of St Leonards, playing at soldiers and golf, and getting caught up in the gossip of town and gown in St Andrews. As William Adam commented: 'No man is worse calculated to sit in a country town and live on capital without occupation.'[72] This prospect was swept into limbo when in 1806 Cleghorn seized the opportunity, denied him earlier, of buying the estate of Stravithie.

15

Stravithie
1806–16

The Stravithie estate of about a thousand acres had been the property of Henrietta, Marchioness of Titchfield, since the death in 1775 of her father, General John Scott of Balcomie. He had been a colourful, thrusting character who was reputed to have made £500,000 solely by gambling: his *Compendium of Easy Rules of Whist* ran into many editions and was still in print in the nineteenth century.[1] But his ambitions had not been confined to the card table: through his mother's connections in Caithness he had first built up a power base there and then turned his political attention to Fife, which he represented from 1768 until his death in 1775. He was the heir of the Scotts of Scotstarvit but he also acquired many other properties in Fife and all these had gone on his death to his eldest daughter, Henrietta, who in 1795 had married William Henry Cavendish Bentinck, Marquess of Titchfield and heir to the third Duke of Portland.[2] He was MP for Buckinghamshire and Lord Lieutenant of Middlesex, with property in Nottinghamshire, Cumbria and elsewhere – so the Fife estates were peripheral to their interests and when they needed money for their English estates another of those in Fife would be sold. Stravithie was in fact the last to go (after Scotstarvit, Balcomie, Berryhill, Dairsie, Sauchop, Lathockar, the Isle of May and Denmiln).[3]

There is no mention in the Cleghorn Papers of the price of Stravithie but Cleghorn did not hesitate when, five years after he had made his first enquiries, it came on the market. He was very aware, however, that it tied up too much of his capital for comfort. In 1806 he was writing to William Adam about the possibility of a post – any post – in government administration: 'I am tired of planting cabbages. My late purchases have reduced my income within bounds almost too narrow for the growing expenses of my family.'[4] But it was not only the possibility of a salary which attracted him: 'I am naturally fond of labour,'[5] he wrote to Adam. Again, in 1807: 'I wish only to eat the bread of labour and I would quit the inactive life of Fife for an employment the gains of which I should be almost ashamed to name.'[6] But this was before Stravithie threw down its challenge and exerted its spell.

That the spell worked with increasing strength was reflected almost unconsciously in his letters. To William Adam he wrote: 'My place is in great beauty. The new access is opened. The lodge is built. The Rivulet is taught to flow in a new Channel – two cascades and a fine lake all in view in the course of the approach to the house . . . '[7] The attachment showed through too when he observed that: 'My habits are now formed to the country.'[8] And that its influence was powerful he acknowledged to his son Peter when he explained that Peter's sons, brought up at Stravithie: 'will naturally and irresistibly form a strong attachment to the property which will continue with them through life . . . and its preservation will act as it never fails to do, as the strongest of all incentives to the Eldest to constant laborious exertions in whatever profession he may be engaged.'[9]

Cleghorn was echoing the same belief right at the end of his life when he said in a letter to his grandsons, aged eleven and ten, in their first term at the High School in Edinburgh: 'If Hugh is diligent at his lessons, he will be able one day to call Stravithie his own and he would not like to sell this pretty place if by working hard in his profession, he may be able to keep it.'[10] Mrs Brampton – the great, great granddaughter of Hugh Cleghorn – has some unsigned, undated verses of the late 1820s which show – with their references to watching trout in the burn, picking wild flowers in the 'birken shaw', hearing the lark above Stravithie glen – how Stravithie had indeed become a much loved element in the lives of the Cleghorn family.

That Cleghorn thought that an estate the size of Stravithie could have been managed in his absence was probably his gesture of private protest to his friend against the responsibilities which came crowding in on him and which in practice he seems to have accepted with gusto. In the spring of 1806 he had already set Robert Meldrum to work opening up a quarry and building dykes.[11] In July he acquired the small farm of Wakefield, on the southern edge of the estate, and transferred his family out there 'during the summer months'.[12]

Judging by the undated plan of Stravithie drawn for Cleghorn by one of his tenants, Alex Brown, there were two buildings at Wakefield, one bigger than the other, on the edge of the steep slope down to the burn (called, on Brown's plan, Tosh burn). Cleghorn must have moved his family out to the smaller of the two – the lack of space left him complaining that he couldn't lay his hands on any papers he wanted – while the bigger one was made ready for them. The move was made necessary because he had sold St Leonards that same July to a lawyer, William Grant of Congalton.[13] What is marked on the plan as Stravithie House were the ruins of the old castle (of which nothing now remains) so it looks as if neither General Scott nor his daughter lived on the estate, and it was Cleghorn who made Wakefield into a country seat, steadily enlarging and beautifying it over the years.

Cleghorn's lawyer in St Andrews, Stuart Grace, also acted as his banker, so the authorisation of payment for work done for Cleghorn was presented by the tradesmen to Grace, and when he paid them he kept the signed receipts and bundled them up at the end of each year. These bundles give an idea of the pattern of Cleghorn's improvements, the earliest receipts being from John Edie for payment 'for work done by me in Repairing of his house'[14] and from John Wishart for renewing window frames and 'windo rops'.[15] It seems that enough had been done for the family to have been ensconced in Wakefield before the winter of 1806–7 set in.

Cleghorn had paid the first stages of the purchase money for Stravithie 'very readily';[16] the final ones were not so carefree. Patrick Anderson was writing to him by the autumn of 1806 with somewhat forceful clarity: 'The Balance of the price of Stravithie may be permitted to remain a term or two but you may depend upon it that money was much wanted by the Family . . . I know you are not fond of entering upon accounts and calculations but the business to be adjusted betwixt [now] and Martinmas really requires to be well weighed because upon the result may depend the securing of the property to the Family.'[17] That this was not an empty threat can be seen by the high number of bankruptcies, foreclosures and sales among landowners at this time. What arrangement was made exactly is not clear but it got the Titchfields off Cleghorn's back. Less easy to dislodge – in fact an incubus for the rest of Cleghorn's life – was the new minister of Dunino, James Roger. As early as March 1806, before the purchase of Stravithie had even been completed, he had thrust upon Cleghorn a demand for a new manse[18] with 'a Mall' leading to it to provide dignity of approach.[19]

Roger had been minister since 1804, presented there through the interest of his cousin, Principal James Playfair. He had been licensed by the Presbytery of Dundee, had been an assistant minister in Angus and tried his hand at schoolmastering. He had also been secretary to George Dempster of Dunnichen and had published work on agriculture and government.[20] On his record he should have been a natural ally for Cleghorn but he was shaping up as a 'character': he had none of the other-worldiness of the country parson; he always wore the most expensive, superfine black cloth, with his coats cut in the swallow-tail fashion and his hair powdered. His nickname was 'the British Linen Co.' because of the enormous white choker under which he buried his chin; he never went to bed before cockcrow, summer or winter,[21] but in spite of his voluminous reading, his sermons were a sore trial to his parishoners. Cleghorn's family later on were going to the episcopal chapel in St Andrews;[22] Cleghorn was also paying rent each year to the Boxmaster of the Wright Trade for a seat in the Town Church.[23] Nearly forty years later, Peter Cleghorn, much more tolerant than his father, was writing sadly to his son, Hugh, in India: 'I hope there is not another parish in the world exposed to such gabble and trash as in this parish.'[24] By simply not going to Dunino church, Cleghorn could escape Roger's 'gabble and trash' – his malice was more difficult to evade.

In 1806 Cleghorn met Roger about the new manse, suggesting that, 'as the two principal heritors have lately submitted to great diminution of income by changing their moneyed capital into landed property,' it would be considerate if the minister 'delayed his demand'.[25] Roger had perforce to accept this for the time being but the prospect of this added expense may have led Cleghorn to carry to the Court of Session a petition which earlier holders of the estates had contemplated: to have Stravithie declared to be in the parish of St Andrews rather than of Dunino. In his 1809 petition, 'that a new scheme of locality may be made up in which no part of the stipend of Dunino shall be localled in the petitioner's lands,' Cleghorn described how he had: 'recovered evidence to prove that his lands of Stravithie originally belonged to the parish of St Andrews and were never disjoined therefrom.'[26] But though he cited Sir James Lumsdaine's arguments of 1709, which went far back in the seventeenth century, Cleghorn failed to convince the court, and the payment of his dues to the church and the expenses of the new manse recur with painful regularity in his accounts.

Much more satisfactory for Cleghorn was the acquisition through Stravithie of a superiority which gave him the right to vote. This was made up by disjunction of valued rent from Stravithie and the mill (£150), on the one hand, and Bannafield, Tosh and Cotton (£276) on the other.[27] Cleghorn never let this right go by default and his comments on the situation at each election show the liveliness of his concern.

Both Wakefield the house and Stravithie the estate began benefiting steadily from Cleghorn's various schemes for improvement. In 1808 Robert Coldstream, probably the most skilful builder in St Andrews at this time and often employed by the University, was busy adding two cellars to the house, one for wine and the other for beer, along with rather engagingly spelt

'Cattocoms', a new office house and seventy-six feet of pavement – all finished, according to his estimate, 'in a workmanlike manner.'[28] In 1810 the major task of re-roofing Wakefield with Easdale slates was carried out[29] and Thomas Fernie, one of the most constant of Cleghorn's tradesmen, was being paid for work on 'the East Wing Hugh Clighoren Esq's hous at Wakefield'.[30] In the next year he was building a draw well, fitting a hearth stone and fixing a marble shelf for game and doing more work on both wings at Wakefield.[31] Also in 1811, Alex Munro's receipt for plaster-work he had done in the house gives us some idea of the layout: in the dining room he had worked on cornice and frieze and enrichments round the recess, providing also a large oval ornament there; the glass in the cupola had needed attention; also, 'the top member of the lobby cornice and the second lobby.'[32]

William MacLean had hung 'the house of Wakefield with bells in the completest manner and with the best materials'.[33] The watchmaker John Hedridge had not only repaired watches and installed a new eight-day clock, but had soldered a cravat stand and a wine drainer.[34] William Foulis had fitted 'eighty-seven balusters for the rail of his stair in the house at Wakefield'.[35] The biggest single item of Cleghorn's expenditure, in the 1811 bundle of receipts, was of three hundred and six pounds for wood, 'for the new buildings at Stravithie'.[36] That these must have been considerable is shown in the tax paid on the number of windows at Wakefield: in 1812 there were fourteen windows,[37] by 1827 there were twenty-seven.[38] The house was also fitted out with water-closets, as is shown in Andrew Marr's account, where one of the items is for panelling them.[39] Marr also carried out a wide variety of odd jobs such as making a pair of lemon-squeezers,[40] putting patent springs on the doors,[41] making a doghouse,[42] building a wardrobe and drawers in the east wing.[43] The Cleghorn family obviously lived in a very civilised setting and they certainly made their home a centre of hospitality, as they had at St Leonards when they were there.

To the improvements which Cleghorn made to the estate of Stravithie there is an unsolicited testimonial in John Leighton's

Fife Illustrated, which was published in 1840, three years after Cleghorn's death: 'Probably no parish in the Kingdom has undergone so great an alteration for the better as Dunino . . . The greatest part of the improvements in planting, draining and enclosing have been made in the last forty years, and they have well rewarded the expense and labour incurred.'[44] Books in Cleghorn's library such as John Thomson's *General View of Agriculture in the County of Fife* (1800) and John Mortimer's *Art of Husbandry* (1718) bear witness to his interest in improved methods of farming. Now he set about putting them into practice. Of planting and draining there is ample evidence in the bundles of Cleghorn's receipts. In February 1809, for instance, Cleghorn bought from John Galloway twelve thousand seedling larch; ten thousand seedling oak; twenty thousand seedling birch; thirty thousand Scots firs; a thousand spruce and five hundred Balm of Gilead, along with gooseberries and black, white and red currant bushes. Then in April a second order asked for two thousand mountain ash, eleven hundred transplanted thorn (these of course were needed for hedging), and more spruce and Scots Firs.[45] Twenty-five years later these seedlings had grown sufficiently in the 'North Planting' for wood to be cut from them for palings and for their branches to be laid 'on the loose bales . . . to break the force of the winds', and the thinnings generally put to good use,[46] such as covering the stones laid for drainage.

The orchard was freshly stocked in 1814. This time William Urquhart, nurseryman in Dundee, sent apple, pear and plum trees, and asparagus,[47] while Jane Watt provided garden seed of onions, early cabbage, pease, beans, spinach, curled cress, radishes, ice lettuce, celery, cauliflower . . . ;[48] the list seems endless. But by 1826 Cleghorn had decided that the garden was not well situated, being too wet, while from 'the Burn fogs, you can have no fruit from the trees and hardly any goosberries and currants from the bushes'. With the improver's gleam in his eye, Cleghorn wrote to his son, to whom he was about to hand over the estate: 'Immediately above it [the existing wet situation] is an excellent one. Would you wish an acre of ground to be enclosed with a proper wall?'[49] The quarrying of stone on the estate, the building of dykes and trenching and draining the ground went on continuously. So much so that Cleghorn, when faced with yet another bill for quarrying, wrote to Stuart Grace to find out 'how so much money comes to be drawn every week'[50] for that purpose – but the quarrying and building went on all the same.

It was in the process of draining the land at Tosh that Cleghorn: 'discovered an apparently inexhaustible quantity of Marl. It lies near the surface. I have already got about fifteen thousand cart loads, and the expense of digging was a few shillings under £50. It has been analysed and is of the finest quality.'[51] This was a bonus, but Cleghorn was also prepared to spend heavily on lime to bring his land into good heart. Not only did he buy it locally, but he had four shiploads sent from Sunderland; the first in 1810, brought by the sloop 'Nonesuch',[52] the second in 1815 in the sloop 'Pallian'[53] and the third and fourth in 1821, delivered from the 'Dunregan' and the 'Phemia of Charlestown'.[54] The receipts from these last two shiploads give some idea of the organisation and labour involved in getting the lime from St Andrews harbour up to Stravithie. It was William Thomson, Cleghorn's own personal servant, who oversaw the whole operation. First he had to pay the shore dues, then hire the tubs into which the lime was shovelled – this meant three days' bread, beer and whisky for the men doing the work. Then the carters had to be assembled and arrangements made with the 'Guy Man' to walk in front and 'call on' the draught animals to encourage them in dragging their loads up the hill. He was given a separate allowance – to wet his whistle – while the carters between them consumed ninety-two bread rolls, drank a hundred and fifty-two bottles of beer, plus whisky (specified in gills and glasses). On top of that there were tolls to pay, quite apart from the cost of the lime itself; all this twice over for the two cargoes.[55] No means of enriching the soil was neglected. Kelp manure was brought up from the sea shore at Anstruther and chopped up for the turnips;[56] there are constant references in Cleghorn's journals to 'driving dung'[57] and spreading compost.[58]

Cleghorn was anxious to improve not only his own place but all the amenities on the estate. The house at Pittendriech was repaired in 1809;[59] in 1810 he was paying for a new road at Wakefield[60] and for another: 'through Stravithie from the Anstruther road to the violet park.'[61] He had to put up the road-builders at Wakefield – for in 1815 he was paying for snuff, 'the greatest part of which has been expended in gratifying the noses of the Captains' Massons.'[62] The roads they built went from the Anstruther Road, 'thro' the farms of Cotton and Kinaldy etc.'[63] and past Bannafield.[64] Cleghorn also paid his share of 'the banking and additions for completing the bridge'.[65] Between 1818 and 1821 he was paying out considerable sums for the improvement of Stravithie Mains,[66] and then in 1821 he turned his attention to Stravithie Mill.[67] In 1822 he was repairing the drains at Cotton and Tosh[68] and at the same time being faced, as one of the two principal heritors, with a major share in the rebuilding of Dunino Manse.[69]

All this had to be paid for and Cleghorn's accounts, with their entries about loans negotiated and interest paid, show some pretty skilful, some might say reckless, juggling with irregularly available resources. But it is clear that he did achieve what he had looked forward to during the trials of his eastern journeys – a life of settled domestic ease with his family and his friends. Madame Clason, an old friend from Geneva, visiting him at Wakefield in 1815, wrote of him: 'Il est toujours le même: gai et de bonne humeur.'[70] His eldest son, John, was building his career in the Engineers in India. He 'has got the best situation in the Corps: Superintendent of the Tanks,' Cleghorn was reporting to Walker. 'He is constantly in Tents and surveys from Kisna to the Coloroon . . . He lives like an Arab and I suppose is now as wild as the sons of the Desert. He can at least save considerably from his appointments and his mode of life admits of little expense . . . '[71] His mother must have been hoping this meant she might see him again – he had been in India since 1794.

Peter, their second son, was obviously endowed with considerable ability. After three years at St Andrews University

(1798–1801), he had studied at Glasgow under Professor James Mylne. From there he won a Snell Exhibition to Balliol College Oxford,[72] where he matriculated in 1804. He had vacated the Exhibition by 1807 and was admitted to Lincoln's Inn. By 1810 he had eaten his dinners and completed his course and was accepted as a barrister-at-law there. But the chances of building up a lucrative practice in London did not come his way and, again through William Adam's influence and recommendation, in 1816 he went out to Madras to practice there as a barrister in the Supreme Court of Judicature.[73]

Cleghorn's wife and daughters took to life in the country with enjoyment and were active in welcoming guests, in going into St Andrews for social occasions and in visiting their wide circle of friends – among whom were the Lows of Clatto, a special favourite being Georgina Low.[74] The family took seriously their duties to the working people on their own estate and in the parish. In March 1808, for instance, they arranged for coals to be given to Isabel Donaldson at Waulkfield; later there were deliveries to Balcaithly and other cottages in the parish. In an undated letter Cleghorn was asking Dr John Lee for a list of medicines: 'We are almost daily applied to by the poor about, for medicines . . . A wish to give relief as well as to save considerable expense . . . makes us often regret that we have no small assortment of drugs which might be given to them without danger . . . I would take it very kindly if at your leisure you would furnish me with a short list of such medicines as are safe and not expensive . . . You will add greatly to this favour if you will have the goodness to take a family dinner here any day convenient to yourself and bring the above list with you . . . '[75]

Cleghorn was also on the committee running the English School in St Andrews, which was flourishing so well that a new building was required; so Cleghorn wrote to Andrew Bell asking if he would subscribe, assuring him that: 'the Teacher, Mr. Smith by adopting your excellent plan, by making the children tutors to each other, superintends the education of two hundred scholars without an usher.'[76] Andrew Bell responded with a subscription and the school was duly built behind Holy Trinity Church (where the District Library is now).

Cleghorn and his family had a wide circle of friends; from Lord Pitmilly and General Durham at Largo, to Professor Haldane in St Andrews University; from his Edinburgh cronies, whom he aimed at meeting at least once a year for their High School reunion, to his London friends such as the Clarkes and George Kempe. His greatest friend, with whom he felt most at home, was William Adam. The two met whenever possible, though Adam was very involved from 1816 as Lord Chief Commissioner of the Jury court in Edinburgh. But as his daughter lived at Charleton, after her marriage to John Anstruther-Thomson, and this was no great distance from Wakefield, opportunities for meeting cropped up to their mutual satisfaction. Or, if they were not meeting, Cleghorn might be firing off one of his salvoes on the economic and political situation. In 1811, when Napoleon's Continental System was hitting the British hard, Cleghorn was writing to Adam:

'Those connected with the land have no right to expect that they are to swim safely over the tempest which has desolated every other interest in the country . . . in the present state of Europe, I should willingly acquiesce in a total prohibition of Distillery from Grain . . . ' and he continues with some trenchant criticism of Percival's measures, ending: 'You may be very thankful that I have been interrupted by my Farm Manager until the departure of the post, otherwise you would not have got off so easily.'[77] For his part, Adam, writing to Peter, spoke of 'the unaltered friendship and confidence in each other through life' between himself and Cleghorn, and it seems he spoke nothing less than the truth.[78]

Another friend in whom Cleghorn took special pleasure was William Tennant, scholar and poet (author of *Anster Fair*) and, in the 1810s, schoolmaster at Dunino. In 1816 Cleghorn wrote a glowing testimonial to his scholarship and his discipline: 'Mr. Tennant sometime ago applied to me as the only Residing Heritor to [give] him Certification of his Moral Character and abilities as a Teacher. I give it with the most perfect fidelity. His moral conduct is exemplary. His manners are firm, mild and conciliating. To a perfect knowledge of the Learned Languages, he unites an elegant and classical taste. And I have known few in this county who possess an equal knowledge of French and Italian languages or a stronger feeling for their Beauties.' Cleghorn then met head-on the problem of Tennant's lameness and went on ruefully: 'Were I to consult my own gratification I would wish Mr. Tennant to remain where he is. He is the only man for miles around me in whose society I feel any pleasure . . . '[79] Tennant did not in fact get that job in Edinburgh but he did move on to Dollar Academy and his place as Dunino schoolmaster was taken by his brother, David. Despite the move his friendship with the Cleghorns grew stronger over the years and he stayed frequently out at Wakefield, Peter describing him as 'the sweetest tempered fellow I ever knew'.[80]

In 1808 Cleghorn was delighted when Adam Ferguson decided to retire to St Andrews, for it meant renewing an acquaintanceship begun when Cleghorn as a youth, had attended Ferguson's moral philosophy lectures in Edinburgh. Ferguson lived for the last eight years of his life with his three daughters in the small attractive house at the east end of South Street, which is now Number 19,[81] on the north side of the street. During these eight years Cleghorn obviously renewed and deepened his friendship with this spirited and indomitable philosopher. That Ferguson was a striking figure was borne out by Lord Cockburn's description:

'His hair was silky and white, his eyes animated and light blue; his cheeks sprinkled with broken red, like autumnal apples but fresh and healthy . . . His raiment consisted of half boots lined with fur, cloth breeches, a long cloth waistcoat with capacious pockets, a single breasted coat, a cloth great coat also lined with fur and a felt hat commonly tied by a ribbon below the chin . . . When he walked forth, he used a tall staff which he commonly held at arm's length out towards the side . . . His gait and air were noble; his gesture slow, his look full of dignity and composed fire. He looked like a philosopher from Lapland.'[82]

In 1810 Ferguson's naval son, John (always referred to by him as 'my little seaman') was on the 'Pandora', which was wrecked in the Kattegat. Ferguson's South Street neighbour, Mrs Stewart, recalled how a student, who was reading the newpaper to Ferguson because of his increasing blindness, faltered when he came on the notice of the wreck, but: 'old Adam simply said, "Go on: read that again."'[83] Cleghorn saw, that for all his outward stoicism, Ferguson felt deeply for his son, so he took what practical measures he could to relieve the old man's anxiety, writing privately to Adam: 'From his great age and unimpaired feelings I would rather wish that his friends would on this occasion think for him than urge him to think for himself.'[84] (John Ferguson did survive but was partly blamed for the loss of the ship.)

The strength of Ferguson's mind and the vigour of his feelings struck all who knew him in these last years. In November 1815 Cleghorn took Madame Clason into St Andrews to see Ferguson, whom she had met perhaps a dozen times in all, over forty-five years. She wrote to her friend about the meeting: 'Á l'âge de 95 années, il a conservé ses facultés spirituelles; enfin juger de ma satisfaction: Il ne m' a point oublié et m' a reçus comme si nous ne venions que de nous quitter . . . '[85]

Ferguson indentified himself with the fortunes of his friends. As Cleghorn said to William Adam: 'The coldness of age had made no inroads on his heart.'[86] The news of Adam's promotion to the new office of Lord Chief Commissioner of the Jury Court in Edinburgh was a source of very great satisfaction to Ferguson. He had after all counted Robert Adam, William's uncle, as his friend and certainly had a high regard for William himself. When Cleghorn heard the news of his friend's appointment, he had at once left for Blair Adam to congratulate him in person, and on returning to tell Ferguson about his visit, found his old friend's strength ebbing away. Cleghorn stayed up with Ferguson all that night, and the next evening, just before nine o'clock, Ferguson

died: 'perfectly calm and serene – rather Sleep than Death.'
Cleghorn writing to tell Adam, went on:

'I really think that the exaltation of spirits excited . . . by his
friend and the son of his friend, being nominated to that new and,
in his opinion, most important situation, had raised feelings of joy
which his feeble frame was not capable of resisting. He had been
in a very uncommon flow of spirits from the morning on which
I left this to meet your Lordship until the day of my return.'[87]
And to Col. Walker he told how he was with Ferguson as he
was dying, and: 'I closed the eyes of my friend and master.'[88]
(This makes it look as if the story in John Small's *Biographical
Sketch of Ferguson*, about his last words being 'There is another
world'[89] is apocryphal.)

Because none of the the male relatives of the Fergusons was
in St Andrews at the time, Cleghorn did all he could to help
Ferguson's daughters. He supplied: 'all the necessary expenses
of the family and hope to be able to do so until their funds
are available.'[90] He went with Dr Daniel Robertson, Professor
of Hebrew, to the cathedral churchyard, 'to select a spot for his
interment. We fixed upon a piece of ground on the north wall
of about nine foot square.'[91] And a grant from the Exchequer
secured it. When Adam's letter, replying to Cleghorn's news,
arrived, Cleghorn read it to the Miss Fergusons: 'It was received
with the most affectionate regard by them and was such a letter as
I expected from you, knowing your Heart as well as I know my
own.'[92] Cleghorn sat down there and then to answer it and ended
hurriedly: 'I am writing in the room with Ladies – interrupted
every moment by women's tongues and idle visitors'[93] – and
indeed if this was in the small panelled room on the right of
the door, it would be difficult not to be distracted by any
conversation.

He drew up a notice which he suggested to Adam should be
put in the Edinburgh newspapers. This ended: 'He was the last
of those great men of the preceding century whose writings have
reflected so much honour on their age and on this country.
And among these none united in a more distinguished degree

a knowledge of Ancient Learning to a perfect Knowledge of the World in which he lived, or more eminently added to the manners of a most accomplished gentleman, the practice and principles of the purest virtue.'[94]

He also consulted Adam on the lines which Ferguson had 'at the age of eighty-nine' (in 1812, four years after he had come to St Andrews) suggested might be inscribed on his tomb. Cleghorn's reaction was: 'It was not a positive command which I should at all hazards have obeyed. It was a wish and that too rather implied than expressed. I am therefore at liberty to consult mutual friends. My impression of that inscription is that it speaks the language and breathes the sentiments of the Stoic School, that it will be understood by very few – and that it will alarm the prejudices of the pious . . . and raise against his memory the sleeping hypocrisy of the Genius of the Place.'[95] Cleghorn enclosed Ferguson's epitaph separately and it does not survive in the Blair Adam Papers but it cannot have been the same as that which John Small quoted from a letter written by Ferguson when he was at Hallyards, before he settled in St Andrews, namely: 'I have seen the works of God; it is now your turn: do you behold them and rejoice.'[96] (That would have been eminently 'appropriate to a country churchyard' and it cannot be said to breathe 'the sentiments of the Stoic School'.) Ferguson's family and friends must have agreed with Cleghorn, and in the event Walter Scott, a great friend of Captain Adam Ferguson, wrote the elaborate eulogy which then was inscribed on the stone now so badly weathering.

Ferguson's funeral was fixed for Thursday 28 February, and Cleghorn signed the burial letters, attended the funeral and, 'to relieve the family,' the two nephews who arrived stayed out at Wakefield.[97] (The South Street house *is* small.) Captain Adam Ferguson, the eldest son, who arrived later, also stayed with the Cleghorns – 'He has just left us to the great regret of our women whom he has kept in constant convulsions of laughter.'[98] He discussed plans for his future with Cleghorn and left him so uneasy about them that Cleghorn ended his letter to William

Adam: 'He seemed to think that retiring upon half pay would lay the Duke of York under obligation by giving H.R.H. the disposal of his Company. I ventured to remark that those in high office pressed by interest and surrounded by favourites, seldom remunerated such obligations. This is a précis of what passed, and if your Lordship views these scheme as I do, you will try to knock them out of his head.'[99]

Cleghorn was then asked by Adam and the Lord Chief Baron to write the life of Ferguson. His reply was prompt and decisive: 'I must decline with Firmness and concern the Honor of writing Dr. Ferguson's life. Writing is a trade which I never practised; nothing of mine ever appeared in print . . . to write a history of a man of letters, it is necessary to know the literature of the age, and I am not a scholar. For thirty years we never saw and were separated from each other by the distance of the globe: he engaged in pursuits of Philosophy and History while my time was idled in foreign countries or spent in the bustle of camps and of cabinets . . . I shall venture to hope that either Professor Playfair or the Rev. Mr. Alison will undertake a task they are so well able to execute.'[100]

Cleghorn was soon writing to Adam to suggest that Dr John Lee be approached to write Ferguson's life since he had known Ferguson personally from the time he retired to Tweeddale and then had followed him to St Andrews. Cleghorn went on to say that Lee agreed with him that: 'It is absolutely necessary to give an account of the Philosophical system which he taught and of that which he most pointedly opposed, and it was consciousness of my incapacity to do justice to this part of his work which made me decline undertaking it . . . Dr. Lee agrees with me that it is essential to be done. Dr. Ferguson, with slight modifications, taught the doctrines of the Stoic School. The system he chiefly opposed was that of the sceptics and Academics . . . [The philosophy of] Dr. Ferguson was a School of Action. Since his time Moral Philosophy has become a School of Metaphysical Speculation in which the Mind is considered rather as a *Witness* than as an *Agent* in the Scenes of Life.'

Full of enthusiasm as ever, Cleghorn was looking forward to Dr Lee's setting out of Ferguson's ideas; he was sure: 'It would be of use to the present age, by withdrawing the rising generation from the Intellectual Rope Dancing of Metaphysics to the Real business of Life'[101] – whatever Cleghorn's inadequacies as a philosopher, he could still turn a phrase with relish! Perhaps the family was lukewarm: at any rate no officially sponsored life of Adam Ferguson was brought out in the years following his death and Dr Lee's work ended up as a brief biography in the supplement to the fourth edition of the *Encyclopaedia Britannica*.

The Miss Fergusons sold their house to Dr Haldane, the closest of Cleghorn's friends among the University professors, so that his visits to Number 19 South Street would have continued for many years to come.[102]

16

Keeping Family and Estate Together
1816–29

In November 1815 Cleghorn was sending light-hearted messages to a friend, through Mme Clason, that as most of his farmers had not renewed their leases: '*Sa santé ait plutôt bonifiée par ce redoublement de travaux.*'[1] But the background to this state of affairs was in fact a severe depression in farming caused by the reopening of British markets to Europe with the ending of the war, the flooding in of foreign corn and a run of poor harvests. As early as 1816 Cleghorn was writing to William Adam to ask for his help in arranging a loan from the Ministers' Widows' Fund, explaining that he would have sold a part of the estate to clear the whole, 'but a purchaser of land is not at present to be found.' Though all his farms were now let, before that: 'they had been thrown into my hands for these last three years and during that time from my Management, from Projects or Improvements, they have been a source of Expense and not of Revenue. Like many others . . . I have been without income while a farmer and am entitled to no rent for the greater part of my land until Whitsunday twelvemonth . . . It is not great debts that distress me. It is a number of little demands . . . I have been so long . . . accustomed to Ease if not to Opulence that these demands prey upon my mind . . . '[2] There is no entry in Cleghorn's receipts to suggest he was able to negotiate this loan; instead, in January 1817, he was thanking Adam for: 'helping me procure a credit from the British Linen Company Bank for £500 and for the Account being at the Branch at Cupar.'[3]

It was not only the landowner who was faced with debt; tenants too simply could not pay their rent. Cleghorn settled with two of his non-paying tenants in 1819. John Doctor of Tosh had not been able to produce his rent since 1816 but he had rendered Cleghorn various services and had supplied oats and grass seed. These were balanced after a roup 'of the Corns, stocking and implements of husbandry' which Cleghorn bought.[4] When Doctor had been paid for these the tenancy was ended. There was more trouble with Walter and James Nicol of Stravithie Mill. In September 1819 there was a formal renunciation of the lease; Charles Grace had to go out to Stravithie Mill to take an inventory of their stocking. A precept of arrestment then had to be obtained – that is, a writ to attach the personal property of a debtor in the hands of a third party till a settlement; the Stravithie Mill roup was held[5] and by 1820 William Berwick was the new tenant at the mill.[6]

Cleghorn had to wage a much more bitter battle with the tenant of Stravithie Mains. In 1806, when Cleghorn had bought the estate, Alex Brown had been the tenant of Cotton[7] but in 1814 a summons of removal had been taken out against him, (as it had against John Duncan, tenant of the Mains). In spite of this, on 24 October 1817, Cleghorn had signed a tack with David Brown, the son of Alex Brown, for Stravithie Mains, at a rent of £600 a year. He too proved unable to pay his rent. In November 1820 Brown was declared bankrupt,[8] and so suspicious of his motives had Cleghorn become that, when a miller from Anstruther asked him to send a cart to carry off meal ground from Brown's oats, he sent a hurried note in to ask Charles Grace whether this could be a trap.[9] David Brown's intransigence arose from the support he was given by a farming club.[10] Cleghorn also believed him to be the tool of Martin and Forsyth, crooked lawyers who had egged him on to 'run the gauntlet of every court in the kingdom'.[11] In January 1821 Cleghorn was writing despairingly to Adam about Brown: 'I have been trying to get quit of him by liberal offers of money. But these have been refused and he continues to occupy a valuable farm without capital, caution or credit.'[12]

With what justification Cleghorn believed that the minister of Dunino encouraged Brown in his defiance, it is difficult to say – but believe it he certainly did. He wrote again, half in jest to Adam: 'I should not have liked to have been before you as a prisoner or Defendant. As there is now no chance of this I may say that our mad and malignant minister has been the Instigator of all.'[13] But in all seriousness he told Peter a year later that it was Roger who had prompted: 'two of my principal tenants to withhold their rents and procured the most unprincipled agents of Cupar and Edinburgh to undertake their cause trusting for remuneration to the uncertainty of the law or to wearying me out by expensive and protracted litigation. They have succeeded in making complete bankrupts of the tenants and in involving me in the most serious difficulties.'[14]

Cleghorn really had no choice but to keep at Brown with all possible legal means at his disposal. Neutral arbiters from Edinburgh were brought in to settle a plan for cropping the farm, but it came to nothing; Brown was served with a petition for a visitation and Cleghorn applied for a warrant to roup.[15] Five months later a roup of Brown's stock and crops was held and in November 1821 an ejectment was served on him, unavailingly. In January 1822 a decreet removing Brown from Stravithie Mains by means of a sheriff's precept was enforced but it was not till February 1823 that Brown agreed to a discharge of all claims against Cleghorn, to whom he still owed £683. Judging by Cleghorn's receipts and notes to Charles Grace concerning them, these crises subsided in the later 1820s; as Cleghorn remarked to Adam: 'A good crop and a demand for labour will more effectually suppress sedition than all the penal laws in the Statute Book.'[16]

That the minister of Dunino reciprocated Cleghorn's distrust is reflected in note from Grace to Cleghorn in 1821 about extending the 'Bond of Caution for you in Lawburrows at Roger's instance', which presumably meant that Roger had obtained a writ requiring Cleghorn to give security against doing violence to him.[17] Roger in his turn ran into financial difficulties, as a result, it is said, of litigation. The Rev. Alexander Macdonald, one of Roger's successors as minister of Dunino, told how Roger was actually arrested for debt and imprisoned in Dundee, but: 'came over on Sundays to conduct worship in Dunino. On one occasion, not having the money to pay his ferry at Dundee, he persuaded a man who was bringing a coffin to St. Andrews to allow him to lie inside. Finding the position quite comfortable, he did not move till they were nearing the town . . . '[18] Certainly in 1826 Cleghorn was given a receipt from Thomas Dryburgh for £79, 'being stipend of the lands of Stravithie, Parish of Dunino Crop 1825, due to me as purchaser thereof from the creditors of the Revd. Mr. Roger as per annexed note of the victual of which Mr. Cleghorn and all concerned are hereby discharged.'[19] Roger, however, remained to plague Cleghorn – who, in 1826, was writing to Peter: 'We are getting a new Kirk at Dunino . . . [the heritors had already built the new manse] . . . I wish we could get a new parson.'

Those aggravations were part of the price which Cleghorn was fully prepared to pay for making Stravithie in time into an economically viable estate and Wakefield the focal point of his family's life and affections, He always spoke slightingly of country squires but his eldest daughter, Rachel, who shared with her father a sharpness of perception and expression, often referred to him in her letters to the others as 'the Laird', no doubt with a note of mockery which was intended to stab but with truth all the same. That his concern with good husbandry was genuine and had become part of his pattern of life is shown in the diaries that he kept in the last two years of his life about sowing and planting, 'country labour' and the weather, and when the harvest began and ended.

Inevitably, family concerns loomed largest in the letters of the last twenty years of his life. In February 1818 his brother-in-law, Col. John McGill, died. Cleghorn wrote of him: 'He has left very few better men behind him. He was perfectly aware of his situation and he died with that decent fortitude and composure which he eminently displayed in all his life.' What he bequeathed went to his sister, Rachel, and her daughters, with the residue going to Jane, the Cleghorn daughter who had been his companion and kept his house in St Andrews for him. This amounted to £2,527, together with the South Street house and other property in St Andrews, which meant that there was one daughter's future that Cleghorn did not have to worry about. Jane and the rest of the family wanted their funds to be secured upon Stravithie, so Cleghorn proposed to consult Adam about 'granting to each of them Heritable Security proportioned to their respective interests'.[20]

Rachel's health was beginning to fail. In August 1819 Cleghorn had to send to Anstruther to Dr Goodsir at two in the morning to attend her, but, he wrote to Grace: 'She is now much relieved by administering laudanum, and we are assured that nothing serious is to be apprehended.'[21] Cleghorn himself was having to consult doctors. In 1820 he was thinking of following medical advice to try the Pitcaithley waters. On a more cheerful note the family were well content in October 1820 to celebrate Jane's marriage to an Edinburgh lawyer, William Campbell, whose family had been connected with the Cleghorns – Aunt Sarah in particular – 'long before any one could remember'. He was obviously no Lochinvar, for Cleghorn remarked temperately to Adam: 'I augur well of this present connection because it affords neither matter of Exultation nor Regret.'[22]

Rachel's health, alas, did not pick up: by October 1821 Cleghorn was grateful if she got a little sleep,[23] but then on 16 October she died. That Cleghorn felt her death deeply is shown by his silence. When he wrote fully for the first time, in March 1822, to Peter, he could not bear to dwell on it: 'The loss to me is irreparable.'[24] And Roger made a point of crossing Cleghorn again: he opposed Cleghorn's putting up 'a very modest monument – a wall a foot high with an iron railing', round Rachel's grave. All this made him long to be free of his commitments and especially of his debts – which could be achieved if he sold up and moved to St Andrews. But before he took action, he asked Peter if he had any thought of putting the money he was making in India into the estate. He went on:

'I have consulted with a few of my most confidential friends and it is the opinion of them all that I should offer you that

part of the property to purchase on which the House stands
and which consists of the farms of Cotton, Tosh, the Mill and
Wakefield.' (This would leave the farm of the Mains to John.)
Having made this proposal – 'the result of mature reflection and
many a sleepless night' – there was nothing Cleghorn could do
but muster what patience he could while packet boats made their
hazardous way to India and back. He even decided against the
distraction of a visit to Edinburgh, which Adam had suggested, to
be introduced to George IV, saying: 'I am old and deaf and in no
public situation.' One of the family – his daughter, Jessie – went
in with Georgina Low to see the King arrive and enjoy the festival
atmosphere.[25]

By the beginning of 1824 Cleghorn had heard from Peter and
John, both of whom had married in India, and neither of whom
wanted 'to fix themselves in this county'. This helped him to
decide definitely to sell the Mains of Stravithie, explaining to
Adam: 'I have all along been fighting to keep the Estate for my
sons but as they have no desire to possess it, it becomes more
imperiously a duty on me to make such arrangements as will
secure my own quiet and above all a provision for my daughters. I
am very thankful that my sons can provide for their own families.
I must provide for the most helpless part of mine.'[26] That this
prudent if somewhat dreary course of action was not followed
by Cleghorn does not come altogether as a surprise, but this time
external circumstances rather than his own natural inclinations
decided him. The first of these was the decision of Peter and
his wife, Isabella Allan, whose family was in Ross-shire, to send
home their two sons, Hugh Francis Clarke (aged five) and Allan
McKenzie (aged four) from Madras to live with their grandfather
and aunts at Wakefield. On the voyage they were looked after by
their ayah, Fatima, and were under the care of Susan Low,[27] being
met in London by Anne and another of 'the Misses' (Cleghorn's
collective name for his daughters). They brought with them to
Fife, to help look after the boys, Jane Dinwoodie, the daughter
of Peter's man of business in London, William Dinwoodie. In
October 1824 he was telling Peter that his daughter: 'who has

been for some time an inmate under the enchanting and hospitable roof of Wakefield, writes to us weekly of the dear Boys who are a constant theme of her praise.'[28]

There is no doubt that the presence of his grandsons at Wakefield changed the whole quality and focus of Cleghorn's life in his last years. His letters reflect how genuine a source of delight, interest and affection he found in them. He was soon regularly reporting to Peter on his sons and the: 'happy progress of their health, talents and temper. No children born and brought up in this country enjoy more perfect health than they: Hugh always stout; Allan gaining in size and strength; they go out in all weather and neither suffer nor feel any effects from a change of climate. They both speak distinctly and correctly.'[29]

Anne and Janet (also known as Jessie and Jenny), with Jane Dinwoodie, supervised the boys' education; 'their Aunt Hugh is never out of the nursery, constantly knitting stockings for them; and for Rachel and me, it is agreed, we are sufficient to spoil the children of a whole parish . . . ' That the children came to enjoy the company of their grandfather seems clear enough: he ends one letter to Peter with: 'I can hardly get a line written – your ragamuffins are tearing me to pieces.'[30] And in another: 'I wish I could send you a painting of the group now lying at my fireside: Hugh and Allan caressing our large bull terrier while honest Lion is extending his paws round their necks.'[31] On a wet day he reported that: 'they are confined to the house, Allan is kicking up a riot from the drawing room to the kitchen. Hugh is lying on his belly with a large map of Europe extended before him at once pointing his finger to any country, capital or river which he is desired to indicate.'[32] Hugh especially 'draws greatly to me and takes his constant station between my limbs . . . '[33] In another letter Cleghorn describes how: 'Allan has chosen his profession. In one of our walks he seized a branch of larch . . . and said he would carry it like a soldier. I asked him if he would be a soldier – No – what would you be – Your man and shoot partridges.'[34] He rarely went out for a walk without his grandsons – one at each hand.

Another circumstance which led to Cleghorn's not going on
with the sale of any of Stravithie came from two sudden deaths
in the family. Only a few months after Hugh and Allan had been
sent home, Peter's wife, Isabella, fell seriously ill and died within
two days – of cholera, on 1 June 1824. This blow left Peter with
two baby daughters – Isabella, aged one, and Rachel Jane, aged
three weeks. In a revulsion of feeling against India he must have
written in a letter to his father about coming home there and
then – because Cleghorn replied with advice on what would be
best if he did come home, and pleading with him not to act too
hastily to his own disadvantage in leaving India: 'You should
betray no desire to return till you have fully fixed the resolution in
your own mind and should previously try a negotiation with him,
your successor, likely to succeed you before you resign.'[35]

Cleghorn discussed the whole question of Peter's future with
William Adam. As a result, on 26 December, Adam wrote to
Peter on the best use to which he could put the money which
he had made and was making in India. The essence of his advice
was that Peter could not do better than invest part of his capital
in the purchase of the Mains of Stravithie: 'By this transaction
you obtain the best possible security for your capital – and the
reflection of how your money is to be employed in this country
must soon press itself seriously upon your attention. The various
schemes which capitalists are engaging in here, you will be
relieved from considering. They are full of risk and but little
chance of their gaining regular returns. Instead of such adventures
(for you will hardly be able to vest your money in land securities
except by purchase), you will have the land with a rise in rent at
the end of the lease.' After more wise reflections, Adam ended: 'I
quite agree with your sisters that your father's situation during his
life should be at Wakefield . . . I can add with real satisfaction
and truth that he seems fair to keep health of body and bigness of
mind to a prolonged period of life.' To this letter Cleghorn added
a postcript on 31 December – New Year's Eve – 'The bairns are
in high health and anticipating much joy from the entertainments
of this evening when they are to be joined by the young Goodsirs

from Anstruther. We have country dances . . . Sandy Kay comes with his fiddle and all is life and joy . . . '[36]

But 1825 brought greater losses to Cleghorn – he had not after all ever met Peter's wife – these were the deaths of his eldest son, John, and his much loved daughter Anne. John had done well in the Engineers in India and had only recently been made a lieutenant colonel when he was struck down by illness. It was hoped that a voyage at sea – from India to St Helena – might help him recover his health. There went with him – not his wife Selina – but a devoted Lascar servant, 'who most carefully attended him and to whom he was strongly attached.' The ship's surgeon too did all he could, as was shown in 'a very full and distinct Report . . . continued from day to day till [John's] death on the 6th of last June.' Cleghorn continued in his letter to Peter: 'You know that John Adam died at sea off Madagascar two days before your brother. There are no situations, says his Father to me, more truly similar or more truly afflicting than ours! He too suffers much but bears it with his accustomed Fortitude. He went to London to meet his son but he is now returned; we constantly correspond and have met on the day of his arrival . . . '[37]

Cleghorn also had to tell Peter of his sister Anne's death. Her health had never been strong and the journey to London to fetch the boys had done it no good. She too had died in June 1825, as had 'old Aunt Sarah' – who had nearly made her century. To soften the pain of the loss of Anne, whom Cleghorn could 'not think of without tears', he set out on a Tour of the West – but every place was filled with sportsmen – 'I needed only distraction and sought for it amid less bustle.' It was characteristic of him to try not to dwell on distress but make himself plan for the future. Anne had been Peter's regular correspondent, so Cleghorn now took this on and tried to concentrate on business matters except when he was reporting on: 'the Dear Children: there the prospect is bright and unclouded.'[38]

The main drift of the flood of advice which Peter received (and not only from his father and William Adam) was that he should stay in India at least another year; that he should invest part of his fortune in Stravithie Mains – nowhere else could it be more secure; that his daughters should be sent home with Selina, John's widow (whether to the Campbells in Edinburgh or to Wakefield was the subject of conflicting advice); that when he did return home, he should continue with his career in law: 'the Business of the Privy Council and India Appeals ought to be the branches of the profession to which you may direct your attention.'[39] Most outspoken of all was Mr Clarke from Chiswick, who, after pointing out the advantages Peter would have in building up a lucrative legal practice in London, went on: 'But you must attain these benefits in the way others do. You must not grub, nor fidget, nor dine at chop houses, nor wear shabby clothes, nor neglect the graces . . . '[40]

Peter let all this advice wash over him, ignored a good deal of it and made up his own mind. He decided to put some of his fortune into Stravithie Mains and sent home money to his father, emphasizing that 'it must be regarded as a debt' so that his father would not go on 'improving with borrowed money'.[41] In 1826 he sent home both his daughters with Selina – this time it was Rachel and Jane Dinwoodie who met them in London and happily bore them back to Wakefield. He paid his sister-in-law £2,000 – she evidently had something of a reputation as a gold-digger. Col. Sim, writing from Madras to Peter, commented: 'Selina has been rather hard on you but it is her nature and nothing else was to be expected . . . ; it is just as well that it is settled.'[42] Peter himself came home in the spring of 1827 and had his first meeting with the children at Anstruther, Cleghorn having taken himself off to Edinburgh for the annual dinner of his High School contemporaries (warning Peter that relations between himself and his daughter, Rachel, were somewhat strained: 'She must direct not only my actions but my thoughts . . . ')[43]

Another difficulty faced Peter: not only his father's debts, which he had been told about, but William Dinwoodie's defaulting on money which Peter had sent home through him. It amounted to £2,561, and as his friend Col. Sim wrote bracingly: 'It is only about a fortieth of your fortune but even that is too much to lose willingly.' Peter was in fact the very opposite of his father in his positive dislike of spending money, so his generosity in response to need was all the more admirable, as can be seen when Gilbert, Dinwoodie's son, wrote to Peter: 'I cannot but express the warm gratitude which I feel for your conduct and forbearance towards my Father.'[44] Peter's other decisions were to see something of Europe and to make no second attempt to build up a legal career in London, however many strings his father was anxious to pull on his behalf.

Cleghorn had talked about removing himself and his daughters from Wakefield once his son had decided to settle there. But Peter went off to Europe and on his return showed no inclination to marry again. He was ready enough to leave his children to the care of his sisters while he picked up the threads of old friendships in Scotland and kept in touch with his Madras colleagues. So what Cleghorn had been dreading – parting from his grandchildren – was never seriously considered. As he had said earlier to Peter, with something less than tact: 'I dread the thought of my Bairns leaving me, I never had any like them of my own getting.'[45]

In December 1827 St Andrews University conferred on Cleghorn an honorary LL.D, trusting that he would: 'receive this academical Honour as an appropriate token of their Regard for one whom they love for his amiable qualities as a Friend, whom they admire for his brilliant Talents and various knowledge and who by his Professional ardour and ability at a very early period of life, shed lustre on their ancient seminary.'[46] This must have brought back memories to Cleghorn and prompted some ironical reflections on the whirligig of time bringing in its own revenges, but it was no doubt accepted in the spirit in which it was offered – his friend, Principal Haldane, being the official channel of communication.

The contrast between Cleghorn's tour of Europe in 1788 and his son's could hardly have been greater. For two years Cleghorn's time had been 'idled away in foreign countries', while within three months, in 1828, Peter had covered much the same ground.[47] Cleghorn deplored his haste: it could prevent him meeting interesting people and those of his countrymen abroad who were his intellectual equals and whose like he would never meet in Fife. But Peter had no social ambitions or enjoyment of polite society as such, and, having worked hard at law to achieve an adequate fortune, he was determined now to go his own way, with Stravithie Mains duly settled on him in return for the money he had sent to meet about half the incumbrances on the whole estate.

In May 1829 Cleghorn was faced with what had been hanging over him for a number of years – an operation to remove a stone in the bladder. He had been making yearly visits to George Bell in Edinburgh to be 'cobbled up' but more than that had to be done in the spring of 1829, so he went to stay with Jane at 21 Society and to face first the formidably painful examination and then the operation itself.[48] For his journey home – no need any longer to 'keep Fife out of my mind as much as I can' – he had the use of William Adam's easy carriage and the care and attention of his coachman,[49] and he stayed first with Dr Goodsir in Anstruther, where he soon began to 'feel sensible benefit from change of air and ready command of exercise'. And he had his greatly valued personal servant, William Thomson, to give him the help needed.[50]

The operation must have achieved its primary purpose but for the rest of Cleghorn's life the wounds of the operation never healed properly and his friends at Clatto found him afterwards 'much changed in appearance',[51] so that the suffering involved obviously left its physical mark upon him. His increasing deafness was his other handicap but neither of these diminished his lively involvement in the concerns of his grandchildren or prevented him from deriving as much pleasure as ever before from books and from his daily walks on the estate.

'Mind Entire and Spirits Good'[1]
1830–37

In his last years Cleghorn seems to have maintained a balance by which he passed his time without it hanging on his hands, and 'without my being a burden to myself or I hope to those around me'.[2] His relations with his eldest daughter, Rachel, were easier. She explained to Jenny (always with that touch of acid): 'As I am determined never to oppose, be persuaded that all is to go on as well as possible – now that the weather is good the day will never appear long to him.'[3] With Peter there was sometimes strain – as Cleghorn wrote to Jane in 1835: 'I have given up even the hazarding of a question when all is mystery and reserve from the Education of his Sons to the Planting of his Potatoes,'[4] (this was after a run of sleepless nights caused by a bout of skin irritation and swelling in his arms and legs).

And the strain was compounded by another financial alarm which left Cleghorn full of self-reproach in case it affected Peter's plans for the education of his sons. In 1831 Cleghorn was suddenly presented – out of the blue for all he had been aware – with a demand for £700 which he owed to Scott and Finlay in Edinburgh. That he genuinely had no idea that any such sum was outstanding can be seen in his letters to his son-in-law. He thought that his account with Scott and Finlay had been balanced by Col. McGill's legacies, his Aunt Sarah's succession, the Carnatic stock and different remittances from India, especially as 'so many years have elapsed without any demand being made or statement of account sent to me'.[5] He was very bitter against himself, and in his letter to Peter on the subject he ended: 'My carelessnesses have been excessive and inexcusable. Would to God I were in my grave.'[6] But when the first wave of distress subsided, his mind as ever took a practical turn and, though it is not dated, there survives in the Cleghorn Papers a list of proposals by which the whole remaining property of the Stravithie estate should be handed over to Peter, 'that is to say all the property now possessed by me and which is bounded by the Burn of Stravithie and Mill Lead on the North, by the River Kenley on the South, by your lands of Stravithie Mains on the East, and on the West by the lands of Kinaldy and Brigton.'[7] But before this the lands should be inspected and valued, Peter being at liberty to refuse the valuation:

'Previous to your acceptance,' Cleghorn continued: 'a list of debts upon the property shall be made out and delivered to you and if you are satisfied that the value of the property exceeds the amount of the Burdens upon it, you will take upon yourself the payment of these debts.' These amounted to about £11,000 in all, half of the sum having been willingly handed over to Cleghorn by members of his family. Thus, '£2000 is owing to your sister, Mrs. Campbell, but at her death, this sum together with heritable property in St. Andrews falls to you or your family.' Other creditors were the trustees of the Surgeons' Widows Fund, from whom Cleghorn had borrowed £2000. If the value of the property he proposed to hand over to Peter came to more than his debts, Cleghorn said he wanted to renounce all right to it: it should be 'divided among your children in such proportions as you may judge proper'. An arrangement on these lines was carried out and Peter took on the whole responsibility of running the estate. He did not get a bad bargain, especially in view of the hazards to which fortunes invested in other ways were subject. Many of Cleghorn's neighbours and friends had been ruined, for instance, when the Fife Bank collapsed in January 1826.[8]

Investing, generally, was a perilous business: 'The Bogs of Ireland, the Mines of South America etc. etc. are attracting companies to find employment for sums lying idle in the hands of the Bank.'[9] The lands of Stravithie were in good heart through Cleghorn's efforts; Wakefield itself and the estate farm houses had been restored or rebuilt; there were 'about 140 acres of wood of all ages – most of it about thirty years', and all this yielding an annual income in 1845 of about £800 a year according to Peter.[10] This may have been meant 'there was little to come and go on' – Peter's phrase – but it provided a way of life which both father and son had chosen and over which neither showed any regrets.

The diaries which Cleghorn kept between January 1834 and December 1836 (and probably before, but these are the two which survive) show how closely he identified himself with the way the land was worked. The Cleghorns themselves were responsible for farming Bannafield, Cotton and Wakefield and the diary noted in a laconic but definite way the pattern of labour on the land and the holidays which punctuated its rhythms. The first of these was a revel for tenants on 6 January 1835, no doubt with a Twelfth Night cake with 'the bean' and pease. Then came old Handsel Monday – on 13 January in 1834 and the 12th in 1835 – when the farm servants were given presents and an entertainment at night with a feast prepared in the Wakefield kitchen. The work during the short days of winter in January and February 1834 was concentrated at Bannafield, for instance, on dividing the west and south parks with hedges and ditches instead of dykes. At Cotton they were carrying off ditch scourings which, mixed with lime, were made into compost. Cleghorn himself had ordered gooseberry and currant bushes from a Dundee nursery and on 24 February supervised their planting. At Wakefield, stones, howked out of the fields, were used to fill in newly dug drains, carts being sent to Tosh for whins to cover the stones. When the ground was frost-bound or too wet, the men were set to thrash grain or pease and then to pass the grain through the fanners.

March and April were the months for carrying and spreading dung – from their own stables and barnyard; or town dung, fish manure or kelp. Then followed the sowing of pease, beans, tares, oats and barley (the wheat having been sown in the previous autumn); then harrowing. March was also the time for lambing, though Stravithie at that time was primarily an arable estate. The beginning of May was the time for planting potatoes. The spring of 1834 was very dry and by 29 May the potatoes were having to be watered from a great barrel dragged out on a cart to the fields – very labour-intensive but in the end worth it for in October Cleghorn was noting what an excellent potato crop they had off Cotton: 'In point of size they are large beyond example.' He also planted, 'back of the Offices,' cuts from two potatoes which his daughter, Jane (Mrs Campbell), had brought back with her from Ireland – 'of a new species there said to be very productive and of excellent quality.' So, obviously, the whole family wanted to make some contribution to Stravithie – but there is no mention of what happened to them. The potato crop of 1835 was by contrast the only failure of the year.

June 1834 saw some of Bannafield being prepared for turnips and swedes: 200 carts of compost and 50 carts of stable dung first, before they were sown; then, in July, stripping, weeding and thinning the turnips, with the drill harrow on them in August. They were lifted in November and December. Sheep shearing was carried out in June and at the beginning of July hay-making began – very poor in 1834, producing only enough seed for the following year.

It was in August 1834 that the family acquired a pony for their new phaeton, the drosky having been their usual form of carriage up till then. In August too the lint was pulled up, slipped into pools on the estate to ret in order to separate the fibre from the rest of the plant. It was then taken out, beaten and shredded. All the farm labourers had their own rigs of lint and other crops round their cottages, which all helped to harvest.

In 1834 they could begin 'shearing the barley back of Wakefield' on 14 August, whereas in 1835 the harvest was not started till the 31st. The Lammas Market in St Andrews was before the beginning of the harvest but, as far as Cleghorn was concerned, his main duty was to provide pocket money for those going in to the Market.[11] An annual ritual, marking another stage in the harvest, was 'the Maiden', the name given to the last handful of corn cut by the reapers. The handful was dressed up with ribbons or strips of silk as a doll and fixed on the wall with the date when it was cut. In 1833 it was only 23 September, in 1834 on the 6th and in 1835 not till 26 September. The corns then had to be stooked and driven to the barnyard or the cottagers' stores, and when this was completed 'harvest home' was celebrated.

For Stravithie the grain yields for both 1834 and 1835 were satisfactory, though the prices they obtained were much lower than some years earlier. In addition to this basic timetable of seed time and harvest, more improvements were undertaken in the Close: the old wash-house and laundry were pulled down and new ones erected adjoining the West Pavilion. Thirteen farm workers were set to dig foundations for the planned six-foot dyke of the new straw yard, carts were sent to Crail for lime and to the North Planting for wood for building new sheds for the cattle, sheep and poultry, south-east of the stables – so that by the end of November 1834 Cleghorn was writing that: 'our outhouse accommodation will answer every object . . . ' Once an improver, always an improver – even Peter, in spite of his caution, was obviously infected by his father's enthusiasm.

It was not until 7 December 1834 that Cleghorn remarked in his diary: 'I am afraid that the affairs of William Campbell will give us much trouble and great pecuniary loss.' Back in 1831 these had not yet been known to the family, so it was with full confidence that Cleghorn had turned to him in his distress at the unexpected demand made on him by Scott and Finlay of Edinburgh. But in fact Campbell was not only in serious difficulties but had been taking unscrupulous advantage of the trust his wife and father-in-law had in him to try to postpone the crash. He had held back any reminder from Cleghorn of how his affairs stood in Edinburgh, as Peter wrote later: 'in order that my Father's mind, being kept in a tranquil state might the more readily enter into Bank obligations for Mr. C. for which we have paid so dearly.'

It seems that one of the things Campbell had done was to deposit the bond for £2,000 (which his wife, Jane, wanted to hand over to her father) with a bank and then himself borrow £1,000 upon it without telling either Jane or Cleghorn, whom he made his security. Peter wrote to Mr Mack, Campbell's partner, in terms of measured condemnation after Cleghorn's death and Campbell's ruin (which followed that same year): 'The more I have considered, the more I am struck with the cruelty and injustice of having kept my Father ever since he had any transactions with' you in 1821 in utter ignorance of how his accounts stood.'[12] Hugh perforce accepted both debt and obligation for the bond, but after his death Peter was plagued with the effects of Campbell's malpractices. But this was the last of the financial blows that Cleghorn suffered and so far as can be judged from the correspondence and diaries of his last years, he was relieved to have transferred his responsibilities to Peter. In September 1834, for example, Cleghorn was writing to the Secretary of the British Linen Bank about the balance drawn by Campbell on this bank, explaining that his son, Peter, was now managing all their affairs, but: 'we are both aware that we are responsible for Mr. C.'

Cleghorn's pension meant he could make his contribution to the running of the household and a list of what he spent over and above this at the back of his diaries shows how modest his personal expenditure was: mainly tips for Hugh and Allan, the odd sixpence or a shilling for gingerbread, his doctor's account and the cost of arranging for someone to return books borrowed from the University Library, or of going into Anstruther. He still worried that he had not left his daughters well enough provided for and so was greatly heartened when, through William Adam and his son, it was arranged that the £200 a year which they together received from the Treasury, would continue to be paid until the death of the last of them. Cleghorn was especially pleased because Peter rather grudged money spent on his own daughters' education – Peter's sisters could now: 'defray with pleasure the expenses absolutely necessary in the education of their nieces . . . ' The contrast again between father and son is quite revealing.

Without doubt Cleghorn's most constant interest and concern in these last years of his life were his grandchildren. Until 1831 the boys were at home, being taught by a tutor, Mr Cruikshank, along with a stepson of Jane's, Robert Campbell, and David, the son of Cleghorn's William Thomson. In this little class David: 'soon became the first boy . . . and after barely three years' labour in Latin and Greek, he was by far the first in the list of competitors for one of the foundation bursaries in the United College of St. Andrews.'[13] The main aim was to achieve a really thorough grounding in classics. As Cleghorn wrote to Dr Bell: 'I have long been convinced that if the foundation is not well laid there, no permanent superstructure is in general ever raised in any of our colleges.' For the next stage of their education, Cleghorn made a list for Peter of the pros and cons of sending the boys in to the High School in Edinburgh. The greatest advantage was the School's good Greek. They also pushed their pupils on well and the boys in the High School were in general of greater ability than those in the mixed classes in the school in St Andrews. The main disadvantages were that it would be less healthy in Edinburgh, more expensive, and the food would be inferior.[14] Peter decided in favour of Edinburgh and in September 1831 Hugh and Allan went to stay with their aunt in Society and started the autumn term in the High School.

The eldest grandson, Hugh, kept many of the letters he and Allan received from the family. Their Aunt Jenny, for instance, reminded them: 'You must write soon to Grandpapa and tell him all you are about and what you think of things in general. It will cheer him to hear from you for he misses you much.'[15] They must have been quite good correspondents for Cleghorn mostly began by acknowledging and commenting on their letters; they did not have much leisure at first, so: 'do your best during the hour of play at Leap Frog and High Spie.'[16] Later on he asked if the boys played at shinty. 'If you take part in that game shall I send you over some nice sticks which William will carefully select?'[17] Cleghorn told them about the comings and goings at Wakefield and usually reported on their pets: 'All the concerns of my Dear Boys here are well – the Ponies and the Rabbits are well cared for. Old Trusty follows your old Grandfather. Young Tartar [the terrier] worries the poultry much larger than himself and Black Tom lies on my knee.'[18] Indeed, Cleghorn often went to feed the rabbits himself because they reminded him of his 'Dear Boys'.

He also gave them news of their sisters. In January 1832 Peter and Rachel were away, 'but Aunt Jenny, your little sisters and I pass our time very pleasantly and never tire. Isabella is a very good and affectionate girl, very grave and sedate. Little Rachel is also very good but full of fun and play.'[19] It was she who attended him 'on all his walks'. Later he wrote: 'I must employ you to get some pretty little books for little Rachy . . . ' (He did not refer to her as 'Tottie', as the others did, but reverted to the diminutive he had given his wife.) 'I have not been able to give her a distinct history of Cocky Doodle Do nor Tom Trip and his Dog, nor of the "House that Jack Built." But you will send over the true history of those distinguished persons and events' – and he enclosed two shillings and sixpence for that purpose. Aunt Jenny had evidently made her protest because he added a postcript that more advanced books should be sent and they were to consult their Aunt Campbell.[20] (Rachel by this time would be seven and a half years old.)

Cleghorn did not hesitate to instil good morality. To Allan he wrote: 'Never tell a lie on any account whatever . . . to lie is the sign of a very bad Boy and a very great coward. And it would break your Grandfather's heart if any of his dear boys were to be either the one or the other.' To Hugh he gave quite practical advice: 'In your play there will sometimes be little contentions and battles . . . never fight with a boy younger or weaker than yourself. But if a boy of your own age or even older strikes you, make no complaint to the Master but strike again. There is nothing dangerous or dishonourable in getting a bloody nose. But always avoid quarrels when you can.'[21] Then he wanted to know what books they read at school and was pleased that Hugh was tenth in Latin in a class of a hundred boys. When Hugh was given his first essay:

'I should like to know what it is. He will converse about it with Mr. Cruikshank. Endeavour to understand it perfectly and not begin to write before he does understand it. Then let him put his thoughts on paper in his own words and not be anxious to say too much.'[22]

Only occasionally does Cleghorn half forget that it was only eleven- and twelve-year-old boys to whom he was writing. He told them in November 1831 that: 'your good friend, old Mrs. Playfair, is dead. She was nearly as old as your grandfather when a much longer continuance in this world is not to be expected. But my Boys now know that the great God who created this world, has created many others. All the stars which you see and which ignorant men think are so many candles to amuse or give us light, are all worlds and most of them much bigger than ours. The Almighty makes nothing in vain and all the stars which you see and the Millions which we cannot see are probably inhabited by rational beings, though probably with powers and dispositions very different from ours . . . '[23] Here he was definitely widening horizons even if in terms of astronomy he was jumping the gun somewhat. In February 1832 he was writing:

'My chief wish for being permitted to live a few years longer is to witness the progress of my dear Boys; but if such excuses were to prevail, the old Ferryman Charon might ride at anchor in his boat and wait in vain for Passengers from this side of Styx.'[24]

By the end of their first year away, Cleghorn and his grand-daughters were longing for the holidays. 'The fishing rods and the flies shall be ready and Dogs for Rabbit hunting and Mr. Fulton has promised to meet you in the North Planting with gun and dog to try to raise a roebuck.'[25]

The boys were at the High School for less than two years, their second being interrupted by their catching whooping cough.[26] When they had recovered they were sent to school in St Andrews where the Madras College, founded and endowed by Dr Bell to practise his monitorial system of education at a secondary level, had been opened in 1833. Hugh concentrated on learning French (for which he was given a prize) and German, arithmetic and mathematics. Cleghorn was convinced he should not 'enter the higher academical branches at too premature an age'. However, in February 1833, Hugh joined the Latin class in the University and remained at College till 1837, when he took his degree in Arts and then went to Edinburgh – where he was apprenticed to the surgeon Professor Syme. In February 1836 Cleghorn was telling Adam that 'I would undertake in the summer to prepare him in Moral Philosophy', and as he was still writing vigorous if somewhat illegible letters, certainly up to July of 1836,[27] it seems probable that he carried out his plan. Allan had less sticking power than Hugh. Cleghorn was writing to him in February 1833: 'I think my dear Allan would mount somewhat higher if he would labour a little more assiduously.' Allan followed Hugh to St Andrews University in 1836 and then went into the army.

The young certainly came out to Wakefield. On 1 March 1834, for instance, Cleghorn noted in his diary: 'Our Boys and eight of their companions remain all night. They will have to be three in a bed.' And on 9 November 1835 he noted: 'Supped 25 this evening.'

Certainly his turn of phrase in his letters to his friends was as pungent as ever and his interest as lively. In 1831 William Adam had evidently asked him for his opinion on the use of the secret ballot in elections. Cleghorn on the whole was against it – because a man might take a bribe from one side and then vote for the other and the only result would be to breed suspicion. 'But I have not thought on this subject and in writing to you I have, as I often do, allowed my pen to dictate my thoughts instead of being directed by them.'[28] But he was quite clear that he was against any sweeping measure of parliamentary reform, which he regarded as a threat to the constitution: 'The Duke of Wellington by pledging himself and his Government to resist all reform, has brought in a set of men fettered by an indefinite pledge which it is impossible for them to redeem . . . a storm is breeding which may blow our present rulers to the devil.'[29]

Cleghorn was behind the presentation of an address to the Crown from the University on the change of ministry occasioned at the end of 1834 by the 'dismissal' of Melbourne (at his own suggestion) by William IV. Cleghorn actually sent Haldane a draft suggesting the form the address might take in upholding the royal prerogative against the radical element in the Whig party which had already forced through a number of sweeping reforms. That Cleghorn could regard the absurd figure of William IV as a bulwark of the constitution could only be explained by his conviction that:

'We are following exactly the steps of the French Revolution . . . Having had good and almost local opportunities of witnessing this fatal process, I confess that it haunts me like a ghost and foretells that this once happy country has the same bloody process to undergo . . . '[30]

But his gloomy prognostications about the British constitution did not prevent him from celebrating with William Adam and General Durham their 'octogenarian dinner'. Cleghorn had already given a hint to Durham that he should 'indulge with moderation or the Duty of Boots devolves on him'. In the event, the occasion was as enjoyable as ever and they parted 'neither sorrowful nor altogether sober'. His diaries show how numerous his other contacts were – through guests who stayed or dined at Wakefield. Sometimes, indeed, he was fairly worn out by visitors. At the end of July in 1834, he noted: 'This month – had much company and I feel myself exhausted in strength and spirits – hope I shall now get rest to recruit.' But a guest whom he found most stimulating was a Lady Campbell. He wrote an account of her visit to his grandsons on 31 August 1835:

'A few days ago Dr. and Mrs. Carstairs with a Lady Campbell dined here; her husband is British Minister at the Court of Persia; she was there several years, saw much and saw it well, during the severe contest of the Civil war between the present Sovereign and his uncles, for the Throne. She has lately come home, having travelled by land some thousand miles with an infant in the Nurse's arms, passing through Armenia and the interesting half barbarous countries between the Caspian and the Black Sea. At the latter, she embarked at Trebizond and landed at Constantinople. Look at the map and show me the course of her journey when you come here. I was never so great a traveller but the countries she visited and their inhabitants were not altogether unknown to me and we made very good company with each other.'[31]

Cleghorn's brief recording of the names of Wakefield visitors shows too what a friend of the family William Tennant had become: he was out there thirty-three times in the course of 1835.

1835 was in many ways a trying year for Cleghorn. It began with another brush with the minister of Dunino over whether Cleghorn gave his share to the poor of the parish since he did not go to church and therefore did not contribute to the church collection for that purpose – a charge which Cleghorn strenuously denied, being supported in this by grateful 'testimonials' from the villager themselves – and the diaries do bear these out.[32] In the spring he could not go out much because of swelling in his arms and legs accompanied by intense irritation, which prevented him from sleeping. William Adam came to the rescue again with a prescription from Dr Short of Edinburgh, with the result that by July the trouble had cleared up. On 7 December he himself had a slight stroke – which affected his speech and his hands (as his diary painfully shows) though it cleared up after a few days.

Despite his problems his interest in the management of the estate and his relish for reading were as strong as ever. As the autumn of 1835 drew on he was writing to Adam: 'I must now confine myself for the winter at my fireside where with the command of books I shall beguile my now short pilgrimage in studious indolence. When my table is well supplied with this species of food, I pay little attention to the arrangement of the dishes.' These ranged from Dr McCrie's *Life of Knox* to studies on the Poor Law, and Dr Cook on patronage and the election of ministers in the Reformed Church. And as he explained to Mrs Wyllie, Peter's sister-in-law:

'The desire of travelling over this world of ours which in my younger days no difficulties could restrain nor dangers appal, is now confined to maps and books.' His youngest daughter, Jenny, was his ally in this – just as she was in the care and education of his granddaughters. It was she who classified Cleghorn's books and wrote to him when she went on holiday with Isabella and Rachel Jane; she who fetched him down to meals and made sure he was not allowed to become too isolated in his study.

In spite of Cleghorn's plans to introduce Hugh to moral philosophy in the summer of 1836, he took the warning of his stroke with some seriousness and asked Peter to go over to Blair Adam with the present he wanted to give his friend, 'in acknowledgment of my affection and gratitude.' It was a box which was originally: 'presented by the Empress Maria Theresa to Signor Domalie, the Venetian Ambassador at the Court of Vienna and upon his death [it] came into the possession of Sir Richard Worsley, our Minister in Venice, who gave it to me. The painting is by Teniers and I am told that it is a good painting of the Flemish School.'[33]

The present did not mark the end of the correspondence. William Adam in the summer of 1836 was amusing himself with his own printing press at Blair Adam and his very first production, called *The Gift of a Grandfather*, consisted of two essays on the 'Study of History' and 'General Reading', which he had taken from a collection of essays made by his mother of all the great figures of the Scottish Enlightenment, among whom William Cleghorn was included.[34] In this connection he wrote to Wakefield asking Cleghorn for particulars about his uncle. This led Cleghorn to reopen his correspondence with Dr John Lee − on whether he had any information about William − with a list of Adam's queries.[35] Adam wrote a preface to the two essays and, in describing David Hume to his grandchildren, remarked how: 'in all he said and wrote and did, when not employed in his unnecessary metaphysical speculation (well named by a friend of mine "intellectual rope dancing") was innocent, playful, moral and most natural in his conversation.' Adam then devoted over a page of his preface to telling his grandchildren about Hugh Cleghorn, (author of the phrase about "intellectual rope dancing"), and his 'frequent, ready and powerful remarks'. Adam described what Cleghorn had done in Ceylon and ended: 'This great service has been but frugally rewarded. My friend however still lives in respectable retirement and we octogenarians often meet and talk old matters over. I know the kind nature of my old schoolfellow so well that I am sure he will not be offended at my thus introducing him to the acquaintance of my youthful relatives.'

Adam sent a copy of this first product of his printing press to Cleghorn with a note which reflects how completely they were at home with each other: 'If your grandchildren are too learned to benefit by the enclosed, they will however learn what perhaps they do not know – what a strange sort of grandfather they had, for you are well and justly libelled in these few pages.' This is in fact the latest note to Cleghorn – dated 25 October 1836 – which survives in the Cleghorn Papers and it is altogether fitting that it should come from his closest friend.

As all his family were at Wakefield at this time, there was no occasion for family letters, so no account has survived of Cleghorn's death. This took place on 19 February 1837. He was buried in Dunino churchyard alongside Rachel's and Anne's graves.

In his diary of 1834, Cleghorn wrote, apropos of his birthday: 'My life has been of some use to my country by adding Ceylon to our Dominions and giving security to our possessions there. But it has been of little use to my family or myself.' He also observed, with some irony, that if he had never stirred from his academic chair in St Andrews, his own income would have been greater than that afforded by his government pension – (he was of course wrong over this: he was taking no account of the life pensions to his daughters which the University could not have provided). But these were irritable reactions to financial constraints: he had too much zest and too many interests to sit and brood in self-pity. Besides, his rarely expressed conviction in an overriding Providence made him embrace his own lot – if at times somewhat wryly; as he wrote to Peter in 1825:

'There is another World . . . Religion inculcates and Reason irresistibly proclaims that all things are under the direction of the Sovereign Creator and Sustainer of Universal Nature.'[36]

Acceptance of that same authority meant that for him principles should not be sacrificed to self-interest and this guided him in maintaining his integrity. His intelligence and boldness made his plans formidably wide-ranging and his criticisms sharply valid but he was generous-minded and not given to brooding on past grievances. His somewhat insouciant attitude to money landed him in his greatest worries but also helped him to launch on adventures which would have made a more careful man hesitate. His 'bigness of mind', in Adam's phrase, meant that he perceived and, as far as his circumstances allowed, helped to promote forward-looking developments in university teaching, in strategic colonial policy and, in the last stages of his life, the practical application of scientific methods to farming. His 'kind nature' – Adam's phrase again – meant that he was valued, loved even, by the young and his many friends found him good company. Certainly all the lectures, diaries and letters which he left are sparked through with interest and evoke a feeling of warmth for the man himself. But he was not one who savoured drawn-out farewells; as he wrote to the Earl of Glasgow:

'Having paid a long visit, I must make a short ceremony and withdraw.'[37]

Appendix

'Plan of Provisional Capitulation'

Meuron's Swiss Regiment, at present in the service of the Dutch East India Company and garrisoned on the Island of Ceylon, belonging as hereditary property to Count Charles Daniel de Meuron and commanded by his brother Count Pierre Frederic de Meuron to whom the revision of above is assured, will be transferred to the service of His Majesty the King of Britain, on the following conditions:.

1 It will receive the pay and emoluments enjoyed by the other European troops that serve in the English establishment in India.

2 If it happens to be discharged at the end of four years or such other period as will be deemed advisable, the officers will receive as a retiring pension for rest of their lives, English half pay according to their respective ranks.

3 The non-commissioned officers and soldiers who on account of wounds or other infirmity cannot continue their service, will receive the same treatment as given in similar circumstances to the other troops of His Majesty or of the English Company in India.

4 With regard to the administration of justice – the police, the discipline and deportment of the regiment as well as all the other advantages assigned to it by the capitulation passed at the time of its formation with the Dutch Company – it will remain on the same footing until the drawing up of a new capitulation which must be discussed in a friendly fashion between the Government of His Majesty of Madras and the Colonel the proprietor or his brother as attorney and that must be done three months at latest after the regiment has passed into the service of the British Sovereign.

5   The Regiment composed of two battalions of the five companies of 120 men can be augmented by means of new arrangements if the well-being of the service demands it.

6   The four heads of the Regiment viz – The Colonel the proprietor, the Colonel in command, the Lieutenant Colonel and the Major, will receive in addition to the pay merited by their ranks, the allowances and emoluments of captains as if they were each at the head of a company.

7   The English Government will pay annually to the Colonel, the proprietor for recruiting the sum of £6000 sterling to be drawn quarterly. The said proprietor will provide recruits necessary to keep the regiment complete and will deliver them at a Continental port assigned to serve as a depot and from where they will be embarked. From the moment of their arrival at the said depot they will be in the pay of the English Government which will compensate the Colonel, the proprietor, at the rate of £25 sterling for every man who perishes at sea or is killed or taken prisoner. The English Government will have the right to appoint a commissioner to inspect and verify the recruits and the Colonel an officer to receive them.

8   As soon as the regiment has entered into the service of His Majesty the King of Britain he will pay to the Colonel, the proprietor, all that the Dutch Company, in virtue of the former capitulation, still legitimately owes, either to the Colonel personally or to the regiment. The titles and credentials which establish the claims of the Colonel, the proprietor, will be examined by the respective commissioners appointed by the Government of Madras in the name of the British Sovereign and by the Count de Meuron on his part. Following on their decision, the money to which he is entitled will be remitted to him by bills of exchange from the Bank of London or in gold coin at Madras just as he chooses.

9   In the same way he will have the option of having each month's pay, as well as the emolumemts and all that is due

to the regiment paid in gold or silver coin by the Treasury of India or by bills of exchange from the London Bank.

10 There will be in the regiment two assistant surgeons and two adjutants not included in the old capitulation but admitted by agreement and paid.

11 The Count de Meuron does not demand any special line of treatment for himself personally. On this point he may rely on the loyalty of the English Government and on the generosity of His Majesty, the King of Britain, but the rank of Major General being due to him for ten years, His Majesty will be entreated to have the 'brevet' sent to him with all expedience before his departure as well as that of Brigadier for his brother, Count Pierre Frédéric de Meuron the Colonel at present in command of the regiment. He declares moreover that he will not take advantage of this rank of Major General to aspire to any command beyond Lieutenant where his regiment will be engaged since he does not wish to arouse distrust in any of the officers now in command in India for the British Sovereign.

12 As he could not, without risking his reputation and causing trouble and annoyance to his family, leave this country before paying his accounts and putting his affairs in order, there will be paid to him from this very moment on the strength of what will be due to him afterwards an advance of £4000, so that he can liquidate himself entirely and so that his hurried departure, the motive of which must remain a secret, cannot have the appearance of a flight nor be interpreted to the disadvantage of his honour.

13 All the expences of this and the return journey for himself, his suite and his equipages will be borne by the English Government who will provide for his maintenance in a manner befitting his rank during his sojourn in India. The Colonel, the proprietor, will be at liberty to take with him as aid-de-camp Captain Bolle or such other officer of the same rank as he chooses. This officer will enjoy the rank, salary,

emoluments and half-pay like the Captains of the regiment and will have his travelling expenses paid in the same way as the Colonel.

14 The Colonel, the Proprietor, will be allowed to return to Europe as soon as he thinks this course is necessitated by the state of his health or by business matters, and he will leave his authority in the hands of his brother, Colonel Pierre Frédéric de Meuron who will take his place in all the commissions and in all the power with which the King has entrusted him.

15 If after some time, experience reveals inconveniences and omissions detrimental to the regiment in this capitulation about to be drawn up, the Colonel, the proprietor, reserves the right to demand that changes, required by circumstances and justice, be effected.

Drawn up at Neufchâtel in Switzerland 30 March 1795, and signed by me, invested with provisional powers to that effect.

Signed
HUGH CLEGHORN
COUNT DE MEURON

The Douglases of Strathenry

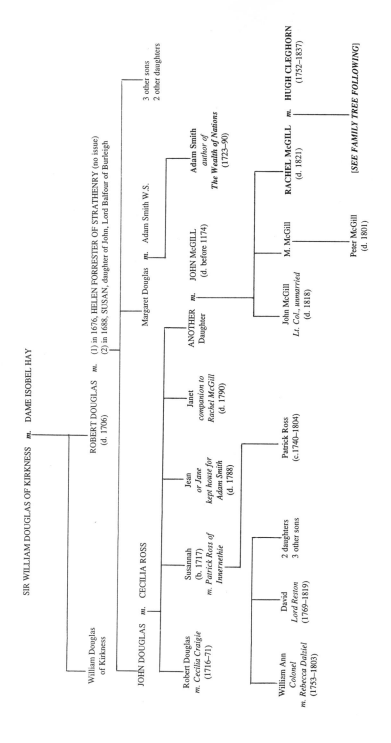

Six Generations of Cleghorns

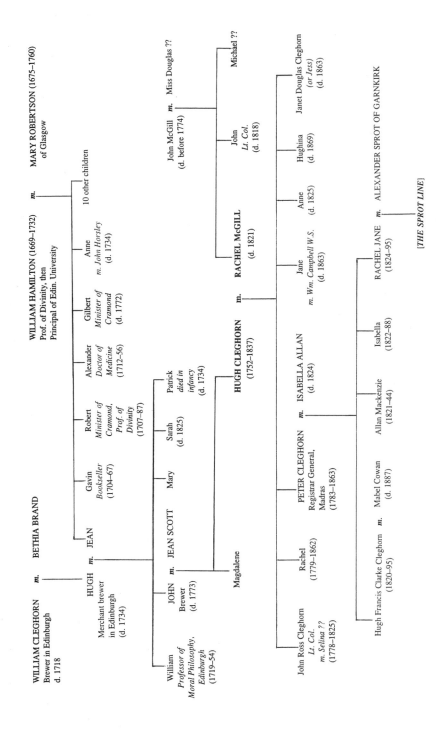

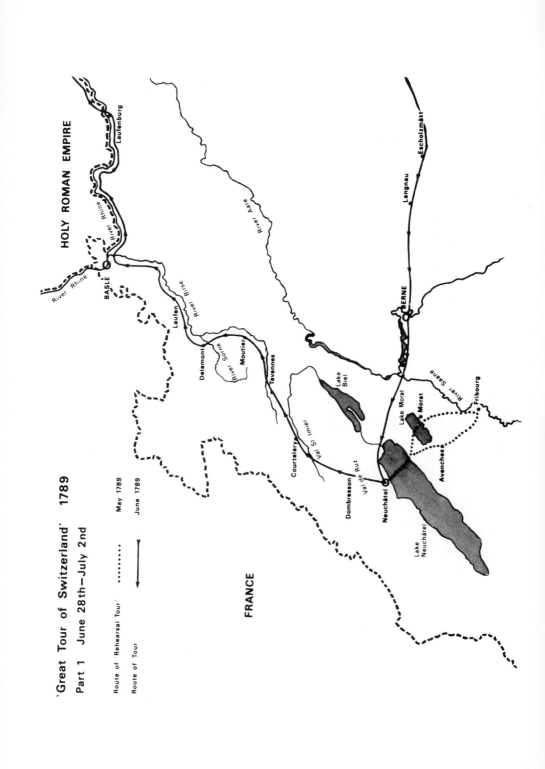

'Great Tour of Switzerland' 1789
Part 1   June 28th–July 2nd

Route of 'Rehearsal Tour' ·········· May 1789

Route of Tour ⟶ June 1789

HOLY ROMAN EMPIRE

River Rhine
River Rhine
Laufenburg
BASLÉ
Laufen
River Birse
River Sorne
Delamont
Moutier
Tavannes
River Aare
Courtelary
Val St Imier
Dombresson
Val de Ruz
Neuchâtel
Lake Biel
Lake Morat
Morat
Avenches
River Saane
Fribourg
BERNE
Langnau
Escholzmätt
Lake Neuchâtel

FRANCE

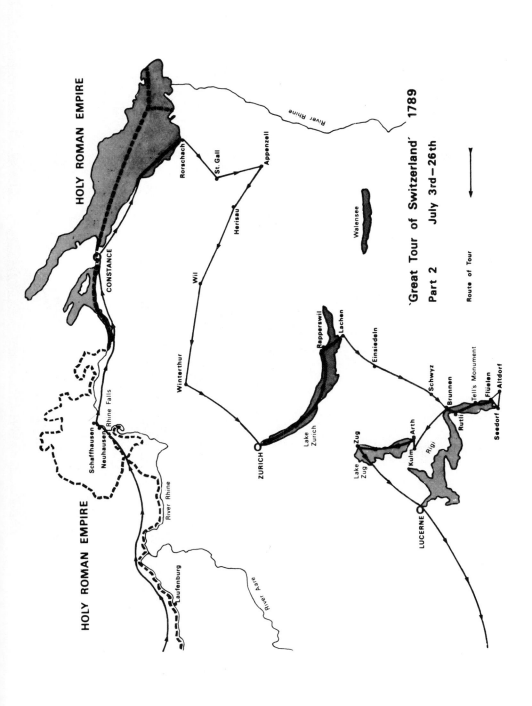

HOLY ROMAN EMPIRE

HOLY ROMAN EMPIRE

River Rhine

River Rhine

River Aare

Laufenburg

Schaffhausen
Neuhausen
Rhine Falls

CONSTANCE

Rorschach

St. Gall

Appenzell

Herisau

Wil

Winterthur

Walensee

Rapperswil

Lachen

Einsiedeln

Lake
Zurich

ZURICH

Schwyz

Brunnen

Tell's Monument

Flüelen

Altdorf

Seedorf

Rutli

Rigi

Arth

Kulm

Lake
Zug

LUCERNE

'Great Tour of Switzerland' 1789

Part 2   July 3rd–26th

Route of Tour

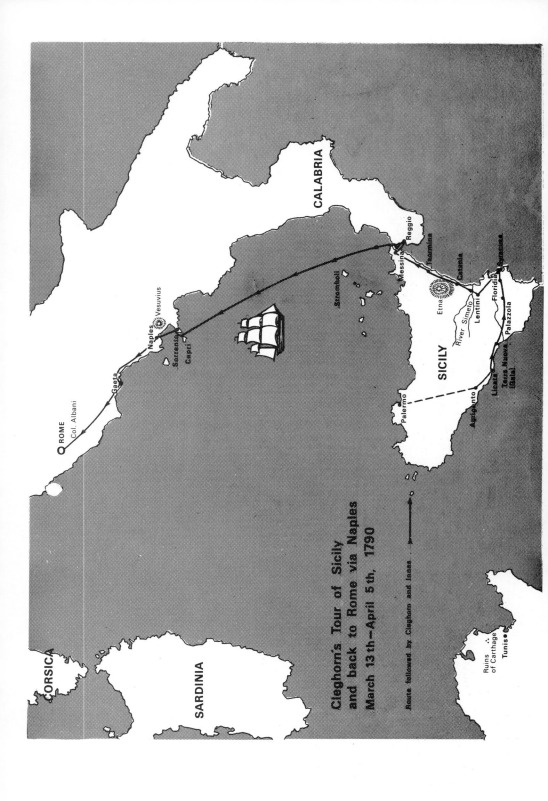

Cleghorn's Tour of Sicily
and back to Rome via Naples
March 13 th—April 5 th, 1790

Route followed by Cleghorn and Innes

CORSICA

SARDINIA

ROME
Col. Albani

Gaeta

Naples
Vesuvius
Sorrento
Capri

CALABRIA

Reggio
Messina
Taormina

Stromboli

Etna
River Simeto
Lentini

Catania
Floridia
Syracuse
Palazzola

SICILY

Palermo

Licata
Terra Nueva
(Gela)

Agrigento

Ruins
of Carthage
Tunise

Cleghorn's First Voyage to the East

Outward   February 24th 1795 — September 30th 1795

Homeward   February 22nd 1796 — March 30th 1797

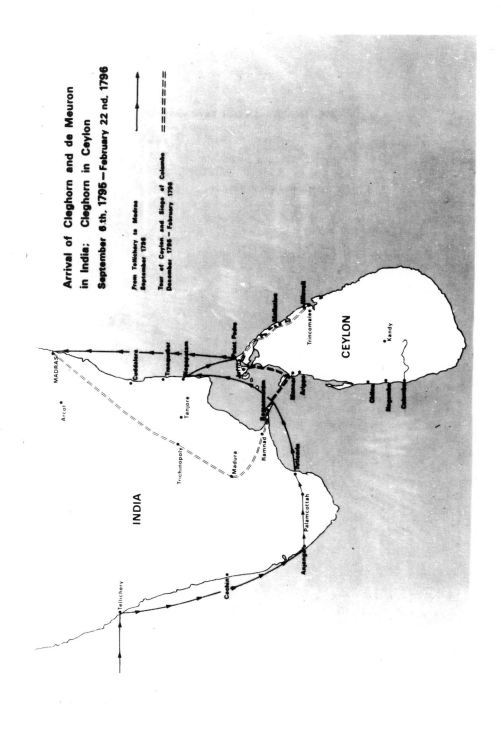

Arrival of Cleghorn and de Meuron
in India: Cleghorn in Ceylon
September 6th, 1795—February 22 nd, 1796

From Tellichery to Madras
September 1795

Tour of Ceylon and Siege of Colombo
December 1795 — February 1796

INDIA

CEYLON

Tellichery

Cochin

Anjengo

Palamcottah

Tuticorin

Ramnad

Madura

Trichinopoly

Tanjore

Arcot

MADRAS

Cuddalore

Tranquebar

Trincomalee

Kandy

Notes

(Abbreviations are explained in the Bibliography)

Chapter 1

1   Scott (1972), p. 316. (My italics.)
2   Southey (1844), Vol. III, p. 718.
3   C.P., Box 2, Envelope 1, #20.
4   N.L.S., Lee Papers, MS 3441 (f122).
5   Burgh of Edinburgh, 1689–1701, p. 21–2.
6   Ibid, p. 214.
7   Grant (1881), Vol. II, pp. 269–72.
8   C.P., Box 2, Envelope 1, #23.
9   See note 5 – pp. 123 & 183.
10 Warrick (1913), Ch. 15, p. 240.
11 Leechman (1789), Vol. I, p. 4.
12 Somerville (1843), p. 64.
13 Wodrow (1842), Vol. III, p. 302.
14 Wodrow (1937), Vol. I, p. 337.
15 C.P., Box 2, Envelope 1, #4.
16 Wodrow (1842), Vol. IV, p. 104.
17 C.P., Box 1, Envelope 2, #8.
18 E.U.L., from typescript letters folded into Alexander Hamilton's *Itinerarium*, ed. A. B. Hart, at the back of the copy.
19 I am indebted to the article by Warren McDougall on 'Gavin Hamilton, Bookseller in Edinburgh', p. 537 et seq., for this information.
20 See note 18.
21 C.P., Box 1, Envelope 2, #10.
22 E.C.A., Cartulary, Number 4, 1748–73, R168.
23 C.P., Box 3, #1.
24 N.L.S Lee Papers, MS 3441 (f133).
25 Mossner (1963), p. 297 et seq.
26 I am indebted for all this section on William Cleghorn to the article by Dr Douglas Nobbs on 'The British Ideas of William Cleghorn, Hume's academic rival', p. 575 et seq.
27 Grant (1884), Vol. II, p. 338.
28 Carlyle (1910), p. 121 et seq.
29 See note 26.
30 N.L.S., Lee Papers, MS 3441 (f84).
31 S.R.O., Edinburgh Marriage Register 1751–1800, p. 143.
32 S.R.O., Edinburgh Old Parish Register of Births, entered under 'Sabbath, 22 March 1752'.

[33] W. Steven, *History of the High School of Edinmburgh*, p. 203.

[34] William Adam (1751–1839), nephew of the Adam Brothers; educated at the High School and the College, Edinburgh; called to the Scottish Bar 1773; MP 1774–81 and 1806–7; supporter of Lord North 1774; he wounded Fox in a duel after a quarrel over a speech by Fox in the House but later became his ally; treasurer of ordnance 1780; called to the English Bar 1782; led the prosecution in impeachment of Warren Hastings 1788; Attorney General to the Prince of Wales; Privy Councillor 1815; Lord Chief Commissioner of the Jury Court 1816; married Eleanora, daughter of 10th Earl Elphinstone; four sons and a daughter.

[35] General James Durham (1754–1835) of Largo; entered the High School, Edinburgh 1764; in the 2nd Dragoon Guards 1769; Major 1794; Brigadier and Major General in Ireland 1804–8; Lieutenant General 1813; General 1830; married twice, the second time at the age of 73 to Margaret, daughter of Col. John Anstruther-Thomson of Charlton; no heirs.

[36] William Robertson (1753–1835); educated at the High School and the College, Edinburgh; member of the Speculative Society 1770–99; admitted advocate 1775; chosen procurator of the Church of Scotland 1779; took his seat on the Scottish Bench as Lord Robertson 1805; resigned 1826; died 1835.

[37] C.P., Box 6, Envelope B, #6.

[38] C.P., Box 2, Envelope 1, #18.

[39] Edinburgh University Matriculation Roll 1623–1774, p. 278.

[40] Ibid, p. 287.

[41] Somerville (1843), p. 12 et seq.

[42] As in note 40, p. 296.

[43] Sher (1985), p. 108.

[44] The Speculative Society of Edinburgh (1905), p. 65, Number 62.

[45] Minutes of the United College, UC 400, Vol. II.

Chapter 2

[1] E.U.L., La/2/241.

[2] C.P., Box 4, #7.

[3] Sher (1985), p. 141.

[4] Statistical Account, Scotland, 13, p. 209.

[5] Southey (1844), Vol. I, p. 710–11.

[6] S.A.U.L.A., UC 400, Vol. II, (30 March 1773).

[7] Cant (1970), p. 92.

[8] C.P., Box 3, #7.

[9] Southey (1844), Vol. I, p. 28.

[10] S.A.U.L.A., UC 400, Vol. II (17 May 1774, 16 May 1775, etc).

[11] S.R.O., R.S. 27/213.

[12] S.R.O., R.S. 27/214/81.

[13] S.R.O., Old Parish Registers, 685 – 1/50.

[14] C.P., Box 5, Envelope C, Letter 67.

15 S.R.O., E/106/22/4.
16 I am indebted to Miss Mary Innes for allowing me to read her paper on Kemback, in which she deals with the career of John McGill of Kemback.
17 Smith, ed. Mossner and Ross (1977), 10 Dec. 1788.
18 S.R.O., CC 8/8/128.
19 E.U.L., La III, 379/162
20 S.R.O., CC 20/4/6.
21 C.P., Box 1, Envelope 3, Letters 6 and 12.
22 C.P., Box 2, Envelope 8, Letter 22 and an undated one.
23 S.A.U.L.A., UC 400, Vol. II.
24 C.P., letter on the back of a page of Cleghorn's lecture notes, Box 3.
25 Boswell (1813), p. 46.
26 C.P., Box 4, #7, 19 March 1790.
27 S.A.U.L.A., Stent Rolls, 865/20/3. Mr Robert Smart was kind enough to draw my attention to this and other valuable sources.
28 S.A.U.L.A., UC 400, 20 May 1780.
29 Ibid, 14 April 1787.
30 Ibid, 2 Feb. 1793.
31 C.P., Box 4, #7, 19 March 1790.
32 Ibid, Box 1, Envelope 2, #12.
33 Bold (1982), p. 7.
34 C.P., Box 2, Envelope 1, #4.
35 Southey (1844), Vol. III, pp. 303–7.
36 S.A.U.L.A., UC 400 May 1777 and May 1778.
37 'Copy of a letter from Mr. Cleghorn to His Grace the Duke of Leeds', W.P.L.
38 S.A.U.L.A., Professor Watson's lectures on Rhetoric.
39 C.P., Box 3, #10. All subsequent quotations in this chapter are from Cleghorn's lecture notes unless otherwise stated.
40 John Millar (1735–1801) as a young man had been strongly influenced by Adam Smith and Lord Kames, through whom he was made Professor of Civil Law at Glasgow University in 1761. In 1771 he published *Observations concerning the Distinction of Ranks in Society*, which, with his *Lectures on Public Laws* and *Historical View of the English Government*, made a great impact on the thought of his day. Many of Cleghorn's points in his lectures were drawn from Millar's 'Distinction of Ranks', as can be seen in the 1771 edition – pp. 79–83, 121, 124, 153, 171, 180, 183, 188, 190, 224, 226, 229, 238.
41 Smith (1904), Vol. II, Chapters 1 and 2. Other references: Vol. I, Book 1, p. 11.
42 C.P., Box 2, Envelope 1, #3.

Chapter 3

1 S.R.O., Blair Adam Papers, Miscellaneous Correspondence and Papers 1830–9 B, from the preface to *The Gift of a Grandfather*.
2 S.A.U.L.A., University Register, 1783–1826.

3 Southey (1844), Vol. I, p. 335.
4 C.P., Box 4, #1, Vol. I, is the basis of pp. 41–6 of this chapter unless otherwise stated.
5 C.P., Box 4, #3, Vol. III. p. 22.
6 W.P.L., Cleghorn's letter to the Duke of Leeds, Dec. 1790.
7 Smith, ed. Mossner and Ross (1977), Dec. 1788.
8 C.P., Box 4, Vol. I, p. 3: William Gibson DD (1753–1828), President of Douai 1781–90, then Vicar-apostolic of the Northern district of England.
9 See note 6.
10 S.A.U.L.A., UC 400/6, 6 Jan. 1789.
11 C.P., Box 4, #3, Vol. II – pp. 46–55 in this chapter are based on this volume unless otherwise stated.
12 Guyot (1958), p. 138 et seq.
13 Mavor (1986), eg. pp. 71, 76, 89, etc.
14 Launcelot Brown – son of 'Capability' Brown, the landscape architect – was an MP at this time.
15 C.P., Box 2, Envelope 1, Letter 21.
16 C.P., Box 4, #5, Vol. III – p. 55 is based on this volume.
17 Ibid, p. 2. Sir James Hall (1761–1832), geologist and chemist; intimate with Hutton and Playfair; tested Huttonian system by studying continental as well as Scottish formations; president of the Royal Society of Edinburgh; MP 1807–12.

Chapter 4

1 Cleghorn's spelling of place names was idiosyncratic to say the least – and not even always phonetic – so Swiss place names have been given their modern form.
2 C.P., Box 4, #5, Vol. III – all quotations from pp. 57–69 are from this volume of Cleghorn's journals.
3 Solomon Gessner (1730–88) was born in Zurich and spent all his life there (except for one year's painting in Berlin and Hamburg) as bookseller and librarian. Most of his poetry was written in the 1750s; it became universally popular because the taste of the period was for the conventionally pastoral and because of its sweetness and melody. *The Idylls* were translated into English and there is a copy of them in the library at Nether Stravithie. As a painter Gessner represented the conventional classical landscape.
4 Johann Kaspar Lavater (1741–1801) was born in Zurich. In 1762 he denounced the painter H. Fuseli for his corruption and forced him to make restitution. In 1769 he took orders and was deacon or pastor in Zurich till his death. He had a great reputation throughout Switzerland and Germany, Goethe being among his admirers until later he accused Lavater of superstition and hypocrisy. At the time when Cleghorn visited him he was incurring some ridicule because of his vanity. In 1799 when the French were entering Zurich he was shot while appealing to them for restraint and he died in 1801 after long suffering borne with great fortitude.

5 Josef Anton von Balthazer (1761–1837) studied in London, Paris and Rome; held various legal posts in Lucerne; helped to found the 'Historish-Politischen Sammlung Helvetika'; gave his own library to Lucerne in 1826.

6 General Franz Ludwig Pfyffer von Wyer (1716–1802).

7 Guyot (1958), pp. 133–4.

8 C.P., Box 4, #4, 'Tour of Savoy', by the schoolmaster of Sallanches, Maxime Effrancey, with an accompanying letter to Cleghorn.

Chapter 5

1 Francis, styled Lord Elcho (1749–1808), son of the 5th Earl of Wemyss (*de jure*). Between 1780 and 1787 he had been MP for Haddington Burghs. In 1787 he was deprived of his seat by a resolution of the Commons as he had become 'the eldest son of a peer of Scotland'. This forced him to retire into private life; he devoted himself to agriculture and did much to improve his estates. His family used the name of Charteris since the 4th Earl had inherited his extensive estates from Col. Francis Charteris. From J. Balfour Paul's *Scots Peerage*.

2 C.P., Box 4, #5, Vol. III.

3 Young (1976), pp. 279–80.

4 Fergusson (1882), p. 482.

5 Thomas Coutts (1735–1822), 4th son of John Coutts and Jean Stuart. He amassed an enormous fortune. His mistress was Susan Starkie, whom he married in 1796 and by whom he had three daughters: Susan (married in 1796 the 3rd Earl of Guilford); Frances (married in 1800 the 1st Marquis of Bute); and Sophie (married in 1793 Sir Francis Burdett – their daughter was Baroness Burdett Coutts).

6 C.P., Box 4, #7, Vol. IV. All quotations from pp. 74–88 are taken from this volume.

7 Skinner (1966), p. 20. James Clarke, born in Inverness, had been sent as a student to Italy by local patrons; at Naples he received travellers from Rome, showed them the sights and arranged for them the purchase of prints and paintings. Described as a 'very modest good kind of man by profession a painter'. In 1788–9 he listed and packed the entire collection of Sir William Hamilton. Died 1799.

8 D.N.B. Sir William Hamilton (1730–1803), diplomatist and archaeologist; between 1764 and 1800 he was ambassador plenipotentiary in Naples; collected Greek vases including the 'Warwick Vase' (now in the Burrell Collection) and the 'Portland Vase'; married Emma Hart; entertained Nelson at Naples 1798; accompanied Neopolitan Court to Palermo 1798; sold his collection to the British Museum.

9 C.P., Box 4, #8, Vol. V. Quotations on pp. 89–90 are taken from this volume.

Chapter 6

1   S.R.O., Blair Adam, General Correspondence C–F, 24 Dec. 1806.
2   S.A.U.L.A., UC 516/1823.
3   Southey (1844), Vol. II, p. 717.
4   This and other quotations in this paragraph are from Cleghorn's letter to the Duke of Leeds, in the W.P.L.
5   Letter from Cleghorn to Dundas, 16 Dec. 1790, in the W.P.L.
6   In the early stages of their careers there seem to be some parallels between Wickham and Cleghorn, though Wickham became a vital figure in Britain's relations with the French counter-revolutionary forces and went on to enjoy a steady career in government service. His own account of this early stage can be seen in a letter to his son: 'I was secretly employed by Lord Grenville . . . in a Foreign Correspondence so early as 1793. This continued till I was appointed Superintendent of Aliens in the summer [of 1794] and I have reason to know that there is no trace of that correspondence, nor was it known, though of considerable importance, to any one but Lord Rosslyn. In the month of October (1794) a circumstance occured that made it desirable . . . that some person of confidence should be sent over on a special mission to Switzerland. The nature and object of this mission was considered so secret and confidential that I never appeared at the Foreign Office at all. It was in 1795 that I was named Minister Plenipotentiary to the Swiss Cantons . . . having in the meantime a separate mission to the armies and conduct of a secret correspondence . . . related to the Royalists in the West . . . ' *Letters of William Wickham*, edited by his grandson, W. Wickham (1870), Vol. I.
7   C.P., Box 1, Envelope 2, #13.
8   See note 2.
9   S.A.U.L.A., UC 400/6, p. 62.
10   Meuron (1982), p. 73.
11   Ibid, p. 76.
12   Ibid, p. 102.
13   S.A.U.L.A. UC 400/6, p. 66 (28 Jan. 1792).
14   Ibid, p. 66 (18 Feb. 1792).
15   Ibid (25 Feb. 1792).
16   Ibid, the Masters' reply.
17   S.R.O., Blair Adam, Gen. Corresp., 1804, C–F.
18   Cobban, 'British Secret Service in France 1784–92'.
19   From memoranda concerning Cleghorn's dealings, in the W.P.L..
20   C.P., Box 5, Envelope A, Letter 25.
21   See note 19.
22   Ibid.
23   S.A.U.L.A., UC 400/6 (24 Nov. 1792).
24   Dr Maxwell Garthshore (1752–1812) and Dr Thomas Merison (army surgeon).
25   S.A.U.L.A., UC 400/6 (30 Jan. 1793).
26   Ibid (2 Feb. 1793).
27   See note 17 (letter dated 1 March 1806).

28 C.P., Box 1, Envelope 2, Letter 15.
29 See note 12.
30 See note 17.
31 C.P., Box 5, #1.

Chapter 7

1 'Copy of Mr. Cleghorn's correspondence from 1795–7 as to the Island of Ceylon', W.P.L.
2 C.P., Box 5, #1, 'Volume of Public Instructions to Mr. Cleghorn'. From pp. 104–11, all quotations are from this volume unless otherwise stated.
3 Andrew Stuart WS (1725–1801); Edinburgh University; member of the Poker Club; counsel for the Duke of Hamilton in the Douglas lawsuit for which he spent three years on the continent (1762–5) investigating the circumstances of the infancy of the Douglas claimant; fought a duel about it with Edward Thurlow; MP for Weymouth and Melcombe Regis, 1790–1801; appointed to the board of trade, 1779.
4 B.L., MS Add 38769.
5 C.P., Box 5, Envelope B, #37.
6 Ibid.
7 Ibid, #38. The next five quotations are from the same letter.
8 Ibid, #39; and the following quotation.
9 Ibid, #40.
10 Ibid, #41.
11 Ibid, #42. William Duff Dunbar was born in Banff; served in the British Army; 1787 married Mlle Gaudot and lived in Neuchâtel in a superb house on the Faubourg; died 1837.
12 Meuron (1982), p. 110.
13 The Circle of Swabia was one of those areas in the Holy Roman Empire created by Maximilian I in 1500 to keep the peace in Germany, and preserved for limited administrative purposes. It lay between the Rhine, the Lech and Lake Constance.
14 C.P., Box 5, Envelope A, #9.
15 Ibid, Envelope C, #53.
16 Ibid, Envelope B, #43.
17 C.P., Box 5, Number 2. Hugh Cleghorn's 'Journal of a Voyage to India by Land', Vol. I. From pp. 112–19, all quotations are from this volume unless otherwise noted.
18 Meuron (1982), p. 111.
19 C.P., Box 5, #4 – 2nd volume of Cleghorn's India journals, p. 56.
20 C.P., Box 5, #1, pp. 45–6.
21 George Baldwin (died 1826); a great traveller; his services accepted by the East India Company; established a direct commerce from England to Egypt; in 1786 he was British Consul in Alexandria; told Cleghorn of a guard against the plague; wrote a number of mystical works.

22 See note 20, pp. 48–50.
23 C.P., Box 5, Envelope A, #12. Copy of an undated letter in French from Cleghorn to 'Madame' – almost certainly Mme Du Peyrou.
24 See note 20, p. 50v.
25 See, note 20, p. 52.
26 See note 20, p. 58.
27 C.P., Box 5, #4 – 2nd volume of Cleghorn's journals on his voyage to India. From pp. 119–27, all quotations are from this volume unless otherwise noted.
28 C.P., Box 5, #1, p. 75.
29 See note 27 – on a loose sheet between pp. 54–5.
30 See note 28, p. 83.
31 See note 28, p. 91.
32 See note 28, p. 95.

Chapter 8

1 C.P., Box 5, #4, 'Voyage to India by Land', Vol. II. This has been used as one of the two main sources of this chapter.
2 C.P., Box 5, #1, 'Volume of Public Instructions to Mr. Cleghorn'. This is the other main source on which this chapter is based.
3 C.P., Box 5, Envelope A, #24.
4 Ibid, #26.
5 Meuron (1982), p. 120.
6 Ibid, p. 121.
7 Ibid, p. 122.
8 C.P., Box 5, Envelope B, #45.
9 Ibid, Envelope A, #31.

Chapter 9

1 The narrative of this chapter is based on the seven volunes in Box 6 of the Cleghorn Papers which Cleghorn wrote between 19 Nov. 1795 and 4 April 1797.
2 Meuron (1982), p. 133.
3 De Silva (1981), p. 187.
4 C.P., Box 5, Envelope A, Letter 33.
5 C.P., Box 6, Vol. III.
6 Ibid, Vol. I.
7 Ibid, Vol. II.
8 Thomas Pitt, 2nd Baron Camelford (1775–1804); commander in the navy, and duellist; passed his early years in Neuchâtel (where at his death he wanted his body to be buried, but because of the war this never happened); then at Charterhouse; 1789 entered the Navy; 1791–4 joined the 'Discovery' with Captain George Vancouver in the survey of North West America; 1793

became Lord Camelford on the death of his father; 1794 he was discharged for insubordination at Hawaii; reached Malacca; appointed acting lieutenant of the 'Resistance'; Nov. 1795 he was summarily discharged and left to find his own way to England.

9   Meuron (1982), p. 154.
10   Southey (1844), Vol. III, p. 520.
11   C.P., Box 6, Envelope A, Letter 9.
12   C.P., Box 6 , Envelope C, Letters 58 & 59.
13   Ibid, Envelope A, Letter 13.
14   Ibid, Letter 12.

Chapter 10

1   The source for this chapter is the *Volume of Correspondence from 1795–1800 between Mr. Secretary Dundas and Hugh Cleghorn Esquire* (in S.R.O., GD51/17/71) unless otherwise noted.
2   C.P., Box 5, Envelope C, #66.
3   Ibid, Box 6, Envelope B, #7.
4   S.R.O., GD51/4/431.
5   C.P., Box 1, Envelope 3, #14.
6   Ibid, Box 6, Envelope B, #11.
7   S.R.O., (S)63, Blair Adam, Box 1798, A–I.
8   C.P., Box 5, Envelope C, #67.
9   See note 8.
10   See note 8.

Chapter 11

1   K.C.A., U471 C39/11.
2   Hulugalle (1963), p. 10.
3   S.R.O., 19516 Melville Papers F43.
4   K.C.A., U471 C27/2.
5   Ibid, U471 C27/6.
6   S.R.O., GD51/17/71. The source for most of the present chapter, unless otherwise stated, is this volume of Cleghorn's correspondence in Register House in Edinburgh.
7   K.C.A., U471 C39/10.
8   I.O.R., G/11/53.
9   Ibid.
10   K.C.A., U471 C28/8.
11   See note 6.
12   K.C.A., 0471 C28/38.
13   Ibid, C28/23.
14   Ibid, C28/6.

Chapter 12

1 The phrase used in this chapter title comes from a letter from Cleghorn to Petrie:
   'I know by experience how severely a man of activity feels upon being reduced
   to a cypher and upon observing the confidence of a Governor given to, and the
   operations of Government directed by any unprincipled time-server who flatters
   his vanity and encourages his folly.' C.P., Box 7, #1. This volume, recording
   Cleghorn's correspondence, etc, on his second Ceylon venture, is the one on
   which this chapter is based, unless otherwise stated.

2 I.O.R., G/11/53.

3 N.L.S., 13603 f119 – letter to Alexander Walker (1764–1831), eldest son of
   minister of Collessie, Fife; to Bombay in East India Company's army; served
   against Hyder Ali at the siege of Mangalore; 1791–2 against Tippū; military
   secretary to Gen. James Stuart in Bombay; 1799 at Seringapatam; 1802–7 at
   court of Gaekwar of Baroda; 1812 Brigadier General; 1822–30 Governor of
   St Helena; his Oriental MSS presented to the Bodleian.

4 S.R.O., GD 51/17/71.

5 De Silva (1981), p. 214.

6 Meuron (1982), p. 156.

7 N.L.S., 13603 f127.

8 Meuron (1982), p. 370, note 9.

9 Hulugalle (1963), p. 22.

10 I.O.R., F/4/130 Collection 2403.

11 William Petrie (died 1816), appointed a Writer then a Factor (1771); then a
   Senior Merchant in Madras 1790; President of the Board of Revenue there; 1807
   acted for three months as Governor of Madras; his indignation at the way the
   Madras civil servants toadied to Sir George Barlow led him to leave Madras;
   1809 Governor of Prince Edward Island: 'I would rather end my days in a pepper
   garden in Penang than be compelled to associate with those who have so cruelly,
   falsely and unjustly calumniated my conduct in Council.' (Extract from letter in
   N.L.S., 1072 f4.) Petrie died in Penang in 1816.

12 See note 9.

13 N.L.S., 13603 f119.

14 Ibid.

15 S.R.O., GD 51/17/71.

16 Ibid, GD 51/3/83/3.

17 N.L.S., 13603 f125.

18 C.P., Box 7, Envelope A, #1 & #2.

19 See note 17.

20 K.C.A., U471 39/9.

21 Ibid, U471 39/2.

22 C.P., Box 5, #4 – on a loose sheet between pp. 54–5.

23 A.L.O.S.A., letter from Cleghorn to Dundas, 5 Oct. 1799.

24 A Pagoda was a gold coin at the time current in South India and Ceylon
   bearing on it the figure of a pagoda – worth approximately forty-five pence

in present-day sterling. A 'Lac' was one hundred thousand – thus, a Lac of Pagodas was worth about £45,000 in terms of our 1992 values.

Chapter 13

1 C.P., Box 7, #1. Correspondence Register – one of the main sources of the beginning of this chapter, especially pp. 222–7 of that Register.
2 K.C.A., U471 C39/2.
3 I.O.R., F/4/130, Collection 2403.
4 C.P., Box 7, #1.
5 N.L.S., 13603 f123.
6 See note 3.
7 C.P., Box 7, #1.
8 K.C.A., U471/C39/9.
9 N.L.S., 13603 f123.
10 A.L.O.S.A., Cleghorn to Dundas, 5 Oct. 1799.
11 Meuron (1982), pp. 162–3.
12 N.L.S., 13603 f129.
13 K.C.A., U471/C29/26 – the report on which the following summary is based.
14 Ibid, C27/29.
15 Ibid, C29/2.
16 B.L., MSS dept., Add. MSS 13867 fol. 72–5
17 K.C.A., U471/C39/7.
18 Ibid, C27/9.
19 Ibid, C39/7.
20 Ibid, C27/12.
21 De Silva (1981), p. 224–6, and *Cambridge History of India*, Vol. V, Ch. 24.
22 S.R.O., Blair Adam, Box 1802, O–S.
23 I.O.R., F/4/129 – for this and all subsequent points from the Report.
24 Southey (1844), Vol. III, p. 720.

Chapter 14

1 Southey (1844), Vol. III, p. 718.
2 C.P., Box 5, Envelope B, #45.
3 Ibid, Box 1, Envelope 3, #1
4 Ibid, Envelope 7, #1.
5 Ibid, Box 5, Envelope B, #44.
6 St Andrews Burgh Reg. Sasines, Vol. X, p. 237. I am indebted to Mrs Catherine Forrest for this reference.
7 S.A.U.L.A., '1788 Inventory of Title Deeds of Number 127 & 29, South Street, St. Andrews belonging to the Trustees of the late Dr. John Adamson'. For this reference I am indebted to Mr Robert Smart, Keeper of Manuscripts and University Muniments.

8   S.R.O., CC 20/7/9.
9   C.P., Box 1, Envelope 4, #3.
10 Ibid, Envelope 1, #3.
11 Ibid, Envelope 4, #3 & #4.
12 Ibid, Envelope 3, #5.
13 C.P., Box 5, Envelope B, #43.
14 S.A.U.L.A., MS 30357/83.
15 C.P., Box 1, Envelope 4, #9.
16 Ibid, Box 8, 1810 Bundle of Accounts.
17 Ibid, Box 1, Envelope 4, #11.
18 Ibid, #25.
19 C.P., Box 8, 1810 Bundle of Accounts.
20 'Inventory of Writs of house and gardens of St. Leonards and Pertinents referred
    to in Articles of Roup, 15 July 1809.' I am grateful to the Headmistress of
    St Leonards School, and to Messrs Pagan, Osborne and Grace, Cupar, for
    allowing me to consult these documents.
21 C.P., Box 5, Envelope B, #42.
22 Ibid, #45.
23 Boswell (1813), p. 46.
24 See note 20.
25 S.A.U.L.A., UC 400/2, p. 587.
26 See note 20.
27 S.A.U.L.A., St Andrews Stent Rolls, B65/20/3.
28 C.P., Box 1, Envelope 4, #10.
29 Ibid, #7.
30 Ibid, Envelope 3, #11.
31 Ibid, #16.
32 Ibid, #10.
33 Ibid, #5.
34 Ibid, #6.
35 Ibid, #4.
36 Ibid, #10.
37 C.P., Box 2, Envelope 12, #1.
38 Ibid, Box 1, Envelope 3, #8.
39 Ibid, #9.
40 Ibid, Envelope 7, #2.
41 Ibid, #4.
42 Ibid, Envelope 4, #4.
43 Ibid, Envelope 3, #7.
44 Ibid, Envelope 4, #1.
45 C.P., Box 5, Envelope B, #44.
46 S.R.O., (S)63 Blair Adam, Box 1802, C–D, 4 May 1802.
47 See note 46 – 18 April 1802.
48 C.P., Box 1, Envelope 5, #3.
49 Ibid, #2.
50 S.R.O., (S)63 Blair Adam, Box 1802, C–D, 23 June 1802.

51   See note 50 – 11 June 1802.
52   C.P., Box 1, Envelope 5, #12.
53   Ibid, #9.
54   S.R.O., (S)63 Blair Adam, Box 1802, O–S.
55   C.P., Box 1, Envelope 5, #12.
56   Ibid, #18.
57   Ibid, #14.
58   Ibid, #13.
59   Ibid, #14.
60   S.R.O., (S)63 Blair Adam, Box C–E (9).
61   C.P., Box 1, Envelope 5, #19.
62   Ibid, #24.
63   S.R.O., Blair Adam, Gen. Corresp. 1804 C–F.
64   Watson (1960), pp. 414 & 416 in the next quotation.
65   This section – pp. 233–8 – is based on a group of fourteen letters in C.P., Box 1, Envelope 6.
66   C.P., Box 1, Envelope 3, #19.
67   Young (1969), pp. 213–14.
68   Hay Fleming, Note Book #15, p. 244.
69   S.R.O., Blair Adam, Gen. Corresp. 1813, N–Z 2, 32.
70   See note 67, p. 214.
71   C.P., Box 8, 1814 Bundle of Receipts.
72   Ibid, Box 2, Envelope 1, #3.

Chapter 15

1   Mitchison (1962), p. 18.
2   Millar (1896), Vol. I, p. 156.
3   Ibid, Vol. 1, p. 357.
4   S.R.O., Blair Adam, Gen. Corresp., 1804 C–F, 1 March 1806.
5   Ibid, 24 Dec. 1806.
6   Ibid, Gen. Corresp., 1807 A–F, 21 Jan. 1807.
7   Ibid, 1818B, 2/199, 9 July 1818.
8   Ibid, 1824, 11 March 1821.
9   C.P., Box 2, Envelope 1, #2.
10   Ibid, Envelope 5, #9.
11   C.P., Box 8, 1806 Bundle of Receipts, 30 June 1806.
12   Ibid, Box 1, Envelope 4, #22.
13   Ibid, #25.
14   C.P., Box 8, 1807 Receipts, 19 April 1806 – 24 Nov 1807.
15   Ibid, 1806 Receipts, Oct. 1806.
16   C.P., Box 1, Envelope 4, #21.
17   Ibid, #25.
18   N.L.S., 14303 f4.
19   C.P., Box 8, 1822 Receipts, R. Balfour's Estimate.

20 *Fasti Ecclesia Scoticanae*, Vol. V, Parish of Dunino.

21 Bold (1982), p. 6.

22 C.P., Box 8, 1816 Receipts, 28 Aug. 1816, 8 Feb. 1817.

23 Ibid, 1820 Receipts, 7 Sept. 1820, for example.

24 C.P., Box 2, Envelope 8, #21.

25 N.L.S., 14303 f4, 8 March 1806.

26 C.P., Box 1, Envelope 3, #21.

27 Ibid, Envelope 4, #18.

28 C.P., Box 8, 1808 Receipts, 8 Sept. 1808.

29 Ibid, 1810 Receipts, 1 Dec.,1810.

30 Ibid, 4 Nov. 1810.

31 Ibid, 1811 Receipts, 19 Jan. & 27 July 1811.

32 Ibid, 11 Jan., Alex Munro.

33 Ibid, 30 Dec., W. MacLean.

34 Ibid, 25 July 1811, John Hedridge.

35 Ibid, 29 May 1811, W. Foulis.

36 Ibid, 19 June 1811, R. Balfour.

37 Ibid, 1812 Receipts, Feb. 1812 (tax for 1810–11).

38 Ibid, 1826 Receipts, 15 Jan. 1827 – assessed tax.

39 Ibid, 1820 Receipts, 1 March 1820, Andrew Marr.

40 Ibid, 9 Feb. 1821.

41 Ibid, 22 April 1819.

42 Ibid, 17 July 1819.

43 Ibid, 1 March 1820.

44 Leighton (1840), Vol. III, p. 83.

45 C.P., Box 8, 1809 Receipts, 15 Feb & 11 Aug. 1809.

46 Ibid, Box 2, Envelope 6, #3, 13 Jan. 1835.

47 C.P., Box 8, 1814 Receipts, 22 June 1814.

48 Ibid, 2 Aug. 1814.

49 C.P., Box 2, Envelope 1, #14.

50 Ibid, Box 8, 1810 Receipts, 26 Oct. 1810.

51 Ibid, 1811 Receipts, 19 Aug. 1811.

52 Ibid, 1810 Receipts, 18 Sept. 1810.

53 Ibid, 1815 Receipts, 7 June 1815.

54 Ibid, 1821 Receipts, 4 & 13 Sept. 1821 – William Darnton (the 'Dunregan'); J. McNaughton (the 'Phemia of Charleston').

55 C.P., Box 8, 1821 Receipts, 14–19 Sept. 1821, William Thomson.

56 Ibid, Box 2, Envelope 6, #3, #4 & #6, April 1835.

57 Ibid, 6 March, 8 May 1835, etc.

58 Ibid, 17 Aug. 1835.

59 C.P., Box 8, 1809 Receipts, 24 Feb. 1809, R. Briggs.

60 Ibid, 1810 Receipts, 4 Dec. 1810, J. Kininmond.

61 Ibid, 1811 Receipts, 3 Nov. 1811, J. Hunter.

62 Ibid, 1815 Receipts, 14 July 1815, John Braid.

63 Ibid, 1820 Receipts, 14 June 1820, J. Masson.

64 Ibid, 21 Nov. 1820, J. Masson.

65 Ibid, 12 April, 17 Nov., 16 Dec., etc.
66 Ibid, 1821 Receipts, 27 March, 5 & 26 May, 12 June, etc.
67 Ibid, 23 July 1821.
68 Ibid, 1822 Receipts, 14 Sept. 1822.
69 Ibid, 'Account Current betwixt Heritors of Dunino and Charles Grace'.
70 E.U.L., DK 7 61/11.
71 N.L.S., 13723 f60.62, 24 April 1818.
72 Addison (1901), p. 79.
73 S.R.O., Blair Adam, Gen. Corresp. 2/131, 24 Feb. 1816.
74 Low (1936), p. 10.
75 N.L.S., MS 3449.
76 Southey (1844), Vol. II, p. 36.
77 S.R.O., Blair Adam, Gen. Corresp. 1807.
78 C.P., Box 2, Envelope 1, #3.
79 N.L.S., MS 3887 f143 (49).
80 C.P., Box 2, Envelope 8, #23.
81 S.A.U.L.A., 865/20/2, Stent Roll 1815.
82 Small (1867), p. 48.
83 Ibid, p. 84.
84 S.R.O., Blair Adam, Gen. Corresp., 1807, 2 June 1811.
85 E.U.L., DK 61/11.
86 S.R.O., Blair Adam, Gen. Corresp. 1816, 2/131, 23 Feb. 1816.
87 Ibid.
88 E.U.L., 13722 f10.
89 Small (1867), p. 85.
90 S.R.O., Blair Adam, Gen. Corresp. 1816, 2/131, 27 Feb.
91 Ibid, 2/115.
92 Ibid.
93 Ibid.
94 Ibid, 2/131, 2 March 1816.
95 Ibid, 1816, 2/115.
96 See note 83.
97 S.R.O., Blair Adam, Gen. Corresp. 1816, 2/115
98 Ibid, 2/128.
99 Ibid.
100 See note 94.
101 S.R.O., Blair Adam, Gen. Corresp. 1816, 2/125.
102 S.A.U.L.A., 865/20/4, Stent Roll 1820.

Chapter 16

1 E.U.L., DK 61/11.
2 S.R.O., Blair Adam, Gen. Corresp. 1816, 2/121.
3 Ibid, 1817, 2/165.
4 C.P., Box 8, 1819 Receipts.

5   Ibid, 'Charles Grace's Business Account with Hugh Cleghorn'.
6   Ibid, 1820 Receipts, 11 Nov. 1819.
7   C.P., Box 1, Envelope 1, #6.
8   Ibid, Box 8, 1814 Receipts, 13 Feb. 1814.
9   Ibid, 1819 Receipts, Grace's account, 1817–19.
10 Ibid, 1820 Receipts, 3 Nov. 1820.
11 Ibid, 13 Nov. 1820.
12 S.R.O., Blair Adam, Gen. Corresp., 1821 A, 11 Jan. 1821.
13 Ibid, 4 Feb. 1821.
14 See note 12.
15 C.P., Box 8, 1823 Receipts. Documents concerning the dispute between Hugh
    Cleghorn and David Brown.
16 S.R.O., Blair Adam Gen. Corresp., 1817 A, 2/154, 2 July 1817.
17 C.P., Box 8, 1821 Receipts, 3 July 1821.
18 The Citizen (St Andrews), Saturday 24 Nov. 1934.
19 C.P., Box 8, 1826 Receipts, 28 Feb. 1826.
20 S.R.O., Blair Adam, Gen. Corresp., 1818 A, 2/193, 25 Feb. 1818.
21 C.P., Box 8, 1819 Receipts, 12 Aug. 1819.
22 S.R.O., Blair Adam, 2/248 (1820), 22 Oct. 1820.
23 C.P., Box 8, 1821 Receipts, 15 Oct. 1821.
24 Ibid, Box 2, Envelope 1, #3, 3 March 1822, and the two quotations following.
25 Low (1936), p. 11.
26 S.R.O., Blair Adam, Gen. Corresp., 1824, 21 March 1824.
27 Low (1936), p. 29.
28 C.P., Box 1, Envelope 9, #1, 4 Oct. 1824.
29 Ibid, Box 2, Envelope 1, #2, 21 Nov. 1824, and the following quotation.
30 C.P., Box 2, Envelope 1, #13, 6 Feb. 1826.
31 Ibid, #14, 19 Feb. 1826.
32 See note 30.
33 C.P., Box 2, Envelope 1, #4, 29 Jan. 1825.
34 Ibid, #8, 10 May 1827.
35 Ibid, #2, 21 Nov. 1824.
36 Ibid, #3, 26 Dec. 1824.
37 Ibid, #6, 16 Oct. 1825.
38 Ibid.
39 Ibid, #20, 17 Aug. 1827.
40 C.P., Box 1, Envelope 8, #13, 10 July 1828.
41 Ibid, Box 8, 1825 Receipts – letter from Hugh Cleghorn to Charles Grace in
    which he quotes from a letter from Peter Cleghorn.
42 C.P., Box 1, Envelope 8, #13, 4 April 1828.
43 Ibid, Box 2, Envelope 1, #19, 17 May 1827.
44 Ibid, Box 1, Envelope 9, #17, 10 May 1829.
45 Ibid, Box 2, Envelope 1, #14, 19 Feb. 1826.
46 Ibid, Envelope 2, #3, 5 Dec. 1827.
47 C.P., Box 1, Envelope 8, #12, Peter Cleghorn's passport and visas,
    9 May – 27 Aug. 1828.

48 C.P., Box 2, Envelope 1, #23, 29 May 1829.
49 S.R.O., Blair Adam, Misc. Corresp. 1820–9 C, 19 July 1829, and the following quotation.
50 C.P., Box 2, Envelope 6, #1, Hugh Cleghorn's Scroll Letters, 1834–6.
51 Low (1936), p. 137.

<h2 align="center">*Chapter 17*</h2>

1 Low (1936), p. 137.
2 C.P., Box 2, Envelope 5, #28, 12 Feb. 1833.
3 Ibid, Envelope 4, #1, 8 March 1833.
4 Apart from surviving letters, the main sources for this chapter are two small volumes containing diaries kept by Hugh Cleghorn between 1834–6, and a notebook of Scroll Letters (i.e. rough copies of what he wrote to his friends) for the same period. They can be found in C.P., Box 2, Envelope 6.
5 C.P., Box 2, Envelope 3, #5, 15 March 1831.
6 Ibid, #2, 13 March 1831.
7 Ibid, #7.
8 Ibid, Envelope 1, #12, 21 Jan. 1826.
9 C.P., Box 1, Envelope 2, #2, 21 Nov. 1824.
10 Ibid, Box 2, Envelope 8, #27, 15 Feb. 1845.
11 Ibid, Box 8, 1819 Receipts, 12 Aug. 1819.
12 Ibid, Box 2, Envelope 7, #9, 17 Oct. 1837.
13 Southey (1844), Vol. III, p. 719 and the following quotation.
14 C.P., Box 2, Envelope 2, #11.
15 Ibid, Envelope 5, #1.
16 Ibid, #2, 1 Oct. 1831.
17 Ibid, #25.
18 Ibid, #10.
19 Ibid, #18, 13 Jan. 1832.
20 Ibid, #20, 23 Jan. 1832.
21 Ibid, #6, 16 Oct. 1831.
22 Ibid, #5, 7 Oct. 1831.
23 Ibid, #21, 20 Feb. 1832.
24 Ibid, #22, 28 Feb. 1832.
25 Ibid, #26, 5 June 1832.
26 Ibid, #30, 27 May 1834.
27 The latest letter in Cleghorn's own writing that I came across is to Dr John Lee, dated 25 July 1836. See N.L.S., MS 3441 f122.
28 C.P., Box 2, Envelope 2, #4, 4 Feb. 1831.
29 Ibid, #7, 1 Jan. 1831.
30 Ibid, Envelope 6, Scroll Letters, 8 Dec. 1834.
31 Ibid, Envelope 5, #33, 31 Aug. 1835.
32 Ibid, Envelope 6, 1834 Diary, 1 Nov. – entry about bringing Mary Lain to Bannafield to give her a home, etc.

33 C.P., Box 2, Envelope 6, Scroll Letters, Jan. 1836.
34 S.R.O., Blair Adam, Misc. Corresp. and Papers 1830–8, 'The Gift of a Grandfather'.
35 See note 27.
36 C.P., Box 2, Envelope 2, #6, 16 Oct. 1825.
37 Ibid, #15, 19 Nov. 1832.

Bibliography

MANUSCRIPT SOURCES (with abbreviations used in the notes).

A.L.O.S.A. – AMES LIBRARY OF SOUTH ASIA
(University of Minnesota, Minneapolis)
Letter from Hugh Cleghorn to Henry Dundas, 5 October 1799.

B.L. – BRITISH LIBRARY
Drafts on:
William Huskisson, 1795–8. MSS Add. 38769.
Frederic North and Sylvester Douglas. MSS Add. 13867, fol. 72–5.

E.C.A. – EDINBURGH CITY ARCHIVES
Cartulary, Charter of December 1760.

E.U.L. – EDINBURGH UNIVERSITY LIBRARY
Matriculation Rolls.
Special Collections: William Robertson's papers.
Letters tipped into Alexander Hamilton's *Itinerarium*, ed. A. Hart, (1907, Annapolis, Maryland).

I.O.R. – INDIA OFFICE LIBRARY AND RECORDS
Instructions to the Governor of Ceylon, 1798.
Letters (Collection 2403) from Frederic North to the Secret Committee of the Court of Directors of the East India Company, autumn 1799.
Report by Henry Smith to the Secret Committee of the Court of Directors on the 1799 Pearl Fishery, 1802.

K.C.A. – KENT COUNTY ARCHIVES
The papers of Frederic North (later 5th Earl of Guilford).

N.L.S. – NATIONAL LIBRARY OF SCOTLAND
The correspondence of Alexander Walker.
The Lee Papers.
John Millar's 'Analysis of Lectures on Government'.

S.A.U.L.A. – ST ANDREWS UNIVERSITY LIBRARY ARCHIVES
Cleghorn Papers (C.P.) letters, lecture notes, diaries, volumes of official correspondence, etc. (These papers have been lent by Major Hugh Sprot.)
Minutes of the United College.
Professor Watson's lectures.
St Andrews Burgh Register of Sasines.
St Andrews Stent Rolls.

S.R.O. – SCOTTISH RECORD OFFICE
  Old Parish Registers of Edinburgh Marriages and Births.
  Register of Edinburgh Sasines.
  'Cess Book of Valued Rental of Edinburgh.'
  Blair Adam Papers.
  Volume of correspondence between Dundas and Cleghorn [GD51/17/71]

W.P.L. – WILLIAM PERKINS LIBRARY
(Manuscript Department, Duke University, Durham, North Carolina)
  Hugh Cleghorn to Henry Dundas (December 1790) with a copy of his paper on
      Ceylon addressed to the Duke of Leeds.
  Hugh Cleghorn to Evan Nepean, 1790.
  J. Reeves to Nepean, 1793–5.

PRINTED WORKS

Addison, W. I., 1901, *The Snell Exhibitioners 1679–1900*, James MacLehose
    & Sons, Glasgow.

Bold, A., (ed.) 1982, *Beggar's Benison and Merryland, Anstruther* (reprint of 1892
    edition), Paul Harris Publishing, Edinburgh.

Boswell, J., 1813, *The Journal of a Tour to the Hebrides*, T. Cadell & W. Davies,
    Strand, London.

Cambridge History of India, Vol. V.

Cant, R. G., 1970, *The University of St. Andrews*, Scottish Academic Press,
    Edinburgh.

Carlyle, A., 1910, *Autobiography*, T. N. Foulis, London & Edinburgh.

Cobban, A., 1954, 'British Secret Service in France 1784–92', *English Historical
    Review*, Vol. LXIX, pp. 226–61.

De Silva, K. M., 1981, *A History of Sri Lanka*, Hurst, California.

Dictionary of National Biography: D.N.B.

Fasti Ecclesiae Scoticanae, Vol. V, 1925, Oliver & Boyd, Edinburgh.

Ferguson, A., 1773, *Institutes of Moral Philosophy*, A. Kincaid & W. Creech, and
    J. Bell, Edinburgh.

Fergusson, A., 1882, *Henry Erskine, his kinsfolk and times*, W. Blackwood & Son,
    Edinburgh.

Grant, A., 1884, *The Story of the University of Edinburgh*, Longman, Green & Co.,
    London.

Grant, J., 1881–3, *Old and New Edinburgh*, Cassell & Co., London.

Guyot, C., 1958, *Un Ami et Defenseur de Rousseau: Pierre Alexandre Du Peyrou*, Édition Ides et Kalends, Lausanne.

Hamilton, A., 1907, *Itinerarium*, privately printed in Annapolis, Maryland.

Hay, Fleming, D., Notebook No. 15, concerning Morison's *Dictionary of Decisions of the Court of Sessions*. (In the Hay Fleming Library, St Andrews.)

Hulugalle, H. A., 1963, *British Governors of Ceylon*, Colombo, Associated Newspapers of Ceylon.

Leechman, W., 1789, *Sermons*. Ed. James Wodrow, A. Strahan & T. Cadell, London.

Leighton, J., 1840, *History of the County of Fife*, Joseph Swan, Glasgow.

Low, U., 1936, *Fifty Years with John Company*, John Murray, London.

Macdonald, A., 1934, article in the *St. Andrews Citizen*, 24 November.

McDougall, W., 1978, 'Gavin Hamilton, Bookseller in Edinburgh', *British Journal for Eighteenth Century Studies*, Vol. I, pp. 1–19.

Mavor, E., 1986, *The Grand Tour of William Beckford*, Penguin, Harmondsworth, Middlesex.

Meuron, G. de, 1982, *Le Régiment Meuron*, Le Forum Historique, Lausanne.

Millar, A. H., 1895, *Fife Pictorial and Historical*, A. Westwood & Son, Cupar, Fife.

Millar, J., 1771, *Observations concerning the Distinction of Ranks in Society*, John Murray, London.

Mitchell, H., 1965, *The Underground War against Revolutionary France: the Mission of William Wickham, 1794–1800*, O.U.P., Oxford.

Mitchison, R., 1962, *Agricultural Sir John*, Bles, London.

Mossner, E. C., 1963, 'Adam Ferguson's Dialogue of a Highland Jaunt', in *Restoration and Eighteenth Century Literature*, ed. C. Camden, University of Chicago Press.

Neil, W., 1927, *The Cleghorn Papers*, Black, London.

Nobbs, D., 1965, 'The British Ideas of William Cleghorn, Hume's academic rival', *Journal of the History of Ideas*, Vol. XXVI, (Oct.–Dec.), No. 4, pp. 575–86.

Paul, J. B., 1911, *Scots Peerage*, Vol. VIII, David Douglas, Edinburgh.

Records of the Burgh, 1689-1724, 1940, Oliver and Boyd, Edinburgh.

Scott, W., 1972, *Journal*, ed. W. E. K. Anderson, Clarendon Press, Oxford.

Scott, W. R., 1937, *Adam Smith as Student and Professor,* Jackson, Son & Co., Glasgow.

Sher, R. B., 1985, *Church and University in the Scottish Enlightenment*, Edinburgh University Press, Edinburgh.

Skinner, B., 1966, *Scots in Italy in the Eighteenth Century*, Scottish National Portrait Gallery, Edinburgh.

Small, J., 1867, 'Biographical Sketch of Adam Ferguson', *Edinburgh Review*, (January), Vol. CXXV, Part 2, pp. 48–85.

Smith, A., 1904, *Wealth of Nations*, Methuen, Fetter Lane, London.

Smith, A., 1977, *Correspondence of Adam Smith*, ed. E. C. Mossner and I. S. Ross, O.U.P., Oxford.

Somerville, T., 1861, *My Own Life and Times, 1741–1814*, Edmonston & Douglas, Edinburgh.

Southey, C. C., 1844, *Life of Dr. Andrew Bell*, 3 volumes, Murray, London, & W. Blackwood, Edinburgh.

Statistical Account of Scotland, 1793.

Steven, W., 1849, *History of the High School of Edinburgh*, MacLachan & Stewart, Edinburgh.

Watson, S., 1960, *The Reign of George III*, Clarendon Press, Oxford.

Watson, W., 1905, *History of the Speculative Society of Edinburgh*, Edinburgh.

Wodrow, R., 1842–3, *Analecta*, Maitland Club, Edinburgh.

Wodrow, R., 1937, *Early Letters of R. Wodrow*, ed. L. W. Sharp, Scottish Historical Society, Vol. XXIV, T. & A. Constable, Edinburgh.

Young, A., 1976, *Travels in France and Italy*, Dent, Everyman, London.

Young, D., 1969, *St. Andrews Town and Gown*, Cassell, London.

Index